'Anne Watts chose a life of dedication ⎯⎯⎯⎯⎯⎯ with human wreckage at its most hea⎯⎯⎯ and sympathetic force she brings to dealing with it sugg⎯⎯⎯ just might be some hope for humanity yet' Clive James

'A magnificent life story. I feel humbled by Anne Watts' experiences' Jennifer Worth, author of *Call the Midwife* and *Farewell to the East End*

'In reading the book, I lived with Anne Watts through her experiences, full of admiration for her grit and compassion. It's the most touching testimony to the pity of war and she is such a natural story-teller' Lyndall Gordon, author of *Lives Like Loaded Guns: Emily Dickinson and Her Family's Feuds*

'Intensely moving' *Daily Express*

'A vivid, humbling memoir' Carle Richardson, *Yours*

'Fascinating' *Bristol Sunday Independent*

'Extraordinary' *Best of British*

'A vivid and moving memoir' *Bournemouth Daily Echo*

'A moving memoir' *Woman's Weekly*

'One way or another, war has shaped and dictated the remarkable life story of nurse Anne Watts ... Now approaching her 70th birthday, Watts has put pen to paper and recorded her truly incredible story as a tribute to the children to whom she brought hope, and the young soldiers whose hands she held as they died. And what shines through the horror, the pain and the utter futility of war is Watts's inspirational devotion, her spirit of adventure and her will to alleviate suffering whatever or wherever it might be ... *Always the Children* is a humbling, terrifying, shocking and yet strangely uplifting story of one woman's selfless devotion and her undiminished determination to alleviate the suffering of her fellow human being. If you only read one book in 2010, make it this one' Pam Norfolk, *Lancashire Evening Post* '[on the nursing memoir genre] Anne Watts's *Always the Children*: A Nurse's Story of Home and War is set to become a notable addition to the genre' Stephanie Cross, *The Lady*

'Anne Watts is no traditional nurse following the path of starch and hospital hierarchy, charting instead a very different route for herself and I have thoroughly enjoyed reading about her diverse and fascinating career. There are some incredible photos too, several very moving . . . Anne's indomitable spirit shines through the most appalling experiences of man's inhumanity to man . . . alongside her darker moments of doubt and fear mixed with anger, compassion and grief at what she witnesses. But there's black humour too, always in evidence in most nursing environments and essential when you've been there. So expect some refreshingly light-hearted moments, much laughter, a wonderful encounter with Bob Hope and a few high-risk mischievous adventures too' *Dovegreyreader*

'Sometimes a person's life story will bring you up short and put things in perspective. This is one such book . . . Anne Watt's memoir has so many impressive elements, it's hard to give it the praise it, and she, deserves . . . her memories of that time are heart-rending and inspirational . . . This is a tale of real courage and devotion to other people's children; the word heroine has rarely been used so pertinently' Abigail Kemp, *Manchester Evening News*

'This is a moving, compelling and deeply inspiring book. Anne has the most incredible story to tell about nursing in war zones around the world. It's not a misery memoir but an uplifting story about what ordinary people can achieve. I heard Anne on Radio 4 and was compelled to buy her book. I cannot recommend this enough!' Bobby Jane, 5 stars, amazon review

'Anne tells her story with humour and compassion. An insight into nursing in war zones, and if ever proof were needed that the innocents are always the real victims of wars, then this book provides it in spades . . . she's a total inspiration' June Jones, 5 stars, amazon review

Always the Children

A Nurse's Story of Home and War

ANNE WATTS

SIMON &
SCHUSTER

London · New York · Sydney · Toronto

A CBS COMPANY

First published in Great Britain by Simon & Schuster UK Ltd, 2010
This edition published 2011
A CBS COMPANY

1 3 5 7 9 10 8 6 4 2

Simon & Schuster UK Ltd
1st Floor
222 Gray's Inn Road
London WC1X 8HB

www.simonandschuster.co.uk

Simon & Schuster Australia
Sydney

A CIP catalogue record for this book is available
from the British Library.

ISBN: 978-1-84739-789-8

Typeset by M Rules
Printed in the UK by CPI Cox & Wyman, Reading, Berkshire RG1 8EX

In memory of my beloved mother
Clara Rosetta Watts

Contents

PART THREE: DISPLACEMENT

PART FOUR: MOVING WESTWARDS

PART FIVE: SQUARING THE CIRCLE

Author's Note and Acknowledgements

My decision to take up nursing as a career sprang from a deep need to express love and compassion, inherited I believe from my generous, warm-hearted, socially aware mother. I couldn't have known at the outset that nursing would also fulfil my thirst for travel, inherited from my salty sea captain father, and nurtured by a wonderful, imaginative geography schoolteacher.

The journey, both professional and personal, that I have taken through life has been constantly challenging, often daunting, sometimes frightening, but the rewards have been infinite. My travels, and my nursing in cultures, climates and circumstances so different from my own, have not only fulfilled my desires and ambitions but given me an enormously privileged insight into the human condition.

I've learned that we have the power and capacity to make this world a better place; that walls of suspicion and fear can be replaced by bridges of kindness, care and understanding. All we – and especially those who govern – need to find is the will to change things: the will to banish the neglect of the poor, the abused and the defenceless in our Western society; to rethink the lousy political decision-making that leads to the destruction and cruelty of war and extreme poverty that I've personally witnessed in Southeast Asia, the Middle East and the Sudan.

Irrespective of a difficult, painful childhood, I seem to have been blessed with the temperament of a free spirit. This has propelled me into situations that more conventionally minded people, wiser and more sensible, might have chosen to avoid. It's certainly been a hell of a ride, but I wouldn't have missed a moment of it.

Marriage and children were never my main focus. I've had my share of love, of romance, and some wonderful friendships with men, but my desires and ambitions were never conducive to settling down. As the saying goes, 'She may have been Miss, but she didn't miss much!'

The choices I made proved enriching and life affirming. Life was not all gloom and doom, not even in the worst areas of conflict and suffering, and I will always be grateful for the opportunities I had to help so many children traumatised by wars in which they were the innocent victims.

Over a number of years, many friends and colleagues urged me to write of my experiences but I was a nurse, not a writer. I had many a story to tell, but I preferred to do so verbally, over a good dinner and a couple of glasses of wine with close friends or family.

In the end, it was my sister Joan who gave me the motivation to produce this book by saying, 'Anne, when you die, your stories will die with you. All those children to whom you gave some laughter and hope; the damaged young soldiers whose hands you held; those extraordinary places you went and the unusual situations you got into and the people whose amazing stories you tell . . . surely they deserve to be recorded in the history of those times? All of it will die with you if you don't write it down. Is that what you want?'

No, I didn't. And so I wrote as much of it as there is space for and, in so doing, I've piled up a debt of gratitude to many people.

Blood seeped from beneath the ragged dressing and mingled with the matted strands of the girl's beautiful blue-black hair. The nurse adjusted the stethoscope and strained to hear her heartbeat. All the rest brought in that morning had died, the youngest of them a cherubic three-year-old. Their bodies, covered by the distinctive Montagnard blankets, which would not keep the rats at bay for long, were stacked outside ready for collection by the tribesmen.

Surely they could save one? Just this one . . . In the last few seconds the girl's faltering, fading heartbeat had seemed to pick up, to become a tiny bit stronger, more regular – even insistent – while the team fought to insert IV lines, desperately attempted to get oxygen into her failing lungs, willed her to live. But despite their efforts, her glazed eyes rolled upwards and with one last, deep sigh she slipped away.

There had been too many deaths this week. No more. No more, the nurse prayed and then, startled by the sound through her stethoscope, she cried, 'But I can hear her heartbeat. There's still a heartbeat.'

Her colleagues looked at her, blank and bewildered, and she removed the stethoscope from her ears. But she could still hear the beat, much, much louder. Jesus! It was a chopper.

'Two of you get to the pad. Go!'

The nurses raced to the rear of the hospital where the Huey was dropping into a hover, the skids barely a foot above the ground, the rotor blades spinning madly. The noise was brain-numbing, the downdraught dangerously close to destroying the bamboo and thatch outbuildings.

The pilot fought with the controls, his co-pilot twisted in his armoured seat, looking over his shoulder. Their handsome young faces, seemingly hewn from granite, spoke of their iron determination to bring their mutilated comrades back from the brink of death.

The interior of the helicopter was an abattoir. Bodies and blood. Three of the Montagnard boys came running with cases of Ringer's Lactate solution, as much as could be spared by the hard-pressed bush hospital. Two of the laundry girls brought old sheets, cotton blankets, anything to help mop up the blood shimmering like a scarlet curtain from the sides of the cargo floor. One of the door gunners was slithering in it, trying to get a foothold as he plugged the sucking chest wound of one of the teenage soldiers.

God, please make this insanity stop.

There must have been eight wounded men. It was difficult to tell for sure because two were gone already, looking like puppet soldiers who had lost their strings, their wide-open eyes staring blankly upwards. A lone severed leg lay towards the rear of the Huey.

The nurses passed the life-sustaining litres of Ringer's to the gunners, who applied large pressure dressings to gaping wounds in a sad attempt to keep spilling intestines inside abdominal cavities. These boy soldiers were drowning in their own secretions.

Would these hasty, makeshift measures be enough to keep hearts beating for the twenty-minute flight to the field hospital in Pleiku? The determination on the so-young faces, the gentleness in those hands unused to such work as they tended fallen comrades, was heartbreakingly heroic.

A voice began to pray: 'Our Father, Who art in Heaven, hallowed be Thy name . . .' What everyone wanted, needed and for an instant had, was a determined belief in a higher power, something divine. These boys needed HELP.

Sister Marie Clare removed the rosary from her pocket, kissed it quickly and pressed it into a bloody palm, firmly curling the fingers around it. 'God speed,' she called, as the Huey lifted steeply into the sky and got the hell out of there.

The two nurses, the three Montagnard boys and the two laundry girls, blood-spattered and drained, looked at each other, turned slowly and made their way back to the hospital.

I had worked hard to follow my star, and this was where it had led me.

1

WAR BABY

My father's face turned a deep shade of purple. He slammed his fist down onto the polished breakfast table, sending nervous ripples across the surface of our milky porridge bowls.

'No daughter of mine is going to spend the rest of her life wiping other people's arses. I will not have it. That is my final word.'

I realised then, as I do now, that no father wants to see his daughter work long, hard, unsociable hours for poor wages. What I didn't realise then was that nurses had not only long been forced to tolerate working in an atmosphere of servility to doctors, but were even once upon a time thought of as little more than camp followers and prostitutes: what sort of woman, it was thought, would want to wash the bodies of strange men?

But we were no longer in the Middle Ages and no tantrum or explosion from my father would shift my decision or shake my determination. This was my point of no return, the defining moment when the rite of passage – part golden idyll, part horror story that had been my childhood – was complete.

Hindsight has led me to realise that, one way and another, my life has been shaped and dictated by war.

My father, Arthur Frederick Watts, born in 1902, grew up with his five brothers and sisters in North Walsham in rural Norfolk. He attended Paston village school for boys (still there as Paston College, a sixth-form college), proud to follow in the footsteps of his lifelong hero, Horatio Nelson, who was schooled in the very same classroom between 1768 and 1771. With his admiration for the hero of Trafalgar, it was little surprise that he himself became an officer in the Merchant Navy.

My maternal grandfather, Edgar Douglas, had also been in the Merchant Navy, but later transferred to the coastguard service in Cumbria, where my mother, Clara Rosetta Douglas – called Clare – was born. Nursing was her vocation, as it would be mine; and it was while working at the Liverpool Royal Infirmary, where she trained and where my father was a patient, that she had met him. He had suffered a bad back injury as a result of falling into the hold of his ship, and it was my mother who nursed him through it.

Liverpool was home port to the Cunard White Star shipping line with whom my father sailed, and it was there that I was born. Within months of my birth Liverpool was in flames, blitzed by German bombers, and my mother found herself and her baby evacuated to rural North Wales. And so it was that the events of World War Two presented me with a childhood lived in the serenity, security and beauty of the Welsh countryside; eight happily rough and tumble years until a serpent slowly took over my own Eden.

At first, my mother and I lived on a farm in Corwen. In the brief snapshots of a toddler's memory, I see a winding country lane, a farm gate leading into waving corn, meadows populated by softly lowing cows.

In 1944 we moved to a little village on the edge of Snowdonia called Pentrefelin and into a big, white country house called Plas Gwyn, which had lots of rooms, a lovely big garden and wonderful surroundings.

Pentrefelin nestled between green fields, seemingly pinned to the ground by buttercups, daisies and clover. Narrow lanes edged with hedges of blackthorn, honeysuckle and sweet briar nudged up against woods of larch, sweet chestnut, oak and silver birch, while carpets of bluebells, primroses and wood anemones took shade beneath their ample foliage. I and my brothers and sisters grew up knowing the names of all our native trees, birds and wild flowers, excitedly marking them off in our little *I-Spy* books.

The large white house was surrounded by fertile farmland owned by Lady Olwen Carey-Evans, a daughter of David Lloyd-George, the former British Prime Minister. Lady Olwen's son, Benjamin, was twelve years older than I, and very much the big boy to our childish gang, but he and I were friends. We remained so, and in later years I looked to Benjamin and his family for advice. They knew both my parents and, when I and my sisters needed know more about our past, Lady Olwen was able to share her recollections of my early life and our family with us. She was a source of comfort and strength, and her family still lives in the same beautiful, wisteria-draped house, surrounded by the fields and trees of my childhood and youth.

To the front of our house lay the main road, which carried little traffic in the 1940s other than the local green buses that took people back and forth between Porthmadog and Criccieth. Only 'rich people' had cars, so not many were seen in those parts.

A few hundred yards down the road from our house was what I called our 'magic wood'. There, everything grew in abundance: the best, the bluest and the thickest carpets of bluebells; the prettiest primroses; the most festive holly with the shiniest dark leaves and juiciest red berries. Best of all in the wood, though, were trees you could climb up and find the comfiest branches to sit in when you needed to get away from troubles at home. You could lose yourself in daydreams for hours in those branches.

The little wooden stile led into the fields that took us up 'the hill'. For years we ran up and down its gentle slopes, and in summer we picnicked on top of it, taking the magnificent views of the surrounding mountains for granted. We walked around the hill, shrieking joyously across fields that were home to sheep and dairy cattle who barely raised their eyes from the serious business of chewing the cud – often on our way to get to Black Rock beach, her sparkling waters belying the chill of the Irish Sea. In winter we sledged down the hill's snowy slopes, screaming with the exuberance that only young children have, impervious to cold and possible danger. Near the small, remote parish church of Ynys Cynhauarn was a lake. How often I swam in those waters with Emrys, one of the three brothers who lived next door. You had to wade in slowly, brushing past bulrushes and water lilies, and trying not to scare off the flocks of mallards, moorhens and wild swans, while the sludgy mud squidged between your toes.

We played out all day, then headed for home tired and bedraggled but happy, and only when our stomachs told us it was time.

Didn't all children grow up like this?

2

HUGS AND SHINY
BUTTONS

My father was away at sea, but I remember him coming home at intervals, wearing his smart Merchant Navy officer's uniform with the shiny buttons. There were always plenty of hugs and lots of laughter.

Each time Daddy came home on leave, there was great excitement. He was a handsome, glamorous figure who represented a different, magical and mysterious world. He brought exotic gifts from faraway places: blow pipes from New Guinea, a boomerang from Australia, a silver-grey horse's-tail switch embedded in an ivory handle from India, used to flick away tiresome flies and mosquitoes. My favourites were two large, comfortable rattan lounge chairs he shipped over from Singapore, which had the biggest cushions I had ever seen, covered in fabric that seemed magically smooth to my child's fingers. I loved tracing the outlines of the beautiful turquoise and rose-coloured birds and flowers which decorated them. I would clamber up onto the squishy cushions, haul myself into a sitting position and gaze at my chubby little legs stretched out in front of me, dreaming about the day my feet would touch the floor like a proper grown-up.

My father regaled us with stories of Raffles Hotel and their famously delicious cocktail, the Singapore Sling. I would sit on his knee and soak up his words, uncomprehending but entranced. Then there were the fresh crates of oranges he brought, a rarity during the war, which he generously shared with each family in the village – a huge treat for everyone.

I have a kaleidoscope of memories of those days in wartime North Wales. Some are fleeting; others are etched into my memory bank and have never shifted.

There were the three German prisoners of war who tended our large garden. They arrived each morning in the back of a military truck and were dropped off at the heavy green wooden gates that led up the driveway to our large white house.

At the end of each day, one or other of them would carry me on his shoulders down the path and carefully set me on the gate, placing my tiny feet between the peeling rungs, and swing me back and forth until the truck arrived to whisk them off again until the next day. All the men in the back of the truck were usually singing, their voices raised in harmony in a language I didn't understand, and would wave at me as the truck drove away.

One of the prisoners, Heinz, would sit me on his knee, hold me close to his chest and softly weep while he spoke of his own little girl, just like me, back in Germany. He always called me *'Mein schatzi'*. He smelled of sweat.

Rudi had a shock of strikingly thick blond hair. One day, he gently and painstakingly fixed the broken wing of an injured pigeon, and I stood and watched as he made a special cage for the frightened bird. He put me in charge of the pigeon while he did so. He wrapped the bird in my cardigan, placed the trembling bundle in my arms and entrusted the little creature to me. Imagine that! I felt so proud and responsible, and I've never forgotten that incident. Sometimes I wonder whether the stir-rings of compassion that grew inside me and convinced me to take up nursing didn't start right there.

Long after the Germans had gone, the pigeon, which we named Rudi, lived with us quite tamely as part of the family. He slept in his cage at night, always with the door open, free to come and go as he wished. He flew around during the day, soaring among the surrounding treetops, but whenever I called 'Rudi, Rudi', even though I couldn't see him, he would flutter down and peck gently at my feet. I so loved that bird and was grief-stricken when he eventually died.

The prisoner named Walther always seemed to be hungry, despite – or maybe because of – being quite podgy. I remember Mum smacking me gently on the hand once because I went into the kitchen and pinched a slice of corned beef to take out to him. He just loved the crumbly meat, and never seemed to mind that I dragged it out of the sleeve of my cardigan, or from my bulging ankle sock.

Farm carts pulled by a horse delivered fresh milk in large silver churns – churns of full-fat milk with thick, pale yellow cream on top. Mum would ladle the milk into jugs and put them in the larder, a cool room just off the large country kitchen. Then, later, she skimmed off the cream for baking or to pour over the strawberries she grew in the kitchen garden. I remember watching wide-eyed as she sometimes churned it into butter. Washdays were a huge production, with bright blue powdery stuff tightly contained in twists of cotton and dropped into the white wash bubbling away in a huge pan on the kitchen range. I could never work out how 'Dolly Blue' made white clothes whiter than white, but it did. Washing was laboriously put through a large mangle several times before being hung out on the long clothesline strung between the apple trees.

Somewhere in this potpourri of a child's memory, was my

grandfather, my mother's father. He was the only grandparent left alive by the time I was born. He was lovingly called 'Gogi'. I remember him as a smell. Warmth, love, security and tobacco all live on in the memory of that smell. He wore a Fair Isle knitted waistcoat and smoked a pipe. To this very day I can close my eyes and see the muted colours of that waistcoat. He would cradle me in the crook of his arm and read stories to me, and I treasured a little china dog he gave me. It was white with black and brown patches, and had a chip in one of his ears. Naturally I called him Gogi. Years later, I learned that my grandfather had passed away peacefully shortly after my third birthday.

I also remember the 'Army ducks' and, of course, the Land Girls. The 'ducks' were amphibian vehicles that used to emerge from the sea at Black Rock sands, just up the road. The soldiers on top of these clumsy-looking vehicles wore red berets and waved to us as they moved in convoy down the main road.

The Land Girls were the young women who kept the farms working and productive while the men were away at the war. Land Girls worked very hard, and the local contingent all knew my mother, who seemed to have an open house, a cheery word and a sympathetic ear for everyone. The girls wore khaki shirts, below-knee trousers and knee-high socks with a bottle-green trim. On cooler days they wore a bottle-green sweater. On their heads, or tipped back behind their necks when it was hot, were their distinctive, wide-brimmed 'cowboy' hats.

I began school at the age of four. There were worries that the small village school might have to close due to insufficient children attending, so numbers were inflated by little ones dragooned in to attend. The daily walk to school was a good mile long and meandered through the entire village. We didn't have a car in those early days and I grew to love that walk over the years.

My journey to school began just as the milk churns were being left at our gate. Off down the road we would go in all weathers. At first Mum walked me to school, but after a few months, as more children nearby enrolled, they would call by for me. This was fun, a gaggle of children, the older ones in charge of shepherding us younger ones. Our route took us past a few houses, then down a hill where the road was bordered with the dry stone walls typical of the area. I was too tiny to see over into the fields and had to wait till we got to the bottom of the hill where there was a five-barred gate. Then I could say hello to the few horses and a small pony that lived there. I always spent a few effortful minutes tugging at thick tufts of grass to offer a juicy fistful to the animals while I chatted to them.

Then it was round the bend past Mr Williams' garden. He was a kindly old gentleman who walked with a bad limp. He grew the most amazing flowers, and often gave me a bunch of sweet peas or yellow roses to take for my mother.

Past the Methodist chapel on the left, and onwards past the little war memorial which sat on a grassy hummock in the centre of the village. The last stretch was past the village shop and post office. The village women often stood gossiping in their doorways, usually with a duster in their hand. They wore turbaned scarves tied around their hair and knotted at the front, and pinafore aprons, and often some of them were on their hands and knees polishing their front doorsteps as if their lives depended on it. These women seemed so ancient to us, but in fact they were only in their thirties and forties.

In springtime we loved watching tiny lambs leaping in the fields; in autumn we kicked and waded our giggling way through the crackling mounds of golden russet leaves, but winter was best of all. That was when you could really let loose, skidding on the black ice in the road, seeing who could slide the furthest without falling over; throwing snowballs at each other, building snowmen and generally finding fun stuff to do on the way to and from school.

The village school had only two rooms, one for the youngest children – under eight years old – the other for the rest. Each room had a huge open fireplace where coal burned in the winter and logs crackled in late autumn and spring. Two crates of small, stubby milk bottles were delivered to the school each morning and left in a hearth in front of the roaring fire. At our morning playtime, each of us was given a bottle of warm, curdly milk. It was disgusting, but we all drank it. The teacher also gave us a spoonful of something that was meant to be orange juice, but it was thick and tasted weird. We picked primroses and later bluebells; juicy blackberries offered themselves up to our pudgy fingers from the hedgerows. We ate them till we were almost sick and took the rest home for our mothers to turn into delicious jam or blackberry and apple pie.

Somewhere in these war years, a group of evacuee children came to our village school. Aged about eight, they seemed a motley crew, wearing funny-looking clothes that didn't seem to belong to them. They were from Liverpool, Manchester and Coventry, and they talked funny too. We circled them warily when they first arrived, not quite knowing what to make of these strange new arrivals. The teacher told us to be kind to them. I remember one boy looked very thin and seemed scared of us and used to cry a lot. The girls wore knitted balaclava-type coverings on their heads, with a large button fastening under the chin. I don't remember them being with us for long, but it was exciting having them in the school for a while.

One day, out of nowhere, great excitement suddenly filled the air. My mother, who was listening intently to the radio, had tears in her eyes and ran to tell our neighbours something. Then there seemed to be lots of people running, jumping up and down, laughing – and crying. But I instinctively knew these were happy tears.

And then the magic words: 'Daddy's coming home soon. Daddy will be home soon.'

A short time later, as evening closed in and the skies darkened, we trekked to the top of the local hill where a huge bonfire had been built. I was carried high on the shoulders of a neighbour. His wife and their three young boys were there too, along with most of the villagers. I remember Mum scrabbling around looking for clothes for us to wear. Now I realise she was looking for something in red, white or blue. My father would still have been at sea. History tells me this happened on 8 May 1945 – VE Day.

To my great alarm and confusion I saw, perched on top of the bonfire, one of the pair of beautiful rattan chairs father had brought home from Singapore. Sitting in the chair was a man wearing a peaked cap. It was an effigy but at first I thought he was real. Once the fire was lit and the flames began to lick around the chair, everyone cheered and danced. Slowly the seated figure toppled into the crackling inferno and people cheered more loudly, their ecstatic faces lit by the flames, yet many were tearful. I remember feeling very frightened.

Years later I discovered this was not, after all, my first Guy Fawkes Night as I had always thought. They were burning an effigy of Hitler. The war was over, and I was a month short of my fifth birthday.

3

SHADOWS ACROSS
THE SUN

October 1945. A milestone in my young life was the arrival of baby Susan. A beautiful golden-haired sister for me to play with. I was ecstatic.

Also very much a part of my childhood in those immediate post-war years were the 'tramps'. I wasn't scared of them – even though they were down at heel, needing a shave, and often smelly – because my mother, and our good friends and neighbours Mrs Jones and Mrs Cole, weren't scared of them or suspicious either.

These tramps would knock on the back door and ask if there was any work. Mum never turned them away. She had a kind word for them and would always find something for them to do like mowing the lawn, clearing the drains of leaves or weeding the large garden, anything that might need attention. She paid them with a hot meal, a place to sleep for the night in one of the outbuildings and somewhere to wash. Sometimes she would find an old shirt or a pair of my father's trousers for them. Everyone did this. This was not unusual, just a part of life then.

Much later, I came to understand that these men must have been ex-soldiers, displaced, unemployed and desperately trying to scratch a living.

At last, towards the end of 1946, my father retired from the Navy and came home from the sea for good. He had served on a number of different ships over the years, among them the *Imperator* which later became the *Berengaria*, the *Verbania*, the *Silver Beech*, the *Brittanic* and others. My sisters and I hold his distinguished service records, but he seldom spoke of his part in the war. His obvious distress when the Battle of the Atlantic was mentioned meant it was a closed subject.

My father's homecoming marked the beginning of many other changes to come. As part of their drive to restore war-battered Britain to prosperity, and in the face of ongoing food rationing, the government encouraged returning servicemen to grow their own produce.

Daddy turned his energy and his many skills to the task. He created a kitchen garden at the back of our beautiful property, where there were already several apple trees and a pear tree. There were also some wonderful gnarled old oaks just waiting for little people to climb up into their welcoming branches. He hung a rope swing with a wooden seat from the straight old pine tree at the front of the house. We loved that swing and played on it for hours over several years to come.

At the bottom of the garden, where a small stream ran, Daddy grew beds of watercress. As well as all manner of vegetables, he also planted a wonderful herb garden filled with fresh parsley, thyme, sage, mint, roots of horseradish, rosemary and bay leaf bushes. No space was wasted: we also kept chickens, turkeys, ducks and two pigs.

Daddy, who did his own butchering, built a refrigerated room, an entire room that you could walk into. No one had seen anything like this where we were, and neighbours came to look and marvel. He based it on the coldrooms in ships and stored whole sides of sheep, beef or pork carcasses there.

He knew all the types of birds that appeared in the garden and surrounding woods and taught us to listen for the first sign of spring, the call of the cuckoo. We learned to recognise the beautiful sound made by the song thrush, and in winter we scattered breadcrumbs for the robin redbreasts and bluetits, but chased away the greedy crows.

At the front of the property was a large lawn, bordered by a privet hedge on one side, a bank of old-fashioned tea roses on the other, and a huge rockery which my father filled with heathers, cushions of aubrietia and tufts of mauve sea thrift. He loved his rockery. At the foot of the lawn he planted a flag pole from which fluttered the Union Jack and the Red Ensign – the Red Duster as he called it. He was so proud of his beloved flags. He taught us all how to furl and unfurl them, how to bend them onto the halyards and how to hoist them up and haul them down. Everything had to be shipshape. Each summer, he strung a badminton net across the centre of the lawn, and hammered croquet hoops into the ground and taught us how to play this seemingly sedate but actually quite vicious Victorian game.

By studying cloud formations, he could tell us what the weather was going to be like in the coming few days and weeks and he was seldom wrong. We knew our cirrus from our cumulus and stratus at an early age.

Everyone called my father 'Captain'. That's how he was known, and how he's still remembered. A naval man to his core, he measured time in watches. There was the middle watch and the morning watch, the forenoon and afternoon watches, and the first and second dogwatches to finish the day. Then it was time for bed and, somewhere, eight bells. 'Come on, eight bells, shake a leg,' he'd say.

Ceilings were bulkheads. At mealtimes he would say,

'Give the butter a fair wind, would you, please,' or the pepper, or the milk. He became agitated if anyone spilled salt, immediately pinching it up and throwing it quickly over his left shoulder, loudly castigating the hapless spiller. 'There are people in this world dying for the need of salt. Do not ever, ever waste it.'

We listened to the radio each evening – there was no television until I was about twelve or thirteen – and Daddy would sit me on his knee for *Dick Barton, Special Agent*. When the distinctive and exciting signature tune played, he would jog me up and down, gaining speed till I collapsed into a giggling heap. Another favourite programme was *Journey into Space*, much spookier and very atmospheric, and Daddy always embellished the stories with amazing sound effects and endings of his own. It was all good fun, and brought the day to an exciting end before being tucked up in bed.

In September 1947, Joan was born. Now we were three sisters and I was beside myself with excitement. I remember sitting on the bottom stair while there was lots of rushing up and down to the large front bedroom on the first floor where my mother lay in bed. I don't think I really understood quite what was going on. My father kept running up and down the stairs, perspiring copiously and yelling at everyone to stay calm, and entrusting me to look after two-year-old Susan. It felt just like the time I looked after the pigeon and I took my responsibility very seriously. Our jolly family doctor appeared, tweaking our cheeks painfully as he puffed upstairs. Then came that magical sound of a baby's first cry. My father appeared at the top of the stairs, red-faced and weeping. 'A little girl. Another beautiful little girl,' he said, and knelt down and gave a prayer of thanks. I remember that as though it were yesterday.

These, I think, were the happiest days at Plas Gwyn. My mother rejoiced in having my father home; he took so much pleasure and pride in what he did, and was at his most nurturing of his children. Like my parents, I relished this time.

Gradually, the way things were began to change. There was major change when my parents turned the large house into a hotel. The area around Pentrefelin was ideal summer holiday country: glorious scenery, beautiful beaches, mountains to climb and valleys to ramble through. The nearby rivers and lakes teemed with trout, grayling and salmon – a fisherman's paradise – and it was exciting having different sorts of people coming to stay from cities all over Britain.

Otter hunters came, men who wore strange knee-length trousers called plus-fours. They had shotguns and big, soppy grey and white dogs called otter hounds, who loved to play on the front lawn. Lined up in the hallway were the tallest, greenest Wellington boots I had ever seen. My father explained that these were hip waders. At the end of each day the men would return with the corpses of the otters they'd killed strung on great loops of string. They were hunted for their fur, to make fashionable hats. When one of the men saw how upset I was on seeing the dead animals, he explained that they ate all the fish in the rivers and lakes, and this was why they had to be killed.

But fleeting shadows had begun to pass across the sun of this golden childhood. As the months went by, my mother seemed different, often tired and not always as cheerful as before. One day while we were out shopping she collapsed in the street and an ambulance was called. Someone said in a hushed tone, 'Someone look after the little girl.' That was me, and I was frightened. Mum's face had turned a strange colour and she was trying to tell the ambulance men to bring me with her.

Another time she collapsed during a church service. Again an ambulance arrived and took her away. I remember sitting with the vicar's wife, tears running down my face, while she gave me tea and talked about Sunday school. All I wanted was my mummy.

There were blurry episodes of visits to hospitals, doctors coming to the house, trips to see specialists in Liverpool. There was the shaking of adult heads, and always we children being shushed off upstairs, outside, into the next room; anywhere so long as we were out of the way. Why did adults always think that children needed to be sheltered from the truth? Children can handle the truth. It's the lies that wreak the havoc.

My mother's health continued to worry those around her. It was like when, after a prolonged period of wonderfully sunny days, a few clouds slowly, stealthily begin sliding across the sky. You don't really notice at first, but at some point you become aware of a chill in the air.

And all the while the hotel grew more established and successful and the workload steadily increased. Waitresses and chambermaids were recruited, but it became obvious to my parents that they urgently needed a chef/housekeeper, and one day a fearsome woman arrived, and took over the kitchen.

Edith Agnes Rigby was originally from Liverpool and was a brilliant cook. She could jug a hare, poach a salmon and cater for a wedding like no one we had ever seen. It must have taken a huge weight off my parents' shoulders, but the cook was a domineering, dictatorial woman with a terrible temper. We all kept well away from the kitchen, which – she made clear – was now her domain.

Mrs Rigby had a little boy called Hugh, just two years younger than I. This was a wonderful addition to our family of three girls. We got on famously and so – aside from the worries about my mother, which we were young enough to push to the back of our minds most times – the idyllic childhood was still intact.

We three sisters, plus Hugh and the three brothers next door, formed a little gang. We climbed trees, and spent hours unsuccessfully but enjoyably trying to build a tree house in the old oak at the bottom of the garden. There was lots of falling off the lower branches into the muddy field below. An old bicycle acquired from somewhere provided endless diversion. One of us older ones would pedal hell for leather, while the youngest, usually poor Susan or tiny Joan, was dragged along behind in a home-made wooden cart attached to the bike by a rope. At the mercy of speed and gravity, the cart usually ended up embedded in the privet hedge, its small occupant hurled in all directions, understandably dazed and grazed. Often, the fierce cockerel chased us mercilessly, his neck outstretched and his feathers creating an alarming ruffle of fury. That cockerel could run faster than any of us and scared the fire out of everyone on a regular basis.

Mummy had a wooden tea trolley, a rich dark brown and highly polished, that she was very fond of. Maybe it was an antique, I don't know, but she treasured this trolley and often served afternoon tea to visitors from it. The rubber-cushioned wheels moved smoothly and silently over the geometric Victorian tiling of the long, narrow front hallway, and always took the sharp right turn into the main kitchen easily.

The trolley had three shelves and one day I got Hugh, aged six, to lie down on the centre shelf and Susan, aged three, on the bottom. Joan only escaped being plonked on the top because she was too little. I wheeled them to the front door, turned around and, mustering all the speed I could, charged down the hallway, turning on two wheels into the kitchen, all three of us shrieking in delight. That's when the trolley collapsed, sandwiching Hugh in the middle on top of poor Susan! After extricating them from the remains of the precious tea trolley, I was given a walloping on the behind and sent off to bed with no supper. It was fun though . . .

During late August and early September the local farms began to harvest the golden crops of corn. We watched the combine harvester driving round and round in ever decreasing squares, scything the corn at its base. As a field was slowly but surely shorn of its crop, the older boys, armed with cudgels, closed in menacingly. They were waiting for the terrified rabbits, now huddling further and further into the diminishing camouflage in search of safety, to make their break for freedom. That is where we younger ones came into our own. When the first rabbits bolted, we ran into the older boys, attempting to give the rabbits time to get away. Sometimes it worked, sometimes it didn't, but we never gave up trying to give the shivering bunnies a chance of freedom.

The trouble was, local shopkeepers and hoteliers paid good money for rabbits, hares, pheasants and salmon, and farmers paid for each grey squirrel tail that was presented to them. So, we were up against formidable opponents.

Many of the local boys walked around with small nets in their pockets and a ferret or two tucked down their shirts. I often watched tearfully as they pegged down the nets over the entrances to rabbit burrows. Two holes were left uncovered, one to allow the ferret access, the other where the boys waited for the rabbit to emerge. It never took long. The scream of a rabbit with nowhere to run is bone-chilling, but at least their necks were swiftly and expertly broken. Dozens were caught like this, providing the older boys with a lucrative pastime.

My father was a good customer and I have to admit we all loved rabbit stew.

And so our childhood rambled on.

4

TOPSY-TURVY WORLD

Occasionally at night I could hear voices raised in anger coming from downstairs. I would sit on the top stair, face pressed against the banisters, feeling frightened but not quite sure why. A sense that all was not well continued to build. Imperceptibly at first, unhappiness was present in the house. Life had been blessed until now, but the atmosphere was becoming different.

Despite these dark moments, we gang of seven – Susan, Joan, Hugh, me, and Wynn, Emrys and Donni from next door – continued to play on our beloved swing, hang upside down from the branches of trees, and bail each other out of mischief. The glories of the countryside were ours for the taking. One springtime we watched in astonishment as a sheep gave birth to her lamb on our front lawn. Daddy timed the whole process from the birth right to the moment the baby lamb stood, trembling, without falling over. It took seven minutes.

The village had its own policeman. He knew us all by name, and was seen as a friendly figure of authority that we all trusted. One time, when scrumping red apples from someone's orchard, we saw him coming towards us. The boys quickly and carefully hid theirs under a hedge to be picked up later; we girls tucked ours into our knickers and walked on nonchalantly. PC Plod knew perfectly well we were up to something, but . . .

Another time, standing at the edge of a fast-flowing stream, we were reaching over and helping ourselves to Mr Williams' delicious apples from the heavily laden boughs that hung low over the back fence of his garden. Suddenly Mr Williams came tearing out of his house and charged towards us, brandishing a rifle. We grinned innocently, calmly dropped the apples into the stream at our feet, and tore off across two fields and over a farm gate to where we knew the apples would come bobbing down the stream and out from the culvert that ran beneath the road. We knew exactly the route of the river and waited patiently. This never failed to amuse us, and we thought ourselves incredibly clever.

Back in the busy hotel, Edith Rigby, the scolding cook from Liverpool, would yell at us in a strange nasal twang that even today has the power to raise my anxiety levels. She seemed to get on awfully well with my father, but no one else dared go near her.

We came to know Mrs Rigby's brother Frank and her sister Eileen, who used to visit at Plas Gwyn. We called them Auntie Eileen and Uncle Frank, and they seemed big-hearted, warm and funny – gentle people quite unlike their hateful relative the cook. We liked them, and looked forward to their visits.

One day, Auntie Eileen asked if Susan and I would like to go to Liverpool to stay with them for a holiday. Would we ever! Yes, yes, yes. Although we lived in the most beautiful corner of North Wales, the offer of a holiday in Liverpool was thrilling. Children love anything different from the norm, whatever it is. I was then aged nine, Susan was five (Joan was still only two-and-a-half) and our instant excitement was huge.

Incredibly, try as I might, to this day I have no memory of

my parents at that moment. Where was my mother – or my father – while all this was taking place? What I do know is that the trip had to take place right then and there, which seemed more than a little strange in retrospect but, at the time, with the trusting naivety of children, we simply went along with whatever we were told. Auntie Eileen helped us throw a few things into a bag and off we went, without so much as a backward glance or a second thought.

We arrived at Birkenhead, where Eileen took us to a large, school-like building, where we waited on a bench while she filled in some forms. This certainly wasn't a family house, and it didn't at all seem like a holiday place. Already bewildered, when Eileen hugged us and, weeping, kissed us and left, bewilderment turned to panic, especially when we were taken off to have our hair checked for nits, and our teeth and fingernails inspected before being shown to a bleak dormitory.

We had been abandoned in a home – what, apparently, was called a home for 'troubled' girls – and it was a long, long time before the sun ever came out again.

This had been planned. Clearly, Eileen had been detailed to escort us to this place. Nowadays, I suppose one would say that Susan and I were placed 'in care'. I wonder why they use that particular phrase. No one seems to care now – and no one seemed to care then.

Time passed in a blur of lessons, scrubbing floors with horrible disinfectant, which I can smell as I write, and inspections of beds, which had to be made just so. Mainly I felt confused, frightened and abandoned. The staff was scary: aloof and cold women who ruled with a rod of iron. No good asking them for answers.

Being younger, Susan was in a different section so I didn't see her often, which only added to the feeling of loss and confusion. There was a girl called Ethel Pollard in my class. She had freckles, wore her red hair in a bob with a large ribbon on one side, bit her nails to the quick and swore a lot. I didn't know what swear words were, and I was warned to stay away from her as she was a very bad girl. I liked Ethel Pollard. She had a mind of her own.

The only staff member I can recall was the headmistress, Miss Beard. She was strict but kindly. She wore tweed suits and smelled of lavender.

My tenth birthday was on 8 June 1950. It was on that day, in this strange place where we were 'on holiday', that my mother came to visit. It was her first visit – and her last. She wished me happy birthday, gave me a silk scarf with a pattern of windmills and Dutch boys and girls on it, kissed me and held me very tightly. 'Remember Anne, I love you more than I love life itself.' Strange words for your tenth birthday, but you don't know that at the time, though something resonates in your child's mind.

Mum held me close for a long time, and I could tell she was weeping. It was all very puzzling, and worse, she didn't take me with her when she disappeared from view, her heels clicking on the highly polished wooden floors of the long corridor. She did not look back.

One day, not long afterwards, I was called to Miss Beard's office where I remember waiting on a large chair, my feet unable to reach the shiny floorboards. Sitting there swinging my legs, back and forth, back and forth, the air seemed chill and heavy. Eventually I was summoned.

I walked slowly over to the headmistress's huge desk. She smiled gently and asked me to sit down, then she moved her chair from behind her desk and sat in front of me. I remember thinking that was unusual.

She said softly. 'Anne, your mummy has gone to live with Jesus. She wants you to know that she is happy now, and loves you very much. Do you understand? She has gone to live with Jesus.'

That's when I shut down. Don't show them anything. Numbness took hold.

Miss Beard said, 'Now we have to tell Susan.' Very clearly, I remember saying, 'No. I will tell her.'

And I did. I don't remember how, but somehow I did, and with no comprehension of what had happened to our world, we two little girls clung to each other for dear life.

I remember nothing else until I was called again to Miss Beard's office. Was it days later, or weeks? I don't know, but I do know I felt frightened. This time she said, 'Your father is coming today.'

Relief. Something familiar to hang on to. We needed to see him so badly. He would take us from this place, I thought. But still I was numb.

My father arrived, walking slowly down the long corridor towards us. He wasn't alone. What on earth was Mrs Rigby, the scolding cook, doing there? Daddy looked awkward; his smile was lopsided, unfamiliar.

Miss Beard said, 'Anne. Susan. This is your new mother.'

That was it.

No hugs, no kisses. Not a smile. Don't show them anything. But I did. I wet myself.

One of the staff grabbed my arm roughly, took me away to get cleaned up and changed, told me I should be ashamed of myself. Everything seemed to be happening in slow motion. No, no, no, I wanted to scream. Maybe I did. All these grown-ups should be ashamed of themselves. Two children hurting so badly and no one seeming to see or care.

But Miss Beard did look sad. I do remember that.

We packed our bags, two children in a state of shock, and went back to North Wales.

5

SURVIVAL MODE

At the age of ten I went into survival mode. The death of my mother shook the only world I had known up till then. Our special place was no more.

All traces of my mother were gone. It was as though she had never existed. The few photographs of her had either been removed or, in group photos in the family album, her face had been neatly cut out with what could only have been a razor blade. It was bizarre and upsetting to see her body in a photo, but no face – her dress standing next to her bicycle, or sitting with us on the lawn. On the few occasions I tried to talk to my father about all this, he answered gruffly, telling me not to listen to any lies about us, always to look ahead in life, never back, and that when I was older I would understand. What I understood was that the subject, like so much with Daddy, was a closed book.

'Get on with life, Anne,' he would say.

And so we did. But Mummy lived on in my heart. No one could touch her there.

I was bullied at school, but wasn't quite sure why. There was some sort of scandal, children ran after us chanting, 'Your mother's an old witch. Your mother's an old witch.' They said it in Welsh, but that didn't make it any less hurtful. Thankfully, I was never cowed by bullying. I would turn on these kids, fight back and stick up for myself even though I hurt inside. Soon, the bullying stopped and time bumped along.

My father legally adopted Hugh, which of course was the right thing to do. He was now our brother and that was comforting. It was nice to have a brother and he was nothing like his mother, who was a cold woman and, worse, a needlessly cruel one.

Edith Rigby, now Watts, seemed incapable of having the slightest interest in our wellbeing. I was at least old enough to have the memory of my mother to help me hold myself together during this barren period, but my sisters were so young and vulnerable, particularly Joan. We were all three made to clean our rooms, wash and iron our clothes, and carry out various chores while being berated at every turn.

My stepmother didn't allow me anything of my own. One day, right in front of me, she smashed my treasured china dog, Gogi, and laughed at my distress.

I loved my books and retreated for hours into the pages of my favourites – *Treasure Island*, *Masterman Ready*, *Coral Island*. I read them over and over again, transported to an exotic world where nothing hurt. One day I came home from school to find them lying in a forlorn heap on my bedroom floor, their pages slashed to shreds. The gloating malevolence lasted days, though nothing was said. We are not born with that kind of cruelty, so where does it come from? I've asked that question many times in my life.

In December 1950, just five months after the death of my mother, flaxen-haired Paul was born. It was only much later, when I did the maths, that I realised it was Edith's pregnancy with Paul that had precipitated the disasters which had befallen us. Now we were a family of five healthy, if not all of us happy, children. I remember Hugh and Paul with fondness and love. If things were left to children, life would be much easier.

I can only think that in the Fifties we were all victims of the times, of generations that had been crippled by emotional ignorance. People were only just emerging from the constraints of pre-war values and morals. Love was often undemonstrative, a don't-touch, remote-controlled emotion. Deep down, way below the surface, the stiff upper lip approach to everything prevailed. I knew my father loved us, but he had no idea how to show it. His niece, Angela, very recently (at the age of eighty-four) told me how her mouth was regularly washed out with carbolic soap for saying things considered 'sinfully inappropriate'. In 1938, when she was fourteen, Angela tried to show off her reading skills by repeating the words on a sign: 'Home for Unmarried Mothers'. For uttering such words, her mouth was painfully washed out with the vile soap, and she was sent to bed with no supper.

My father, of course, grew up in that climate of thinking and with hindsight I realise that wartime service had affected him too, changed him. He seemed to have developed a destructive streak and, despite the misery he had caused my mother, the tragedy of her death, and his marriage to Edith, over the years he continued to have affairs with various women, including members of staff at the hotel.

Because I understand all this now, I can forgive him much – but not everything. The consequence of his behaviour was the destruction of our childhood.

The hotel, however, prospered steadily. My stepmother's cookery skills won two further AA stars for the business, and she worked hard. Indeed, the one thing she seemed to enjoy was working with food, but her professional satisfaction did nothing to dampen her fierce temper, which was often exacerbated by crippling bouts of migraine.

Joan and I were singled out for the worst of Edith's tongue lashings and cruelty, but never within the hearing of our father.

It just made me tougher. I would survive this.

I studied hard for my Eleven Plus examination. Daddy taught me logarithms, insisting I would never get on in life if I failed the dreaded Eleven Plus. My stepmother did all she could to make it difficult for me to do my homework or follow my father's strict guidelines. While he preached the importance of hard work and diligence, she undermined this at every turn, telling me that he had never wanted daughters and longed for the day he would have only sons. I wept with nerves and exhaustion over those bloody logarithms, sailed through my exam, and have never come across logarithms since, thanks be to God!

But the Eleven Plus brought one of the happier interludes in my life around this time when Daddy took me to London as a reward for passing my exams. The first stop was Nelson's Column in Trafalgar Square. I remember how emotional Daddy was when speaking of the Admiral with such pride and respect. He then took me to the Cenotaph, where he tipped his trilby and bowed slightly as we approached the beautiful memorial. He became emotional again as he talked of the many young men who had been killed in wars, and how we must never forget them.

From there to Buckingham Palace, by which time I was beginning to wilt with the overload of history lessons, the power of my father's emotion, and the sheer amount of walking we had done. While Daddy was deciding where we should go for a spot of lunch, a man walked out of one of the palace gates. I was immediately fascinated, believing he must be someone very important, to be coming out of the palace.

He had long, wispy white hair straggling over the velvet

collar of his long black coat. I had never seen anyone who looked, or dressed, like this. He appeared to have stepped out of the pages of a Hans Andersen fairy tale and seemed very old to me, but when you are eleven, anyone over the age of twenty-five is ancient.

While I stared, my father stepped forward, politely raised his hat and said, 'Excuse me, but could you be so kind as to give me the correct time please? My watch, I think, is slow.'

The man stopped, looked at Daddy in evident astonishment then smiled. Chucking me gently under the chin, he said, 'For goodness sake, to think you could have asked me any question at all, but you asked me that.' This was not the reaction my father expected, and even I thought it strange. Then, addressing me, he said, 'Do you know, little girl, what my work involves? I am responsible for winding up all the clocks in Buckingham Palace. What do you think of that?'

Throwing back his head he laughed, gave Daddy the time, reassuring him it was as accurate as Greenwich itself, and, after chucking me under the chin again, hunched his shoulders into his warm coat and headed off across the Mall. Of all the wonderful things I saw on that first visit to London, that was the incident that most grabbed my imagination, and how I regretted that I'd been too dumbstruck to ask the wizened clock winder how many clocks there were in Buckingham Palace. Nevertheless, when I got back to Wales that was the one story I couldn't wait to tell my sisters and my school friends.

Another, later, excursion with my father in these post-war years was a visit to Liverpool to visit my birthplace – Huskisson Street, near Sefton Park. Since I had no memories or knowledge of the place, the visit clearly meant more to him than it did to me, and he was visibly upset by the deterioration of what had once been a pleasant area. What he told me had once been handsome Georgian houses looked run down and dejected, with broken windowpanes and paint peeling from dismal front doors.

When I was fifteen, a chance conversation with one of the hotel chambermaids revealed that my mother had hanged herself. I remember forcing myself to remain completely expressionless and continue to make up the bed we were preparing. I must have punched those pillows many, many times. Don't show them anything.

But I could see from the maid's expression that she realised she had told me something I had not already known. From that day forward, I vowed that I would never allow anything to hurt me so deeply again.

I coped by going for long walks to the nearby beaches. I often hitched rides to the foot of Snowdon at weekends, and grew up climbing this beautiful mountain many times. Her moods suited mine. I would return in the early evening, weary but calm. I did this solitary journey dozens of times. The stark beauty of the mountains soothed my grief, and to this day I enjoy long, solitary walks and am completely content with the world when surrounded by nature.

6

LIGHT BULB MOMENTS

The idyllic part of my childhood ended brutally. That's life. We all moved on. When handed lemons, you make the best damned lemonade in town. At difficult times, when tensions at home became unbearable, the cheek-pinching family doctor or the vicar and his wife helped calm my tearful outbursts.

Where was my father in all this? He was there, focused on the business. He never intervened in any difficult situation between his daughters and his wife, seeming to blot out any discord or unhappiness by working hard, tending the garden, and encouraging us in his bluff, undemonstrative, Edwardian way. We loved him, and he loved all of us, but there were no more hugs and kisses; all displays of affection had disappeared with my mother, who was never mentioned again other than in an occasional derogatory aside by the cook, and never, ever within the hearing of my father. Life continued in a constant round of school, doing chores in the hotel when we got home, and concentrating on surviving the scolding and jibes of my stepmother.

Edith, I now realise, must have been a deeply unhappy woman. She acted as though she despised us – particularly Joan and me. Her hostility towards me was so extreme that when my periods started she told me I was a dirty animal, whom no one would ever love. Joan and I strongly resemble our mother, both physically and in character. No doubt that must have been like a red rag to a bull for our stepmother. Tough.

Susan, however, Edith treated a little differently. This was explained many years later when another bombshell was dropped into the vision of our past with the revelation that Susan had been adopted. We learned that a married cousin of my mother's in Norfolk had fallen pregnant during a brief but passionate wartime affair with an American soldier while her husband was away. Desperate, she had contacted her Auntie Clare, my mother, who suggested that when the time was right her niece should come to Wales, where she would deliver the baby. That baby was Susan, whom my parents then adopted. I've always been thankful that they did because Susan has always been, and still is, a wonderful sister, without whom our lives would have been the poorer.

Despite the torrent of abuse at home, I entered my teens attending Ysgol Eifionydd, then the grammar school at Porthmadog. Moving on from the village school was a big step. For a start, there was no more walking to school with the little ones, but a daily bus journey, and in a proper school uniform: a horrible box-pleated gymslip in brown with a gold sash, cream shirt and striped tie. But I felt very grown-up.

We had sixpence a week pocket money, but it had to be earned. Each of us had specific chores, which had to be completed before school. Mine was dusting the banisters and brushing down two flights of stairs. School shoes had to be spotlessly cleaned with Cherry Blossom polish and were inspected before we left the house. Anything not done to satisfaction and we were fined a penny off our pocket money.

Before leaving for school, we stood in a line and were given a large spoonful of a thick, gloopy, disgusting white substance called Scott's Emulsion, followed rapidly by a spoonful of cod liver oil and malt. This brown substance came in a large brown bottle and had the consistency of treacle. We had to take it 'because it's good for you'. Now, over fifty years later, I Googled both mixtures to see exactly what it was we were fed all those years ago. They were potent mixtures containing vitamins A and D, calcium and omega 3 'which promote natural resistance to infections, build strong teeth and bones'. I have to admit that all five of us have certainly enjoyed and maintained good health.

On returning from Sunday school each week, the big treat for healthy, hungry children was afternoon tea around two huge plates of hot toast, spread with dripping freshly scraped from the bottom of the roasting tin. This was truly delicious and there was usually a scuffle for the last slice.

Thanks to two of the teachers at the grammar school of Porthmadog, I got through those important, formative years. Miss Whittaker, the domestic science mistress, was outwardly a tough, scary woman, but with a soft centre – a good ally to have in your corner. She guided me through the confusion of hormonal change and its accompanying teenage angst, a minefield for which there was no help at home. Miss Whittaker gave me the practical help with my periods that was denied me by my stepmother and wrote strong letters to her, trying – unsuccessfully – to break through Edith's wall of barren emotional intransigence.

Then there was Mr Pritchard, the geography master.

We all have moments in our growing up when we begin to sense that there are things in this world which go beyond the simple questionings of childhood. Two occasions when a light bulb switched on inside my head stand out in my mind as defining moments in my life. The first was when I was barely eleven, the second when I was just sixteen.

At school, geography was the one subject I looked forward to with real pleasure and expectancy. Mr Pritchard was one of those teachers who make lessons three-dimensional and fire the imagination of young students. He brought continents, far-away countries and the fascinating peoples who lived in them to vivid life. His lessons added even more colour and another dimension to my father's tales of his travels, which had always captivated me.

My first light bulb moment came during one of those geography lessons, when we were about to start studying Africa. Mr Pritchard announced a guest who, he said, would like to meet us all, and flung out his arm towards the classroom door with a dramatic flourish.

The whole class was stunned into silence as an amazingly tall and stately black woman walked gracefully into the room, dressed in colours I never knew existed. Bright flame-coloured orange was shot through with golden yellow; lime green melted into toffee caramel browns, and somehow there were tinges of violet emerging from the riot of shades. On her head she wore a matching turban with a spectacularly tall, fan-shaped arrangement that stood defiantly to attention above her round, dimpling face. Her smile lit up the room. I had no idea teeth could be that white. On her feet were sandals with a strip between her toes made of snakeskin. A large ring on her finger was carved from ivory.

This was rural North Wales in 1951 and none of us had ever seen such a wonderfully exotic person. All we could do was marvel at the sight of this striking woman. Then she pointed to her homeland on the large wall map of Africa and, as she began to tell us about Nigeria, we hung on her every word. We learned of yams, sweet potato and plantain; of scarlet hibiscus blossoms and purple jacaranda; of neon-yellow trigger fish; of tropical storms that light up the sky and fiery sunsets to take the breath away. She spoke of a landscape and a life, of sights and sounds and tastes so different from our own, we could only listen as if in a dream.

Here was a living representative of the richness which was out there, someone other than my father, who actually came from the colourful world he always spoke of with such passion. I had always dreamed that I would travel, had secretly determined I would be a part of this exciting world I could see so clearly in my imagination; but from that magic day in Mr Pritchard's classroom, an intimation became a certainty.

7

MOVING ON WITH ELVIS

The 1950s was an eventful decade, particularly in the life of a teenager. We were caught up in the nation's grief at the death of King George VI in 1952. Sixteen months later, in June 1953, when I was thirteen, I was swept up in the solemnity, ceremony and celebration of the Coronation of Queen Elizabeth II.

Happily for me and my siblings, by the time of this great event my father had bought a television set. We were awestruck by this new piece of technology, which he said would be the most important tool for education ever invented. It was large, boxy and brown, and Daddy explained with great seriousness what each of its many knobs was for and how we were never, ever, under any circumstances to touch any of them. The first image I saw was of Muffin the Mule and, despite the snowy interference peppering the screen, I was transfixed.

When the Coronation was televised, our neighbours were invited in to watch with us. It was quite an occasion in our young lives, and I still remember how proud and excited we were as we ate our way through piles of sandwiches and cakes while gazing wide-eyed at the flickering black-and-white screen. Daddy, ever emotional, could hardly hide his tears, while the

Union Jack and his beloved Red Duster flew proudly from our flagpole outside. Later we giggled our way into the fancy-dress carnival in the village. I was a gypsy girl, with huge brass rings stitched into the sides of my red headscarf, and thumped on a tambourine in time to the marching; Hugh was a pirate, and Joan and Susan were little Dutch girls. Paul, not yet three, was a bit too young to be anyone but himself.

Then father bought a car, and yes, it was a bottle-green Morris Minor 1000 Traveller. The excitement this generated was immense. I even remember the registration plates – FND 413.

The decade moved on. In 1953, BBC television showed the first *Panorama* documentary and in 1954 launched its first daily TV news programme. Billed as an illustrated summary of the news, it was read by Richard Baker to a visual accompaniment of still photographs and maps; and for escapist entertainment there were exciting and scary plays like *The Quatermass Experiment.* Then, in 1955, ITV arrived, bringing us the first TV commercials, or adverts as we called them then: Friday night is Amami night (shampoo) and fabulous pink Camay (soap) set to awful jingles that annoyingly kept on playing in your head. The game show *What's My Line?* was popular, and *Dixon of Dock Green* was a huge favourite.

One morning in 1955 we were all sitting around the breakfast table with the radio news on. Suddenly Daddy ordered us to hush up and listen: an important announcement was coming from Buckingham Palace. Princess Margaret had been forced to choose between love and duty. She chose duty, thus ending the romance between her and the handsome but previously married and divorced Peter Townsend. My father jumped up saying, 'Good for you, Margaret. I didn't think you had the courage. Good for you.' Then he sat down and blew his nose violently, thinking we wouldn't notice the tears in his eyes.

I couldn't see why this was good news, and went back to my

porridge. The only explanation we got was 'When you are older, you'll understand these things.' A few years later, Prince Charles was rumoured to be interested in a European princess. That time father said, 'That's impossible. She's a Roman Catholic.' There was no explanation for that which made any sense either. Growing up and falling in love was sounding like a pretty complicated business to me.

As I did my studying in 1956 I would have been listening to Elvis singing 'Heartbreak Hotel' and 'Don't Be Cruel', both of which must have had a certain resonance for me! I loved everything by The Platters; 'My Prayer' sent me into teenage ecstasies, as did the Four Aces singing 'Love Is a Many-Splendoured Thing'. Guy Mitchell was 'Singing the Blues' – well, weren't we all! 'Sixteen Tons' by Tennessee Ernie Ford was a winner and, when feeling a little melancholy, Roger Williams' 'Autumn Leaves' always sorted me out. Music from our teenage years is evocative in the same way certain smells are. They immediately take you right back . . .

And then there was 'Rock Around the Clock'. There was no way you could ignore Bill Haley and the Comets, and that really did worry parents in 1956. I was only allowed out once a week, to attend the village old time dancing club where I certainly learned to waltz, tango and foxtrot 'properly', with a man holding you firmly and leading you. It was only much later, when I hit the student scene in Manchester, that you twisted like crazy but barely touched your partner.

At school I enjoyed badminton and played a good game so, at sixteen, Daddy finally allowed me to join the local sports club. Using badminton night as the excuse, I hatched a plan to see the movie *Rock Around the Clock* with a couple of friends from school. No self-respecting teenager could afford to miss it, but parents locked up their daughters when it was advertised at the local 'flea pit'. There were reports in the press of teenage rioting in the USA wherever this film was shown. Seats, it was said, were ripped up in theatres, and wildly dancing kids spilled into the aisles. Rock and Roll was sexy, loud and anarchic, and spoke to teenagers like nothing had before.

Excitedly and with some subterfuge, we climbed the steps of the Coliseum in Porthmadog, paid for our tickets and went into the small cinema where, it seemed, all our classmates were too. However, I was the only one dressed for badminton! Members of the local constabulary had been drawn in from several outlying areas to deal with possible trouble. That meant six in total, including our own village copper. I shrank into the seat, but he saw me. 'Anne Watts, does your father know you are here?' but he smiled and left me alone. The six plods walked slowly up and down the aisles, their eyes scanning the audience carefully all through the movie but, apart from some energetic toe tapping and a bit of hand clapping, we were not the rioting type.

And so I moved through my adolescent years. There were the usual teenage hormones and mood swings to cope with: I even, for heaven's sake, found myself blushing when boys I'd grown up with flicked spit balls at me in class! Much harder was the struggle to ignore the daily barrage of abuse from Edith at home while trying to keep up at school, as well as having to learn the many practical skills required to run a busy family-owned hotel.

Along with my sisters and brothers, I became adept at dismantling bunk beds, putting up double beds, lugging mattresses from one room to another. This was a job usually done on Saturdays, which were always hell. In the Fifties, guests booked their 'bucket and spade' holiday fortnight a year in advance, and regulars often requested the same rooms. And always the holiday week ran from Saturday to Saturday. Sometimes there was a wedding reception thrown in, just to keep us on our toes. My father seemed to thrive on pressure, but it made me a bag of nerves. I hated it.

At school we learned cooking, home economics and sewing to O-level standard. At home we were all proficient at washing dishes, making beds, waiting on tables and generally able to deal with all sorts of people. Plucking and gutting chickens and ducks became second nature; I could skin a rabbit or scale and clean a salmon without turning a hair. I was less adept at cooking, though I learned a lot from watching my stepmother; ill-tempered and vindictive though she was, there was no denying that she was brilliant around food. Occasionally, her mood softened and she would take time to describe a favourite recipe. Surprisingly, given her narrow outlook and sour demeanour, she was a very well-read woman and an armchair traveller, gleaning knowledge from the many books she loved to read. In one of her more human moments she told me her dream was to one day visit Tashkent in the USSR.

Lunchtime desserts in the hotel were usually queen of puddings, jam roly-poly and custard, treacle tart with its distinctive latticework of pastry strips, and blackberry and apple pie, which was a favourite. We gathered juicy blackberries on our way home from school or church; apples came from our own trees. Evening desserts, however, were a much grander affair. A special trolley was wheeled out with great solemnity, displaying an elegant charlotte russe; a stately pavlova filled with cream and raspberries; yummy Viennese Hazelnut gateau; a traditional trifle, or fluffy orange soufflé. There was always a good choice for guests.

One of the waitresses was a very efficient German lady called Hilda. Everything she did was carried out quickly, efficiently and with good humour. Hilda was tall and thin with a haggard, lined face, but we all loved her. She doted on me, and I remember feeling uncomfortable at the intensity of the hugs and kisses she rained down on me, particularly at Christmas or birthdays. One day she explained why she was like this.

During her days in Berlin, she was happily married and

gave birth to a son. He was born on 8 June 1940 – exactly the day I was born in Liverpool. Some time in 1943, while running to an air-raid shelter clutching the hand of her toddler son, they became separated in the panic and crush of people. She never, ever found him. Her husband did not survive the war, and eventually Hilda left for Wales, where she had a distant relative. Over the years she spent whatever she could on advertising in German newspapers and such like, seeking information on her lost child, never giving up hope that he was alive somewhere. She measured his progress through mine.

The cruelties of war take many forms, not always the most obvious, as I was to learn.

My father, while certainly something of a mess emotionally, was a fair and generous man in many respects. One day, I heard raised voices coming from the reception area. It was Daddy speaking with one of the guests. The man, a retired colonel who had stayed at the hotel before with his wife and four children, was complaining that Hilda had been the waitress on duty on this, the first day of his holiday. 'I will not have my family served food by a Jerry,' were his angry words. 'Either she goes, or we go.' Daddy politely showed him the door, and would not take a penny from him.

I always admired him tremendously for that.

8

FIRST KISS

With my dreams of travel firmly rooted after my first light bulb moment, aged eleven, in Mr Pritchard's geography class, my second revelation came when I was sixteen and attempting to study for O levels. Like most teenagers, I found it almost impossible to crack the books unless the radio was on. One day, while twiddling the dials to find some music, through the static I accidentally found Radio Free Europe. I was riveted by what I was hearing until my father burst into the breakfast room. 'Turn that damn noise off. If you paid as much attention to your studies as you do to this rubbish, you might get somewhere in life,' and with that he switched off the radio.

I asked him quietly why people in Hungary were begging for help, and why they were being shot in the streets of Budapest by Russian soldiers. He looked at me intently for a moment, then turned the radio back on and sat down, listening with me. We could clearly hear shots being fired and voices begging for help to be sent. 'They are killing us. Help us, help us.' Then silence.

Why were we not going out there to help? I asked my father what was going on. He looked sad. 'When you're older you will come to understand a little of how this world works. It's not fair or kind to everyone. You'll learn this.' He turned the volume down but left the radio on, patted my arm and told me to concentrate on my studies as he left the room.

So: there were still terrible events going on in the world. They were not over after World War Two, as we had believed, or the end, in 1954, of the rationing – food, clothes, petrol – that I'd grown up with since earliest childhood. There was more. If we truly were meant to be one family, looking out for each other, how come young men and women could be heard begging for help – heard by a young schoolgirl thousands of miles away who, in that moment, felt the first stirrings of discomfort? Why could we not help these people? In that second light bulb moment I knew that, whatever I did in life, I would in some way try to help others less fortunate than myself. I couldn't just sit there listening to such naked need and ignore it.

The Hungarian Uprising, which began with peaceful student demonstrations against the Soviet Occupation and their interpretation of Communism, culminated in three thousand deaths. Twelve thousand dissidents were arrested and imprisoned, almost five hundred were executed, and two hundred thousand escaped to the West.

People were hurting in this world in so many different ways and I felt a burning determination to help – as I so wished I could have helped my mother in her pain and grief. I knew then with absolute conviction that, like my mother, I would become a nurse. It was time to get serious about my studies.

1956 was turning out to be quite some year. My determination to take up nursing as soon as I had passed my O levels meant I had to really knuckle down to studying for the exams.

Meanwhile, there were some glamorous distractions from all these serious issues. The gorgeous ice-blonde movie star, Grace Kelly, married Prince Rainier of Monaco in a real fairy-tale-come-true wedding. We schoolgirls were obsessed with ideas of romance – Princess Grace's and our own – and when my father actually gave me permission to go to the New Year Ball held each year by the local old-time dancing club, I was beside myself with excitement.

Peter, the handsome seventeen-year-old son of a local police officer had asked if he could take me to the ball. Once the huge decision to let me go was finally made at the summit meeting deemed necessary to discuss the matter, the wheels were set in motion to choose a dress. To my absolute astonishment, my usually hostile stepmother enjoyed choosing a dress for me at Bonne Marché in Liverpool, where we went annually to get kitted out with school uniforms and 'sensible' winter coats. On this occasion, standing awkwardly in front of the store's changing-room mirror in a strapless creation into which I'd been thrust by Edith and a saleswoman, I seemed to mutate from gawky, blushing schoolgirl to promising young womanhood.

The dress was a multi-layered froth of blue and grey organza with hints of large blue flowers and green leaves beneath the filmy top layer. I had to admit it was pretty, but I was terrified to raise my arms because I felt sure the bodice was going to fall down. But Peter was tall, and I'd *have* to raise those arms if we were going to get any dancing done! Of course my fears were needless.

The panic of getting ready was a new experience for me, but was the rite of passage that every woman will recognise. A pale green pair of soft leather kitten-heeled shoes finished off the outfit, but my stepmother made the mistake (her only one on this occasion, to be quite fair) of deciding that this was the evening I should wear my first pair of stockings. I practised by walking around wearing my new suspender belt all day, hitched front and back to the stocking tops. It felt terrible. When I sat down, one of the suspenders snapped open. I thought I'd done myself, and anyone within a range of a few feet, a serious injury, the ricochet was so sharp. How on earth was I going to cope?

But there were more important things to worry about. How was I going to keep the blasted bodice up? My breasts were OK, but they weren't as full as the dress suggested. I experimented with various handkerchiefs and borrowed some from my sister. Six were too many, four not quite enough. Then I remembered the roll of cotton wool in the first-aid kit in the kitchen. Four hankies and some cotton wool, a minor adjustment here and there, and it didn't look half bad – even a hint of cleavage if you didn't look too closely and used your imagination. Hair done, new shoes more or less firmly on over the silky stockings, but I knew I'd soon kick them off anyway; I always did when I danced. The *pièce de résistance* was a splash or three of Evening in Paris perfume, smuggled in to me by Mrs Jones from next door, a loyal friend to my late mother and always a staunch ally to me.

Peter arrived, looking so very handsome in his borrowed evening suit with maroon satin cummerbund. I didn't see his embarrassment at the too-long sleeves, or the trouser legs hastily tacked up two inches by his mum; well, you don't, do you, when caught up in the agonising ecstasy of your first grown-up date? Peter spent the requisite polite length of time speaking with my father in the lounge, man to man stuff. Then I made my entrance, trying to breathe in more than I breathed out in an effort to keep my breasts in just the right place for the fit of the bodice.

I was rewarded for this supreme effort by the appreciative look on my escort's face, and the apoplectic look on my father's! Good. I'd got it right.

We left in the chauffeur-driven car hired by Peter's father and purred off into a magical evening. We won a spot prize, a bottle of wine, which we were too young to be trusted with – so it was a box of Black Magic chocolates we waltzed away with instead. My suspender belt only pinged twice, no one was permanently maimed – and I was given my first, dreamy, grown-up kiss.

Perry Como, Pat Boone and Fats Domino sang me through 1957; and the Hit Parade was essential to every teenager's life. I wept through films like *An Affair to Remember* with Deborah Kerr and Cary Grant; *Bridge on the River Kwai* left us all whistling to 'Colonel Bogey' and the gorgeous Harry Belafonte sang 'The Banana Boat Song' over and over, but never too many times for me. Knock-knock jokes drove everyone mad, and I had my tonsils removed.

O levels came and went. My seven passes allowed me the entry I needed for nurse training.

9

FOLLOW A STAR

There was only one obstacle to my ambition: my father flatly refused to sign the papers consenting to my enrolment for the four-year training course in nursing at the prestigious Manchester Royal Infirmary. But I was not going to budge. My decision was a natural progression of what I felt at a deep level: my feeling of connection with the world; my natural instinct to express love and compassion.

If my father wanted to lock horns on this one . . . well, that was easily fixed.

I borrowed money from Mrs Jones next door, wrote Daddy a letter, and took myself off over the border to stay with a trusted uncle and his family in Norwich. The stand-off between father and daughter lasted three months.

Eventually he relented and signed his consent, declaring theatrically, but not without a characteristic tear in his eye which I pretended not to notice, 'If you want to throw your life away, on your own head be it.'

I put in my application and was invited to attend for interview in Manchester in early February of 1958. I travelled to Manchester by train, accompanied by my father who had booked us into a small hotel for two nights – the first time in my life I stayed in a hotel outside of the one that was our home, and it felt quite strange being a guest. I was extremely nervous about my interview, anxious to make a good impression, and apprehensive about the possibility of not being accepted on the course. My state of mind wasn't helped by the clothes that Edith and Daddy had insisted I wear – a suit that I considered hideous, with an even more hideous hat on my head – but at least by then I was used to stockings and adept at ensuring the seams were straight!

However, once settled in, my anxieties became secondary in the face of the tragedy that shook the city. By a ghastly coincidence, my brief stay coincided with the Munich air disaster, the crash which struck the plane carrying the Manchester United football team home from Belgrade via a refuelling stop at Munich. Twenty-three of the forty-four passengers died, among them eight of the players. Newspaper vendors were visibly shocked and upset as they shouted the headlines to the stunned Mancunians, who wept openly in the streets. Miraculously, Sir Matt Busby survived, as did nine of the 'Busby Babes', including Bobby Charlton, but the impact of this tragedy, the witnessing of an entire city in shock, both took the edge off my nervousness and came to overshadow my memory of my interview.

To me, on this first visit to the Manchester Royal Infirmary, the hospital seemed like a city within a city, a world of its own. The long, draughty, open corridors were teeming with what felt like regiments of people – patients and visitors as well as staff – hurrying about their business. Senior consultants, followed by packs of what were obviously medical students, senior nursing sisters, junior nurses wheeling trolleys of medical equipment, porters pushing patients in wheelchairs. This was the world I was hoping to enter.

The nurses all looked so competent and confident, and so

smart in their attractive, pale green cotton uniforms with starched bibbed aprons crossed over at the back and secured with tiny buttons. As I was to learn, first-year student nurses had a single stripe of white tape displayed on the right-arm short sleeve of their dresses; second years wore two stripes and third years three. On obtaining your SRN (state-registered nurse) certificate at the end of three years, all stripes disappeared and you gained a dark green belt with the MRI badge on the buckle.

But what was really special was gaining your 'strings'. This meant you had successfully survived four stiff years of intensive training and had successfully graduated from this top-class university teaching hospital. 'Strings' were heavily starched tapes tied at the top of your head and secured with clips, but hidden by the starched cap placed on top. The carefully prepared, regulation-size frilly bow was worn beneath the chin.

On the day of my interview, my father and I made our way through the hospital across to the School of Nursing, a forbidding, grey stone edifice set apart from the main building. With classrooms filled with rows of dark wooden desks and chairs, it seemed uncomfortably like the school I had recently left – except that the walls were adorned not with maps, photographs and schoolchildren's artworks, but with charts and diagrams revealing the intricacies of human anatomy. And that wasn't all: learning tools included a generous display of human skulls and complete skeletons.

The senior tutor who conducted the interview looked like she had stepped straight out of a Victorian tale. Her unyielding bonnet was perched on her head, stiffly starched cotton strings met beneath her chin in a prim bow, and her dark hair was pulled back into a tight bun. With her thin, pursed lips, she was an austere figure, and I did wonder if she had ever known the thrill of a kiss. My father, however, who paid particular attention to the rules and regulations of the nurses' residence where I would live if I was accepted as a student, was very impressed with this woman. She assured him that curfews (ten p.m.) and late passes (one a month – in by eleven p.m.) were strictly enforced; visitors were carefully vetted, security was tight, and 'Sister Sporne's girls' were quite safe. It was only once I was in residence that I learned it was known as the 'Virgin's Retreat'!

We travelled back home on the steam train, the clickety-clack, clickety-clack of wheels on the track lulling me into a reverie about my future in which I relived my impressions of the hospital and re-ran the interview, wondering whether being a part of those hallowed halls would ever become a reality.

In due course, the letter I had been waiting for arrived. I had been accepted by the nursing school and would start my training on 6 October 1958.

The first six months of training passed in something of a blur. There were twenty-nine of us at the outset, sorting our friendships and learning the ropes, not to mention the stringent rules that governed our lives. I had entered a new world and a strange routine, which took some settling into. Fortunately, I was no stranger to hard work – and being a junior trainee nurse is as hard as it gets.

Initially, our lives were dominated by the classroom. There were interminable lectures and hours of studying for weekly written tests in anatomy, physiology and other subjects that needed book-learning; we were instructed in professional behaviour and hospital etiquette, and were schooled in the terminology of nursing. On the practical side we were taught how to set up instrument trolleys for various procedures, how to give blanket baths, take pulses, temperatures and blood pressure, deal with bedpans and urinals, and a dozen and one other vital skills.

Discipline was rigidly enforced and some of the girls threw in the towel before the first six months was up. Admittedly, at that early stage we were the lowest of the low in the hospital hierarchy and there were times when I, too, felt I just wanted to leave. But pride kept me going. I had fought so hard for this opportunity and I just had to stick it out and, besides, it wasn't all unrelieved drudgery and gloom: we at the nurses' residence were given lots of free tickets to various shows and concerts and films, and we could go to the Saturday night dances at the university's student union if we wanted to. And when we had some time off, a group of us would sit for hours in a coffee bar with orange walls called The Mogambo, talk about life and think we were pretty cool!

10

MISS HUGHES

At the end of six months we were considered ready to be turned loose on the wards.

My first ward assignment was to a female surgical unit. I was eighteen and, although I looked outwardly competent and unflappable in my uniform (we all did), in truth my heartbeat was in overdrive with the anxiety of the first few weeks. As the junior on the ward, I was naturally the one who got stuck with all the messy jobs, but like any apprenticeship that was the way to learn. I seemed to spend most of my time in the dreaded sluice room, scrubbing and sterilising bedpans and emptying trays full of dirty swabs that had been used to clean the mouths of seriously ill patients.

Many of the women had cancers, or tumours, as they were called then. People found it very difficult to say the word 'cancer', which carried such negative connotations. Women were not yet educated to recognise early symptoms and were reluctant to see a doctor, often because they were shy, so in those days early detection was unusual. As a result, it was not unusual to see very gross breast cancers that a woman had hidden from everyone, even herself. The smell of cancer is one you never forget but, thankfully, in the developed world today such advanced tumours are generally a thing of the past.

The first of the many significant and valuable lessons I learned over the years was during that surgical unit experience.

All the wards then were the long Nightingale wards of thirty beds: fifteen each side, with two side wards reserved for the very ill or dying. The sicker you were, the higher up the ward you were placed. To be moved into a single side ward near Sister's office was not good.

One afternoon, the unit was terribly busy and – very unusually – Sister actually came into the sluice room and said, 'Nurse Watts, I need you to relieve Staff Nurse Wilson in side ward two. She has not had any lunch yet.' This was a big step up in responsibility. I shot up the ward, cheeks flushed from the hot steam of the bedpan washer, and rather nervously went into side ward two. The staff nurse barely glanced at me as she pushed past, removing the mask she was wearing and tossing it into the bin. 'Thank God you're here,' she said. 'I'm starving, and I've got to get out of this stink. I'll be back in forty-five minutes.'

'Can you tell me about the patient, please?'

'Read her notes,' was the curt response and off she went, leaving me feeling somewhat apprehensive and nervous.

I went over to the bed where the seriously ill woman lay. She was barely a bump under the bedclothes, but her eyes were wide open. 'Good afternoon, Miss Hughes. I'm Nurse Watts and I'm here till your nurse returns from lunch.' The woman's face looked like a skull with paper-thin, yellowed skin stretched tautly over it, but her eyes were extraordinarily bright and piercing. The small room smelled of faeces. I moved to the side of the bed behind her and peeked under the sheet. The large pad beneath her buttocks was clean and dry.

I sat close to her so that she could see me, and reached for her notes. The lady was forty-eight. Aside from her alert eyes she looked double that age. She was a pharmacist by profession. I was so impressed. A lady pharmacist? Good for her, she must be very clever. As I sat reading, her arm slowly emerged from under the sheet. Her nails were too long, like talons. She gripped my arm with her bony fingers. 'Please. The pain is too much. I need something.' Then she vomited.

I knew then where the smell was coming from. The fluid she brought up was faecal – and she was fully aware of what was happening to her. I was horrified. I saw she was watching me but I was not at all sure what to do. I put some rubber gloves on, reached for her mouth tray, and gently began swabbing her mouth and tongue with the pink Glycerine and Thymol swabs; then I changed her pillow and placed a clean pad beneath her cheek and chin. I began talking to her, asking her about her pharmacy career, telling her I had never met a female pharmacist before. I expect I was babbling, but I knew I needed to take her thoughts away from where she was. At the same time I was witnessing something I could never have imagined in my worst nightmares. Yet I felt very close to her and instinctively knew not to wear a mask to hide my face. Multiple tumours were destroying her bowel and stomach and she knew it.

But why did the senior staff nurse I was relieving not understand this? She was so much more experienced than I. Was it possible there could be bad nurses? Uncaring nurses? Despite looking so competent, were they really that cold and clinical? Where was the 'respect and dignity to be upheld at all times for the patient' which I had just learned in the classroom? It had never occurred to me that there might be nurses unable to respond to that most basic of human needs: the need to be cared for. I knew this woman, Miss Hughes, was not cared for. She veered between cajoling, wheedling, demanding and hissing at me: 'Please. Needle. The pain is too much. Call yourself a nurse? You will never be a nurse. Get my needle.'

When a junior doctor popped his head around the door, I

quietly asked him to look at the orders for Miss Hughes' pain relief. The four-hourly intramuscular Omnopon was relieving her agony for maybe twenty minutes, before the next wave of agony rolled in. For three hours and forty minutes she had to tough it out till the next dose was due.

The doctor was sympathetic and took the chart off to the office. I heard raised voices, and a few minutes later a senior registrar came in. He immediately pressed a mask to his face before glancing briefly at Miss Hughes, then said to me, 'Why are you in here, you are too junior for this.' And he left the room.

I followed him out into the corridor. 'She surely can't be allowed to suffer like this. Can you not change the order?' He explained, as though talking to a small child, that it was too dangerous to increase the dosage. 'Do you want her to become addicted?' I had to screw up every ounce of courage to say, 'I want her to stop knowing that she is vomiting faeces.'

He just turned away and, addressing my superior, said, 'Sister. Explain to your junior, will you.' And off he strode.

I spent the next thirty minutes cleaning Miss Hughes' mouth and cutting her fingernails. Pushed carelessly to the back of her bedside locker, I found the remnants of her life: a half-full pot of Pond's cream, her hairbrush and a scent bottle. I massaged her hands with the Pond's cream; I cleaned up her hairbrush and tidied her hair as best I could; then I sprayed a little scent – Californian Poppy – on her wrists, behind her ears, along her breast bone and a little on her pillow. The irony of that was not lost on me. Omnopon is a derivative of opium, extracted from poppies. The narcotic properties of morphine and codeine were used for severe, intractable pain. In the days when I trained it was given sparingly because of the fear of addiction, but morphine addiction was the very least of Miss Hughes' problems. It apparently was beyond even a senior doctor to breach an order and either increase the dosage or shorten the period between doses. That was just the way it was.

I went through every emotion on the scale from compassion through fury to impotence and grief. I began doubting my ability to confront situations such as this, but finally accepted that I could only do what I could do. Staff Nurse Wilson strolled in from her break and, virtually ignoring me, headed for the box of masks, hastily tied one over her nose and mouth and said, 'You can go.' I went over to Miss Hughes and told her I was leaving, that her nurse was back from lunch. The look in her eyes followed me out of the door, down the corridor and into the sluice room, where I belonged.

Miss Hughes died two days later. Hers was not a good death. But she was such a pivotal part of my development; of my understanding of the pure essence of what nursing is, can be and must be. I wish I could have told her that, but somehow I think she knew

I had walked into that room a naive and trusting young girl. I left it older and wiser.

11

HELLO, WORLD

The musical *South Pacific* opened at the Odeon, with Rossano Brazzi and Mitzi Gaynor, and we all rushed off to see it at the first possible moment. That film was still on at the same cinema four years later, with coachloads of people being bussed in regularly from all over Lancashire to see it. Even now I associate that film with my entire training period in Manchester.

Each Christmas the hospital held a formal ball. At the end of my second year, I was lucky enough to be able to go. A friend had had an almighty falling out with her fiancé, so at the last minute she not only gave me their tickets but lent me her beautiful blue satin evening gown. I took Ian, my rather over-earnest boyfriend of the moment, who was a fourth-year medical student and a nice guy, even if he was a bit of a drag. One of the live bands playing that night was Kenny Ball and his Jazzmen. They were magnificent and brought the house down, and I became a huge and lifelong jazz fan that night. Their 'Midnight in Moscow' is still a big favourite of mine.

Training followed a set pattern: secondment to a specialisation, followed by a three-month stint of classroom study before the next specialisation. In this way, I was assigned variously to medicine, paediatrics, orthopaedics, gynaecology, surgery, casualty and neurosurgical nursing. I loved them all. Yet throughout four intense, and intensive, years, the subject of death was avoided. There was no instruction or help at all on how to answer the questions of a dying patient; or how to sort out your own feelings about painful and often shocking situations. Children under the age of twelve were not allowed to visit, not even if the patient was their parent or sibling.

In the gynaecological theatre, at the end of a morning's 'uterine evacuations, I would stand in the sluice room looking at the large glass suction bottle that held the remains of the twelve-week-old foetuses. Six little ribcages, twelve arms and legs, and six baby skulls. My job was to place the remains into special bags ready for incineration. Although the Abortion Act did not come in to effect until 1967, terminations were carried out when a woman's health was endangered by carying to full term.

Nowadays there's hot debate about the right of a woman to choose. I certainly agree with the pro-choice view, but it is sad to note that the number of abortions carried out in the United Kingdom has grown to shocking proportions and continues to rise. It's dispiriting, too, that young women having unwanted pregnancies now include the young teens, and abortions are treated pretty casually in popular TV soaps. As I join in these discussions, the vision of those jars comes back to haunt me.

The hardest secondment was probably the neurology unit. Sister Ruth, who ran the unit, was loved and respected by everyone, and I learned so much from her. She was the epitome of what a nurse should be and very different from the stiff, starchy dragons who ran much of the hospital. She was gentle, kind and strong, with an air of calm serenity. Nothing was ever too much trouble for Sister Ruth. She was first to arrive and last to leave each day, and she always went the extra mile both for patients and for student nurses. The work on that unit was heavy, but she made it bearable. It was the only clinical area where twelve-hour shifts were worked – seven a.m. to seven p.m., or, on the dreaded 'graveyard' shift, from seven in the evening until seven the next morning.

The night-shift rota ran for fourteen nights, back to back, and we did it without question. The reward was six whole days off at the end, almost a full week of freedom, but it was a killer rotation. I look back and wonder how we ever got through it. The worst part was when you hit the sixth or seventh night and knew that another seven nights stretched ahead interminably. That was when you hit the wall of pain and felt like giving up. We all used to get a bit punch-drunk, I think. Sometimes, despite being dog-tired, instead of going to bed we would go into Kendal Milne – *the* Manchester department store in those days – where we would try on beautiful hats until we got thrown out. Why we thought that was funny beats me, but the week off was great.

It was during those leave times when I went home that I became aware of how very different my world had become from that of my old school friends who had remained in North Wales. They seemed so young to me, and it was with some sadness that I realised I was moving on, ever further away from my childhood and youth, and these visits became increasingly less frequent. Instead, I often went climbing and rambling in the Lake District and the Yorkshire Dales, where I marvelled at the wild beauty of our country. And I learned to ski in Scotland. Four of us went to Grantown-on-Spey at a time when the Scottish Tourist Board was widely promoting the fledgling ski industry, and special travel and hotel rates were offered to impoverished students. A group of us spent two weeks there and loved every minute of it, from the early morning snow ploughs clearing our way to the ski slopes, through our lessons with the Scots, Norwegian and Austrian instructors, to our carefree evenings in the local hostelry.

*

Three years of backbreaking hard work and study culminated in the state-registration exams. To my huge relief, I passed the exams and was now well on my way to being a fully qualified nurse. Only one more year of training awaited me, to be spent working in a clinical area of my own choice. I decided to go to the Sick Infants Unit at St Mary's Hospital for Women, part of our hospital group, a facility which housed sixteen cribs occupied by premature babies, or babies suffering with cardiac anomalies such as Fallot's tetralogy – blue baby syndrome – where septal defects interfere with blood flow.

One morning, we were told that the babies were to be transferred to other hospitals and the unit was to be prepared for the arrival of new admissions for a research study.

It was October 1961 and I was about to meet my first thalidomide babies.

At the time, little was known about thalidomide, and I still remember how shocked I was to see the unit filling up over several days with babies born either without limbs at all, or with stunted, flipper-like limbs. Many of these tiny creatures were otherwise perfectly healthy and strong; they cried lustily, fed well and thrived. Others, however, had multiple, irreversible deficiencies of heart and brain, leading to death within a few hours or days.

My shock was also tinged with alarm. I was planning to study midwifery once I had completed my general training and was fearful of what was happening out there to cause such devastation in innocent babies. I tried to imagine how you could possibly find the words to tell an excited young mother that her newborn baby was seriously deformed or liable to die. Gradually more information came to light, and eventually it was confirmed that the cause of what we were dealing with was the drug thalidomide, which had been prescribed for nausea in pregnancy.

The first few cases were born in 1959, but numbers peaked

between summer and December of 1961, when the NHS officially stopped prescribing thalidomide during pregnancy. I was witnessing the high rate of birth defects at its very peak. Though accurate statistics are difficult to obtain, it is thought by the Thalidomide Trust in Cambridgeshire that approximately two thousand babies were born in the United Kingdom, of whom five hundred and four have survived into the twenty-first century, many having lived happy and fulfilled lives.

The staff in the Infants Unit – from consultant specialists to their junior doctors and from senior sisters to junior nurses; from the almoner there to support parents to the laboratory and X-ray personnel – the entire team caring for these little babies worked closely together, surrounding them with love and warmth.

I completed that final year, was presented with my bronze Manchester Royal Infirmary 'penny', which I have worn with pride throughout my nursing career, and went on to study midwifery.

Then, one morning in 1965, I opened my bedroom window and shouted out loud, 'World: ready or not, here I come.'

12

NEW HORIZONS

The hunger, born in Mr Pritchard's geography class, to experience worlds and cultures different from my own had only grown stronger with time; and now that I was a fully fledged nurse and midwife, my desire to help and nurture the sick, especially children, was the focus of what was to be my working life. More than ready to spread my wings, it was first stop Canada.

Why Canada? Because we had family there my father was happy to let me go and, although I had stood up to him in pursuing my training, had long left home and had come of age, I still seemed to need his approval – or, at least, to avoid his disapproval.

In April 1965 I arrived in the beautiful city of Vancouver, and very soon secured a position at the Vancouver General Hospital, or VGH as it was known. Assigned to the ER, I gained what proved to be invaluable experience in the field of emergency medicine. At the same time, I was living a new, different and thoroughly enjoyable life. For the first time ever, I lived in a flat in a large apartment block; I acquired a very nice Swedish boyfriend with whom I went skiing and sailing, and generally I had a lot of fun outside of work – the kind of carefree fun that young women in their twenties in the 1960s were supposed to have. It was a far cry from rural Wales, or the constraints of the nurses' residence in Manchester, and I was as happy as I could have wished to be.

After a year or so, however, I grew restless – a little puzzled and discontented. Yes, I was in a different – and more comfortable – milieu to that of the UK, but when all was said and done, Canadians were hardly exotic, and there were enough Brits around complaining about the weather to make me feel sometimes that I'd never left the British Isles! Where, I began asking myself, was the *real* Canada? The country I'd learned about at school. Where were the grizzly bears, the gold prospectors, the lumberjacks, the Eskimos? I wanted to get into the heart of the country and to learn about its indigenous peoples and those who had settled in a harsh environment and made a go of it.

With magic synchronicity, it was during this time that I came upon an advertisement for a nurse to work in Cassiar, a place of which I'd never heard. A close look at the map and I knew that this was what I was looking for: an isolated but thriving asbestos-mining community of some two thousand souls, way up north in British Columbia on the border of the Yukon. Off I went, and this time my spirit of adventure, and my natural curiosity and interest in different peoples and cultures, was well satisfied until July 1967, when it was time to return home and see my family.

Back in the UK, browsing through the *Nursing Times* one morning and idly wondering whether I ought to find and enrol for some specialist further nursing courses, I happened to glance at the job vacancies section. An advertisement caught my eye:

Save the Children fund requires more nurses for their expansion programme of a rehabilitation and training centre for widows and orphans in Qui Nhon, South Vietnam.

During my teens, I had donated a penny a month from my precious sixpence a week pocket money to the Save the Children Fund, and often used to wonder what happened to all those pennies meant for 'the poor children of Africa'. I pondered over the ad, thought about Vietnam, where bitter war was raging, and made the phone call that would change my life.

Part Two

DESTINATIONS

London, September 1967. The headquarters of SCF, the Save the Children Fund, which brings hope, comfort and encouragement to children in areas of conflict, fear and deprivation. A huge map of the world is mounted on a wall. It is covered with green triangles, red dots and yellow squares marking places as far-flung as Biafra, Bangladesh and Southeast Asia.

A red dot is placed on Qui Nhon, South Vietnam. It is a coastal town lying 360 kilometres north of Saigon. It is a war zone. Sick and wounded children, innocent victims of violence and politics, need help.

Several interviews later I'm selected, briefed, inoculated, kitted out.

Don't take anything leather, it'll mildew. Don't take anything synthetic, it'll be too hot. All clothing must be absorbent and loose-fitting to keep prickly heat at bay. Ideally, everything should be cotton – but cotton is expensive and hard to find in 1967 Wales.

Temperatures, I am advised, will be way above 110 degrees Fahrenheit, with humidity at 90 per cent plus, but that is meaningless when you come from the cool, clean air of North Wales. I have to get there, and learn the hard way. I'm given a plane ticket and two hundred pounds in travellers' cheques. Two weeks later I'm flying to Saigon, via a stopover in Bangkok.

People haven't stopped asking me if I'm scared.

Scared? Excitement stirs in the pit of my stomach.

I stand, limp and dishevelled, on the tarmac at Tan Son Nhut airport, Saigon, and gaze with a pronounced sense of unreality at the vast military sign on the front of the camouflaged terminal building:

In the event of a mortar attack do not panic, do not run.
Lie face down and cover your head with your hands.
Await further instructions.

In the relentless heat, my limbs are finding it difficult to function normally and sweat leaks from pores I'd never known I had.

OK, whatever you say ... Thus, silently, I address the warning sign and begin walking across the shimmering tarmac. Inside the terminal building I'm swept along towards a row of desks manned by grim-faced men, uniformed and heavily armed. The air hums with tension, and despite the heat and fatigue my senses feel almost painfully acute. Everyone is shouting at everyone else, and a sense of urgency seems to propel all activity. Later, I learn that the airport is frequently mortared, with loss of both civilian and military life. For now, more by the grace of God than good management, entry formalities are completed.

Clutching my documents in sweat-sticky hands and trying to keep track of my luggage, I negotiate various confusing orders while attempting to ignore the profusion of weaponry all around me.

Then, through the crowd, I notice a doughty-looking woman striding in my direction. As she comes closer, I spot the logo stitched to the pocket of her pretty, light-blue suit: the red and white of Save the Children. Immediately, I feel calmer – and safe.

'Anne Watts,' she says, with a warm smile and an outstretched hand. 'Welcome to Vietnam.'

13

SAIGON

Bridget Stevenson. Seventy years old, straight of back, sure of purpose. The quintessential Englishwoman. An experienced SCF administrator, Bridget was responsible for us, her 'girls', as well as for the purse strings of the project in Qui Nhon. She would become friend, confidante and mentor to everyone in the team. I will always remember her indomitable spirit with respect, admiration and love.

With her arm firmly linked with mine, Bridget steered me out, through the crush of humanity, into the harsh sunlight and a battered little blue and white taxi that spun us off into another world.

Saigon: a blur of sight and sound where military trucks bulge with young Vietnamese soldiers staring impassively at the chaos around them, weapons at the ready; American jeeps with handsome young men in fatigues at the wheel tear along the crowded streets, ferrying senior officers; incongruous amid the streams of traffic, tanks. With their long, lethal gun barrels pointing ahead, they prompt the fleeting thought that perhaps they're there to blast a route through the impossible congestion!

Sputtering mopeds precariously carry what seem like entire

families balanced above the petrol tank; bicycles are ridden by wiry little men, calf muscles straining as they pedal their impossibly wide, dramatically high loads of anything from bamboo to exotic fruit to bales of cloth, or squawking ducks crammed into raffia cages – all destined for the market.

A flurry of beautiful young girls comes cycling by, their long, black, silken hair streaming out behind them. They wear the traditional *ao dai*, a split tunic dress worn over loose-fitting trousers that permits freedom of movement while retaining modesty. All are dressed identically, white tunic over black trousers, and look for all the world like a flock of graceful swans, impervious to the chaos surrounding them. I also spot the garishly painted faces of other, once pretty, girls, servicing soldiers of several nationalities. Survival is the name of the game.

Then there are the cyclos. These vehicles must surely rank as instruments of torture for newcomers to Southeast Asia. A battered carriage, seating one passenger comfortably, two at a push, sits low down, in front of the driver, who pedals furiously from behind. That first ride, where the passenger doubles as the front bumper while the driver charges towards oncoming military traffic in a war zone, is a bowel-loosening experience.

Every now and again, the deafening cacophony of sounds threatens to overwhelm me, and the stench of open sewers assails me, bringing nausea in its wake. The heat and the humidity are god-awful, and my clothes, damp and clinging, feel strange. All familiar terms of reference are gone, and it dawns on me that this is what is meant by culture shock, as if the mind and spirit need time to catch up with the body. And yet I feel perfectly calm, not at all frightened, and find myself wondering what my sisters would make of all this.

The battered little taxi screeches to a halt outside a dusty, bedraggled building on Tu Do Street. I see a tired tangle of cables bearing unlit light bulbs, draped forlornly around a sign that says Majestic Hotel. This is where Bridget has reserved rooms. The place strikes me as partly tawdry, mostly sad.

A gaggle of hawkers surge forward with their pathetic wares of chewing gum, cigarettes and mysterious bits of green leaves I can't identify. I'm horrified to see that many of the crones have blackened teeth. I don't understand what they are saying and I just want to get out of this cloying bloody heat! Quickly realising there is to be no sale here, some of them spit, and a strong stream of deep-crimson sputum lands inches from my feet. God, what is this? Is TB tearing their lungs apart? No. This is betel juice, which the locals chew and which gives them a mild 'high'. Bridget takes it all in her stride, maintaining her particular brand of British dignity while barking at the hawkers to get back. She pays the cab driver and serenely guides me up the steps of the hotel.

My breath is taken away by the sweep of the lobby. There is no air conditioning, only large, creaking ceiling fans move the sluggish air around, but they give a comparative respite from the oppressive afternoon heat. There are several arrangements of exquisite fresh orchids at the main desk – beautiful, highly polished teak. I feel as if I'm checking into the pages of a Graham Greene novel. A smiling Vietnamese receptionist greets Bridget warmly and welcomes me by name. In a daze of exhaustion, excitement and sheer relief I sign in and am shown to my room, waved off with Bridget's cheerful 'Get some rest, dear. We'll meet in the dining room at eight.'

My room is vast but simple, its functionalism lightened and brightened with yet another impressive display of orchids and a bowl of exotic fruit on a coffee table. The bell boy, shuffling backwards while bowing and holding out his cupped palm expectantly, shows me the bathroom. He is beginning to irritate me, and all I have on me is a British half-crown. He pockets it quickly but flashes me a look of disdain tinged with confusion.

After a shower, I collapse on the huge, hard bed and sleep fitfully, lulled by the ceiling fan whirling slowly above me, until it's time to dress and meet Bridget for dinner. Later in the evening, she and I go for a short stroll. The hotel is transformed in the sultry night. The droopy, daytime façade is blotted out; the light bulbs now on are brightly coloured, cheerful and welcoming. The streets teem with life. American soldiers are everywhere, spilling in and out of neon-lit cafés and bars, always with – or looking for – girls . . . More culture shock, followed by a glass of mint tea and a much-needed deep sleep.

Over the next two days, all necessary formalities are completed at a bewildering array of government departments, followed by a visit to the British Embassy and a welcome cup of decent English tea. The British Ambassador, Peter Wilkinson, is charming, as is his wife, Mary, whom I will get to know very well in the coming months.

So many new and foreign sights, sounds and sensations; so many impressions of places and people unlike anything I've known before. Impossible to believe I've only been in Saigon for two days. Impossible too, despite the military presence everywhere, to believe what terrible death and destruction was being visited upon this country.

14

THE BLACK POUCH

The morning of my third day, and it was back to the airport; time to leave Saigon and journey north to Qui Nhon.

Bridget and I had been assigned seats in a huge military plane, the like of which I had never seen before.

The Hercules C130 transport plane is considered to be the workhorse of the air in times of conflict. Despite looking heavy and cumbersome, it is capable of landing and taking off in rough terrain and requires only a short runway. Seating is hammock-like, low-slung canvas webbing placed along the sides of the plane so that lines of men sit facing each other, weapons between their knees, kit bags under their seats. The cargo is carried in the central body of the fuselage.

We settled in, surrounded by young American soldiers. One kindly offered me a can of fizzy drink, which I dislike, but I was already feeling so dehydrated that I gulped it down gratefully. We were unable to see out as the plane roared into the air, and the noise was indescribable. Before long, nausea set in and, halfway through the three-hour journey, only sheer pride prevented me from bringing up my breakfast.

An officer barked orders as the plane began its descent, and the soldiers leaned forward, placing their heads as close to their knees as possible, their hands covering their heads protectively. Bridget followed suit and prodded me to do the same, which I did, but wondered why exactly this was necessary.

Later it was explained to me that those planes often picked up ground fire on landing or taking off. Those in the tail section were particularly vulnerable.

Guess where we were sitting.

We landed with a thud and the aircraft shuddered to a halt, accompanied by the scream of its brakes. The noise was overwhelming and we let out a gasp of relief once we were grounded. The young soldiers shouldered their weapons, hoisted their kit bags and, remembering their manners, stood back to let us through with murmurs of 'After you, ma'am, after you.' Bridget led the charge down the ramp of the tail section, straight out into heat which, to me, felt like charging into a blast-furnace. She forged ahead in her 'Follow me, everything's under control' fashion, while I prayed that I could continue to avoid throwing up.

We waited on the runway till our bits of luggage were unceremoniously thrown out of the back of the C130. Trying to appear attractively nonchalant, I lugged my rucksack while two obliging young soldiers hauled our other bags. We wended our way towards the airport buildings. Buildings? A couple of Quonset huts and a bamboo and thatch lean-to. Long lines of khaki-clad servicemen were snaking back and forth across the tarmac, some embarking, others disembarking. 'Hurry up and wait' seemed to be the order of the day. The arrivals had a gung ho air and looked ready for anything; those leaving seemed older – tired, worn, expressionless.

The Americans wore khaki fatigues and peaked, baseball-type caps, but those officers going on leave were in smart dress uniforms, light beige with pale blue braiding at the shoulder. But there were many Vietnamese soldiers milling about, too.

Attached to the ARVN (Army of the Republic of Vietnam), they wore black/khaki camouflage with floppy bush hats, and blue kerchiefs at their necks.

The noise around us was unrelenting. Huey helicopters, Chinooks and C130s clattered and roared incessantly, some taking off, others landing. Every now and again there was a loud, heavy thump, which startled me at first, but I quickly learned the difference between incoming and outgoing mortars. You don't hear incoming. Automatic weapons fire rattled away sporadically somewhere to my right . . .

Where had my world gone?

At the entrance to the small terminal hut, a tight group of soldiers waited, some sitting, some standing, a few lounging. They seemed separate somehow, isolated from the main crowd of men. They wore combat fatigues with black T-shirts showing under open shirts. Around their necks they sported loosely knotted black kerchiefs, black braided bootlaces or woven, multicoloured chokers. Floppy bush hats were tipped back behind their necks or pulled down low over their eyes. Some wore metal bangles on their wrists.

The body language of these men immediately struck me as different from the others around us. They looked as though they wouldn't take orders from anyone, and made no effort to conceal the fact that they were staring hard at us. One man in particular stared intently at me. There was something other-worldly about him, not quite right around the eyes, and I began to feel very uncomfortable. The only way forward was to pass through this small group. Bridget took a step back and placed a protective hand on my elbow, the other firmly in the small of my back, guiding me through. But the strange one stepped forward suddenly, intercepting us. He spoke to me.

'Hi. I've been waiting for you. This is for you, baby. Take care of it for me.' He pressed an object into my hand and forcibly closed my fingers over it.

Hot and flustered, I barely registered what was happening. Two soldiers stepped forward, smiled apologetically, and manoeuvred the weird guy away. It all happened so quickly, with Bridget prodding me forward the whole time. Everything was strange, confusing, overwhelming. Not for the first time, I was drenched with sweat, but at that moment I wasn't at all confident that it was only because of the heat.

After our military travel documents were stamped, we exited to see a beaming, middle-aged Vietnamese man, in crisp white shirt, dark tie and smart grey trousers, excitedly jumping up and down and waving at us. On his breast pocket was the red SCF logo – something reassuringly familiar in this insane place.

'Welcome home, Miss Bridget.' He pumped her hand up and down vigorously. 'Welcome, Miss Anne. Welcome to Qui Nhon.' This was Mr Bom, senior driver at the Children's Centre. Fussing like a mother hen, he cleared a way through the crowd, settled us into the back of his ancient Peugeot, loaded our bags and took off, hitting every pothole in sight.

We bumped along a dusty highway, damaged by the constant flow of heavy military traffic. Immediately to our left, the South China Sea lay sparkling in the sunlight; palms swayed in the offshore breeze, and fishing boats bobbed in the water close to shore. Further out, we saw some American naval vessels: Qui Nhon has a large, deep natural harbour, which gave it strategic importance during the Vietnam War. I was beginning to realise that, no matter what the landscape, visible reminders of this war were everywhere.

To our right we passed by a crowded shantytown. Tin shacks cobbled together from salvaged Budweiser, Coca-Cola and Fanta cans bore tacky signs, giving them names like Miami Nights, California Dreamin' and Coconut Grove. Ragged curtains or strips of coloured plastic partially covered the doorways of such establishments, where gaudily made-up women and disturbingly young girls lounged outside touting for business. Soldiers in varying states of drunkenness and undress staggered between the shacks. We skirted this miserable place for several hundred yards, swerving to avoid children – most of them naked from the waist down – playing among the mounds of garbage or squatting to relieve themselves. Pigs roamed in this squalor, as did mangy dogs and surly men, some carrying guns. The stench was terrible, the heat suffocating.

For the first time, I was fearful of what I'd done by deciding to come here. I seemed to have stumbled into some kind of hell, and felt a clutch of serious doubt as to the wisdom of the choice I'd made. As if sensing my state of mind, Bridget explained that we were in a large refugee area, swollen daily by thousands fleeing the intensifying fighting to the north. We would, she said, soon arrive at the Children's Centre. Exhaustion made me light-headed and nausea threatened to return. I was thankful that my long journey was coming to an end. It was then I became aware that my fingers were still curled firmly around the object given to me by the disturbed soldier at the airport. I opened my hand and saw it was a small black leather pouch.

As I began to tug at the black lacing that held it closed, Bridget made to take it. 'It's nothing, just give it to me,' she said briskly, but I hung on; I wanted to know what it was. The contents that spilled into my palm looked like dried apricots and bits of shrivelled leather. In fact, they were – or once had been – fingers, several of them, and two ears. I was struck dumb with shock and horror as Bridget gently took the pouch from me, explaining that it was the practice of some soldiers to collect enemy body parts as trophies. I thought of the young soldier who gave me the pouch, and I suddenly and very clearly recalled the look in his eyes: staring into the middle distance, focusing on something we couldn't see; something that nobody should ever see.

I had only been in the country for three and a half days, and I had already had my first experience of the thousand-yard stare.

15

WIDOWS AND ORPHANS

The wide wooden gates swung open. A small man, whip-thin body swamped by his baggy shirt and trousers and wearing a pith helmet several sizes too large, held the gate open and saluted as we bumped into the walled compound in a swirl of choking dust. His nut-brown, wrinkly face, eyes twinkling, creased into a broad grin as he greeted Bridget. This was Cu, handyman and gardener.

The large compound was mostly bare, with two long, single-storey, whitewashed buildings along two sides, forming an L-shape. Each building was ringed by a concrete walkway. A few potted plants struggled in the heat, and a beautiful scarlet bougainvillea curled around a wooden trellis and up onto the roof of one of the buildings. One end of one building was given over to our living quarters and Bridget's administrative office; the remainder of that building and all of the second building constituted the Centre that housed the children.

We were greeted by Jean Ringe, the head nurse, who introduced me to my other nursing colleagues, Ruby Burkhill and Lily Ho – all three women friendly, all three looking tired beneath their welcoming smiles. I was taken to a whitewashed room furnished with a bed, mosquito net draped to one side; a bedside table on which someone had thoughtfully placed a small glass containing a stem of scarlet bougainvillea; a chair, a wooden table, and a chest of drawers. In one corner a few coat-hangers dangled from a metal rack and a small mirror hung on a nail in the wall. The window was without glass, but was screened with mesh to let the air in and keep the mosquitoes out, and was barred to keep things secure.

The room was simple, functional, and would be my home for the next sixteen months. The hideous journey to Qui Nhon was banished from my mind. I was thrilled to be there.

Next I met Tinh, the cook, who proudly showed off her kitchen, a small room with two kerosene stoves on the floor. Woks and pans were stacked on a couple of shelves, a row of large knives and ladles hung on the wall, wooden chopping boards on a table covered in colourful, washable plastic. Several large metal bowls kept under the table were used for washing the dishes, as well as the fruit and vegetables. How Tinh managed to turn out such delicious meals in this small space was something I would continue to marvel at in the months to come.

I was introduced to her cooking by way of a welcoming meal, enjoyed in the homely living-cum-dining area of the compound, in the company of my new colleagues. Jean Ringe, whose aura was one of crisp efficiency, was a vivacious brunette, who had previously nursed in Cyprus and Malaya. Ruby Burkhill, from Yorkshire, was a petite, pretty, pixie-faced blonde with a quiet, pensive air. Lily Ho, the only resident trained Vietnamese nurse, had completed her nursing education at the French Catholic hospital in Saigon, and was a delight. Lily had a ready sense of fun and immense inner strength, and with her French, English and Vietnamese language skills she was the backbone of the team. As I would learn, she was the one who kept us all going when things got really tough.

Over supper, my companions gave me a crash course in necessary domestic basics. Water for drinking had to be boiled and left to cool. It tasted pretty awful at first, but I soon learned that you can get used to anything, especially when you see how little others have. Sometimes Kool-Aid, the coloured fruit powder, was added to the water in an effort to give it a marginally better flavour; sometimes there was Budweiser beer, donated by visiting Americans.

There was no electricity at that time and we used kerosene lanterns for light. The toilets and bathrooms might have seemed primitive to some, but they were adequate for our needs. Each area had a large stone jar containing water, with large scoops with which to wash, rinse and flush. The jars were topped up regularly by Cu from the well just outside our building.

These, then, were the off-duty staff quarters of the SCF Children's Centre at Qui Nhon. The rest – the working part and the reason why I was here – would have to wait until morning. Just as well; I was exhausted.

The Centre was situated up against the perimeter of the airport, which could at any time become a target for attack. The din of military air traffic was almost continual, day and night, and despite my exhaustion I had a poor night's sleep.

However, after I'd 'showered', put on my crisp white uniform, and pinned on my Manchester Royal Infirmary bronze 'penny', anticipation, adrenalin and pride took over. The MRI penny was awarded to all successful graduates of the four-year nurses' diploma programme. Princess Alexandra, cousin to the Queen, had presented everyone in my class with the bronze medal. Carved into the face of it was the image of the Good Samaritan helping the Jewish man at the side of the road, with the motto: *Tu fac similiter* – 'Go thou and do likewise'. I loved my penny.

After a breakfast of strong French coffee and deliciously fresh, warm, crusty baguettes brought in by Tinh from the market, I felt heaps better and ready to start work.

16

SETTLING IN

Nothing can prepare one for coming face to face for the first time with the ghastly evidence of what war does to a civilian population. The Centre at this time housed fifty children. Of these, 70 per cent were war wounded; the remainder were ill with a variety of tropical diseases or chronic medical conditions.

While everyone bustled into their busy daily routines, Jean walked me slowly through the Centre. Jean's live-in team – Ruby, Lily and now me – was augmented by two locally trained Vietnamese nurses who came in from the village where they, and the Centre's domestic staff, lived. Also from the village, and critically important to the enterprise, came young women who worked under our supervision as nursing assistants.

The first room we entered held the babies. Row upon row of tiny mites. Many were undernourished, and suffering from pneumonias, anaemias and all manner of skin infections, from impetigo and scabies to rat bites. They mostly came from orphanages in the area that had been overrun with orphaned, lost or abandoned children in the chaos of the fighting. On the outskirts of the town, where there were US Navy, Army and

Air Force bases, the South Korean Tiger infantry division was stationed, along with South Vietnamese troops.

The streets of Qui Nhon were, consequently, thronged with soldiers who frequented the bars and brothels. Many of the bar girls became pregnant by American men and their mixed-race babies came to be known as Amerasians. The girls and their babies were often targeted by Vietcong infiltrators – the Communist National Front for the Liberation of South Vietnam did not take kindly to local women consorting with the enemy, and the penalty was death. Thus, mixed-race babies were frequently left in the orphanages for their safety, and the safety of their mothers. Each week, sick babies came to the Centre from the orphanages, while those well enough to leave medical care were sent back.

The second room we came to housed the toddlers, the majority of them horribly maimed by war: multiple limb amputations, napalm burns, blindness or paralysis caused by shards of shrapnel or, more directly, by bullets. The surgical notes of one three-year-old boy read: 'Trans-section of base of penile urethra, with loss of both testes, following village attack by helicopter gunship.' He had the scrappy remains of a mutilated penis into which a permanent catheter was inserted to drain off his urine. The nurses named him Be Trai – 'little boy'. Every three hours, he would go and lie quietly on his bed, looking up at us with large, trusting brown eyes as he waited for the stab of pain in his bladder as one of us removed the wooden spigot from his catheter and slowly drained off the small amount of urine that struggled through his scarred urethra. He seldom cried, just gave a little whimper as the spigot came out.

Even as a nurse who'd witnessed the tragic deformities caused by thalidomide, and had worked with severely ill babies and children, this introduction to such cruel and avoidable suffering was shocking and painful. I had to summon every ounce of discipline and training to withstand what I saw, and knew I would have to deal with daily.

Close by, in the next building, were the older children, up to the age of fourteen. These boys and girls helped each other out as far as possible. Most were survivors of multiple blast injuries which, with the cruel ingenuity of guerilla war, might have been caused in any number of ways: booby-trapped cola cans at a roadside, or a grenade tossed into a busy marketplace; landmines set to explode under public transport vehicles or in rice paddies; deadly gunships firing into villages, sending shrapnel flying in all directions to lodge in spinal cords, eyes and brains.

Many children were left paraplegic or quadriplegic – paralysed from the waist down, or with three or four limbs affected, the paralysis extending from the upper chest down. Limbs were lost, either at the scene, or later in surgery. Burns were common, caused by napalm, or domestic fires as kerosene stoves were overturned, or inflicted in the deliberate torching of flimsy villages.

Medical conditions were several, and none were rare. Chronic, untreated malaria; gross anaemia, often leading to a hugely swollen spleen and heart failure; tuberculosis; chronic hepatitis; hookworm, usually picked up by bare feet constantly immersed in water in the rice paddies or exposed along dusty roads. The omnipresence of malaria, and the whole panoply of tropical diseases, as well as the trauma of conflict, was devastating. No National Health Service here.

Ken Shapiro, an American correspondent writing for the *Stars and Stripes* military newspaper, described the SCF Centre as 'the Oasis'. It was indeed a refuge, a place of peace and calm, which had been set up with two objectives: to provide nursing and convalescent care for children, thus relieving the hard-pressed local hospitals and orphanages, and to provide vocational training in childcare, and practical skills such as tailoring, for widows and young women in the area, thus providing them with work and enabling them to feed their families. When I arrived, the Centre had already been open for a year, with incredible strides made by the first nurses who came. Local conditions were far from easy, and the fluctuating security risks had slowed progress. It was now planned to expand the intake of children from the original fifty to eighty or more, and to develop the services further.

The creation of the Centre had been instigated by the local provincial hospital, where a surgical team from New Zealand worked – six nurses, two surgeons, one anaesthetist and a physician. But even patients lucky enough to be operated on and treated by this excellent team could die on the wards because of overcrowding, unsanitary conditions and insufficient skilled staff for aftercare. And, as is sadly usual in times of war, all available resources, both human and material, went to the military, leaving civilians with very little. SCF in London were approached to support the provincial hospital by setting up a rehabilitation centre for children, helping to nurse them back to health after surgery and thereby alleviating the overcrowding of the hospital's wards.

Once the project was approved, an appropriate building was found, and three nurses were sent out to Qui Nhon to open the Centre and get it up and running. As their tour of duty came to an end, replacements were needed – of whom I was one. There were only two British teams in the entire country at that time: The Children's Hospital in Saigon, and the SCF team up country in Qui Nhon.

There were four different places from which the children were sent to us: the three local orphanages; the government provincial hospital, where the New Zealand surgical team worked; the Holy Family Hospital, funded by the Roman Catholic

Church; and the American 85th (and later the 67th) Evacuation Field Hospitals in town.

The Holy Family Hospital was impeccably run by a staff of Americans, Canadians, Indians and Sri Lankans – all of them nuns. The administrator was a nun; the surgeons, physicians and nurses were nuns; the microbiologist, the lab technicians, the radiologist and radiographers were all nuns. If somebody had an outpatient appointment at ten a.m., they'd better BE there at ten a.m. or lose their spot. Despite the sweltering heat, these remarkable women wore full habit, long white robes and aprons, beautifully laundered, their wimples starched.

Many children were referred to us from that hospital to convalesce, to get nursing aftercare and encouragement to walk; to eat Tinh's good food and, most of all, to be loved. I was more than a little in awe of the nuns at first. The closest I'd ever got to a religious order of this kind was watching Audrey Hepburn in *The Nun's Story*, one of my all-time favourite movies!

The orphanages, too, were run by nuns, Buddhist or Catholic, and they never had enough staff to cope with the constant influx of babies and children. The sisters did a valiant job, but they had few supplies, little equipment and insufficient funds to enable them to deliver the standard of care and protection these children needed. Pneumonia was common, and babies were often fed by having a bottle propped up by a piece of cloth, the teat placed in the mouth and the baby left unsupervised as other hungry mouths were dealt with. Babies frequently choked, inhaling the milk, and most infants didn't even have a crib. They lay side by side on straw mats on the floor, leaving them vulnerable to rat bites during the night. A few were put in the small baskets that could sometimes be found in the marketplace.

When I first visited the orphanages, I was still thinking

like the English nurse I was, coming from a country where gleaming stainless steel and sterilising equipment was taken for granted, and where each baby had its own cot. I was used to places where a sick infant could be fed intravenously, and where there were enough trained nurses and auxiliary staff available to accurately monitor and record any changes in heart rate, temperature, skin colour or respiration; where medications and feeds were regularly administered, and recorded on well-maintained charts. Where I had come from, babies were regularly changed, bathed and kept plump and sweet smelling . . .

This was just not going to happen in Qui Nhon. With the number of infants for which each one of us was responsible, there simply weren't enough hours in the day, enough nursing help, or anywhere near enough equipment. On each visit to an orphanage, we brought back any sick babies to the Centre, at times so overloading ourselves that we risked being unable to give them adequate care.

It became clear that the conventional approach of nurses or nuns caring for each baby individually simply wasn't going to work. Some lateral thinking was needed. So, we put our heads together and came up with a scheme whereby we dragooned the older children in the orphanages into groups, each headed by one of the eldest girls. They might only be eight, nine or ten, but that was old enough. Each girl that we thought capable of the responsibility was put in charge of six babies and taught how to hold them, bath them, mix their feeds, give a bottle, sterilise the bottles and teats. There was never enough water, and the source was not always clean, so sterilising tablets were used. We showed the little girls how to care for some of the skin problems by dabbing on Gentian Violet, and taught them which conditions to refer to the nuns. Over a relatively short period, things improved and became more manageable. The flow of babies, toddlers and abandoned children into the orphanages was constant and the nuns barely had time to breathe, but at least some of the problems eased, and we visited regularly. Eventually, we were able to get hold of some cots to raise the babies off the ground.

The American 67th Evacuation Field Hospital, our fourth source of children needing care, was where I learned how kind Americans can be, and how generous. They were ready to share valuable resources and skills whenever possible. Of course, US personnel always took priority, but when wounded soldiers were flown in by helicopter from villages and areas under attack, wounded children were often also evacuated, ending up in the casualty clearing station of a field hospital somewhere. As soon as they possibly could, the doctors treated these children, surgically when necessary, but they had to be moved on.

The 67th Evac. participated in the Medcap (Medical Civilian Aid Program), going out to villages and holding clinics. American military nurses were restricted to base, and we civilian nurses often volunteered to go with Medcap teams, so children also came to us this way. The flow of casualties was steady, space and resources were at a premium. The American army nurses loved having children around, but it was not what they were there for, so the little casualties were transferred to us. The American nurses also visited the Centre when they could, following up on any child they were particularly concerned about or attached to, and always offering to help. This was great for our morale too.

Anyone arriving at the Centre for the first time and seeing those children at play would have been hard put to imagine a more cheerful and confident bunch. Yet most had suffered serious, sometimes appalling, injuries, often complicated by emotional disturbance and malnutrition. With us, they received the love and care from the nursing staff, but love and concern also came from a more unlikely quarter: the young soldiers, American, some Korean and a few Australian, all of whom were based in and around the area, and who would come by and visit the kids.

17

MODERN CONVENIENCES

Living conditions at Qui Nhon were simple but adequate. Our clothes washing was done at the well in the compound. In the monsoon season, the rain came gushing and sheeting down with unbelievable force. The heavens truly did open, and I often went outside in my bikini, shampooing my hair in the rain. I felt like Mitzi Gaynor in *South Pacific*. It was wonderful.

One day, Frank and Jay, two American army captains, both helicopter pilots, came to visit the 'oasis' they'd heard was being run by 'round-eyes', the local term for Westerners. Because there were so few round-eyes in the area, they found us easily, but when we showed them around they were shocked at the way we were living. They simply couldn't understand how we could possibly get through the day without a Budweiser, Coca-Cola or Scotch, laced with ice cubes. Or, at the very least, without Tony Bennett singing 'I Left My Heart in San Francisco', which was played constantly on the jukeboxes in their officers' clubs. We assured them that we were perfectly OK, but they just couldn't handle the fact that, for the most part, all we had to drink was the rather tepid water we boiled and left to cool – no fridge of course – but, frankly, we preferred that to the Kool-Aid powdered flavours that were kindly put our way.

Some days later, I was sitting in the shade of the porch, feeding babies, along with my new colleague Pat – Patricia Ashe – a gorgeous Elizabeth Taylor lookalike, and a wonderful dedicated nurse, who'd recently arrived from Scotland. Suddenly, Frank and Jay reappeared, pulling a large machine on a trailer.

They came to a halt in front of us, and Jay asked, 'Where would you like this, ladies?'

We had no idea what this was. 'Well, I don't know . . . what is it?' I replied.

It was a fifteen-kilowatt generator, large enough, they explained, to give us some limited electricity. We asked where it was from.

'Ma'am, redistribution of army goods. Don't you worry about a thing.'

'But it belongs to the Navy,' I pointed out. I'm not a sailor's daughter for nothing; besides, it wasn't khaki, but dark blue!

Ignoring our admittedly half-hearted protests, they quickly installed the generator at the far end of the compound, sandbagging it to help muffle the awful noise it made, though – as we noticed the serial numbers had been carefully scratched out – I suspected it was just as much to hide it from view.

Over the next few days an amazing collection of modern conveniences appeared, courtesy of these two men. Tinh and Cu were delighted. When a huge old refrigerator was installed in the kitchen, you'd have thought Tinh had won the state lottery. For ages afterwards she rushed about, serving ice on just about everything. And when a pump appeared at the well, Cu was over the moon, filling endless buckets of water from the new tap and almost drowning the flowers he tended. We girls were thrilled with a shower system of sorts that was rigged up for us, one of several helpful gestures to make our lives a little easier, but the really big day was the day the ice cream came.

We were asked by some other visiting soldiers if we'd like

some ice cream. Would we ever! And which flavour would we like! I still remember thinking how there must be something to this good old American know-how after all. A choice of ice-cream flavours in that hot, dusty, alien war zone seemed like a fantasy, but the very next day a refrigerated military truck arrived. Two young soldiers jumped out and began offloading four huge catering tubs of ice cream, two chocolate and two of vanilla.

We had no way of keeping it cool. Even one of these huge tubs was far too big for the ancient fridge. 'Just one tub will be more than enough,' we said, and tried to explain why, but this turned out to be another 'redistribution of army goods' situation. The whole lot had to be offloaded all at once, with no questions asked. Which it was.

Something had to be done, and nobody who was at the Centre that day would ever forget what happened next.

We gathered everybody on the premises on and around the porch, trying to keep in shade, which was difficult. There were about ten young soldiers present, and forty children and toddlers. Those kids who were bedridden had been carried out, some of them in their beds. Vietnamese nurse aides were cuddling sick babies; a couple of Buddhist nuns who happened to be visiting from their orphanage were present, as well as an American nun surgeon who'd come to see some of her small patients from the Holy Family Hospital.

Solemnly we started handing out spoons and bowls, of which there were not enough to go round – our valuable ice-cream was melting quickly. Some of the smaller children shyly stuck a finger into this stuff, which they had never seen before, and tentatively licked at the white and chocolate mess. The wondrous look on their faces as they tasted ice cream for the first time triggered a signal for the bigger children. Within a minute, using their hands as scoops, everybody got stuck in.

Have you ever seen a chubby nun, in full white habit, sitting on the ground eating chocolate ice cream with her fingers? Or GIs in combat fatigues gently helping little children with no arms to get their share, and guiding the fingers of blind children to the delicious stuff? Soon, everybody was covered in sticky mess and laughing helplessly when, into this ecstatic gathering, drove a high-ranking US general, whose visit we had completely forgotten about. His look of disbelief turned into a smile of understanding and, together with his young driver, he joined in the fun. Those tubs were demolished in no time at all.

A few weeks later, when we'd grown rather accustomed to our newly acquired comforts – morning showers and sporadic bouts of electricity – we received a visit from the military police. Pat and I were once again feeding babies out on the porch when two police officers jumped out of their vehicle, faces stern, backs straight. 'Do you mind if we take a look around, ma'am?'

Carefully not looking at each other, we nodded. They walked slowly around the compound, examining very, very closely the generator, the pump, various taps, and the treasured old refrigerator. Tinh and Cu were quaking in their shoes as the MPs made notes on clipboards, watched by little clusters of silent children.

After an age they came back to us and asked us where these items had come from. We looked blankly at them, and then at each other.

'Were those guys Australian, did you think?' said Pat.

'I don't know. They could have been Kiwis. Definitely from down under, I'd say,' I replied. Of course we were dreading that they might confiscate everything, but more importantly we didn't want to be the cause of trouble for people who'd done nothing but show us kindness.

Not for a minute did we think they believed our feeble

efforts to mislead them but, as so often happens, the tension was broken by the children. Initially wary of the policemen, two or three of the littlest ones now came slowly forward, sucking their thumbs and staring soulfully up at the two men, who worked hard at not noticing them. Then three-year-old Be Trai, who had a habit of sidling up to a soldier and hanging on to a fistful of combat-green shirt-tail, did just that to the sterner-looking of the two men. It was hard not to notice the suspicion of a grin on the face of his colleague. Eventually the MPs threw their clipboards into the jeep, turned smartly on their heels and left. The only unmilitary gesture I observed was a rolling of the eyeballs heavenward as they drove out, a group of children running behind them in a tangled mass of cheerful noise.

We never heard another thing about the whole business.

18

SATURDAY NIGHT
AT THE MOVIES

We received an invitation from the Sisters at the Holy Family Hospital: 'Why don't you come round on Saturday night and see one of our movies?'

I wondered what kind of film they would be showing. Did they want to recruit us? I felt mildly discomfited by the thought, but my friend Pat, the Elizabeth Taylor lookalike and a Catholic herself, laughed at my misgivings. Anyway, we liked and respected the nuns, and decided it was only polite to accept their invitation.

So one Saturday night in October 1967, our driver, Mr Bom, took us to the hospital. We were met by Sister Elisabeth, a very pretty, very hip, guitar-playing nun with a sweet voice. She led us up several flights of stone stairway and out onto the flat roof. It was just beginning to get dark and we were a bit mystified. A large and motley assortment of chairs, some of them the sort of canvas loungers you might take to the beach, had been arranged in neat rows, facing a large screen and with an aisle left in the centre. A 16mm projector on a tall stand stood in the aisle.

I had never been to an open-air film before, though I'd read about the drive-in movies they had in the United States. Out in the balmy, tropical night air, this seemed a good place to start, especially as, courtesy of the ever generous US military, a supply of beer, soft drinks and potato chips had been laid on. 'Help yourself to a drink, anything you want, and find yourselves a seat,' Sister Elisabeth instructed.

More soldiers began arriving, then a few of the New Zealand doctors and nurses turned up, as well as some Korean and European civil engineers who worked in the area. Lastly a sprinkling of American personnel from the 67th Evac. arrived in dreadful Hawaiian shirts and a flurry of friendly joshing. Between reels, we all chatted amiably. Mike – Captain Michael Samuels – was a general surgeon, who cornered me and asked after some of the children at the Centre who had been his surgical patients. I liked him immediately. He was not only tall and good-looking, but his kind eyes were alive with interest, concern and compassion. We had a chat about all sorts of things. Mike's calm demeanour made me feel that he would be a good man to have around in a crisis, and the easy camaraderie between us was a comfort in strange times. This was beginning to look like fun . . .

After the nuns sat down and made themselves comfortable, sinking into their billowing white habits ready for the show, the cans containing the film were brought in, to a buzz of anticipation. It turned out this was the hottest ticket in town, any town: Warren Beatty and Faye Dunaway in *Bonnie and Clyde* – a new release even back in the States. We sat back, sipping cold Budweiser and eating crisps, riveted by what was, for its time, a very violent film, in which several characters were brutally gunned down and the audience was not spared the sight of blood.

The irony was not lost on me. Here we all were, watching this in the cradle of a cruel war, and doing so for *enjoyment*. Now and again the rattle of machine-gun fire that was not coming from the screen could be heard; the boom of mortar fire made our nerves jump; red tracer bullets periodically sliced into the night sky beyond the screen and into the twinkling stars. This formed the backdrop while we sat, unable to tear our eyes away from the mesmerising duo of Warren Beatty and Faye Dunaway. How, I thought to myself, could I ever tell friends and family about this, let alone be able to explain how we could recline on a lounger, sipping beer, and relishing faked violence while the real deal was going on around us? There was a strong sense of unreality about this whole occasion, and I felt some unease creeping into me. This evening had little to do with my expectations of living in an impoverished country during a major war.

This was where I got to properly understand the word surreal.

I wondered then, and have wondered many times since, how a war can be fought with well-stocked bars, jukeboxes, pinball machines, candy, ice cream and the latest movies shipped over for the entertainment of the troops. Of course I realise that morale has to be propped up before and after young men go out to kill other young men, but it has always seemed so at odds with the reality of the situation. The Americans appeared to take the United States with them wherever they went, as far as I could make out, but my mixed feelings about it were made more so by their tremendous generosity from which I and my colleagues at the Children's Centre often benefited.

The Saturday night movies at the Holy Family Hospital became a regular event, providing us with a welcome little slice of social life. One time, when we saw *The Sound of Music*, either the projectionist was confused or the reels of film had been stored in wrongly numbered cans, but we saw the second reel first, the fourth reel second, the first reel third and the third reel last.

Yes, war is hell – but we sang along heartily just the same.

19

WEDDING RINGS

Day and night at the Children's Centre Huey helicopters clattered urgently overhead, flying their precious cargo of shocked, injured and dying soldiers into the 67th Evac. The soldiers were often little more than teenagers from places such as Oklahoma, Pennsylvania and Idaho, but more recently from Dak To, Anh Khe and Phu Cat.

I was astonished to learn that numerous senior medical and surgical specialists had been drafted into this war, just as the young GIs had. Many were married with children, and had been enjoying lucrative private practice or eminent careers at centres of medical excellence all over the United States, responsible for teaching medical students. I had assumed that medical careers in the armed forces were a matter of choice. Who, I wondered, was left to care for the sick and injured back home in the US when such experienced personnel were being drafted because their collective skills were so urgently needed.

The work of the army doctors and nurses met the highest standards of the day. The medics spent their time stabilising wounded men prior to their being medevaced out, either to Clark Air Force Base in the Philippines or to Okinawa, Japan, for further assessment and treatment. From there, some of the lads were sent home in a freedom bird, their bodies partly salvaged, their minds often shattered. The walking wounded were patched up and sent right back to fight again. The medics, when time permitted, visited the children to check on progress and decide on further treatment: when further skin grafts were to be carried out on extensive burns, whether broken limbs were healed sufficiently to remove the cast, and so on. But sometimes, doctors visited children just to hold them, comfort them and breathe in the memory of their little ones back home.

A few of the doctors, however, came to the Centre regularly every week, and I found myself especially looking forward to Mike's appearance, thinking about his dark eyes and steady gaze. One day, he turned up unexpectedly, and I could tell from his grim expression that he was angry about something. Nevertheless, he insisted on feeding a three-year-old boy his fish soup and rice. The child had one arm and had been blinded. Gently, lovingly, Mike fed the bereft child until the last grain of rice was gone, visibly relaxing when the child smiled trustingly and said, '*Cam un bac si*' – 'Thank you, doctor.'

Then Mike explained his anger. His hair was longer than regulations permitted, and his CO had ordered him to get it trimmed and report for inspection at nine o'clock the next morning. It was the absurdity of the situation which had infuriated him. He had been operating on seriously wounded young men, attempting to salvage what he could of their ravaged bodies, for forty-eight hours without respite. Then he had to go and get his hair cut! Suddenly, he had had to remove himself from the madness of the situation, and so he came to see the children.

I could well understand how he felt; at the same time, I also understood that his commanding officer, crazy as it seemed, was attempting to maintain a semblance of order in a situation that defied order.

Mike had brought his beloved ukulele with him. After he'd

got matters off his chest, he went back to the wards where, surrounded by giggling children, he played them some music,
sang them some songs and tucked them up in their beds. He
left for his base looking much better than when he'd arrived.

A few days later Mike called by to ask me to a Christmas
show. He had no idea what kind of a show it was, but hey! –
this was a war zone and who cared? Nobody mentioned his
short haircut.

Come the day, I was excited about going. I had to be ready at
16:00 hours. Should I wear the baggy shirt or the white T-shirt
with my jeans? No point driving myself nuts, just wear the
baggy shirt. Any kind of make-up in the steamy tropics just
melted off the face, so getting ready was hardly a major oper-
ation.

Then a call came through to say that no one at the casualty
receiving bay would be able to attend the show, as they were on
standby to take in multiple casualties imminently. A Chinook
had come down with loss of life and all medical staff were
on standby to deal with the injured. OK, no show, but I wasn't
staying where I was. I had the Vietnamese driver take me round
anyway.

It was one of those moments when you know that what
you're seeing, hearing and smelling will be etched into your
memory bank forever. In the casualty bay, rows of gurneys were
lined up with military precision, each laden with a blackened,
misshapen corpse. In the eerie silence medical staff, some in
scrub suits, others in fatigues, looked tense and weary. The few
I recognised seemed older, their faces pale and pinched with
sorrow. Nothing could be done for the twenty-two men who
had been disgorged from the wreckage. The twin-rotor, heavy-
lift Chinook helicopter, carrying its battle-weary passengers to
a concert, was rumoured to have suffered mechanical failure.
Could it have been shot down? All its passengers had perished

on impact, and these experienced, dedicated surgical teams, always ready to deal efficiently with any emergency, were instantly redundant.

While I stood quietly in the entrance, feeling like an intruder, a pretty, ashen-faced nurse walked past me carrying a stainless-steel tray on which lay a collection of about ten twisted, blackened little objects. Wedding rings. Cut off the fingers of the dead. Now they lay on that shiny tray, each one a symbol of someone's love, mute testimony to the pity of war. How many babies had been orphaned in that moment? How many wives and mothers were soon to learn what we in that place knew?

But by God, all male medical personnel had regulation-length hair.

The show that had caused the excitement was the Bob Hope Christmas Show. For security reasons no one knew for sure where it would be held, or if it would be held in the Qui Nhon area at all.

The soldiers in the Chinook had been selected randomly and quickly from some hell-hole to be flown to the show as a surprise treat. Now that there was little to do other than ID and bag the bodies and hand over to the 'graves registration' guys, the casualty receiving teams were free to attend. Nobody felt like it, but then the pretty nurse who had carried the rings said, 'We should go for them,' and so about ten of us took a deep breath, pulled ourselves together and went.

We were soon enough caught up in the extraordinary sensation of being among a few thousand troops sitting on the ground, gathered to see the legendary comedian who was clearly loved by these men and women so far from home. The sweaty atmosphere was charged with excitement and antici-pation.

When the great man appeared, the huge audience welcomed

him with rapturous applause, whooping, hollering and cheering. They stopped immediately he signalled for silence, and he launched into his familiar, corny routines. He was hilarious.

Bob Hope held everybody in the palm of his hand. The troops loved him for not forgetting them, and for bringing them Miss World, Raquel Welch and Joey Heatherton, a sexy, blonde American actress, dancer and singer who wore revealing outfits on stage and had appeared in movies with Perry Como, Dean Martin and Frank Sinatra. To say the temperature soared when Raquel Welch walked onto the makeshift stage in a white, crocheted mini-dress, her thick, chestnut hair tumbling over her shoulders, doesn't begin to describe the reception she got. They went totally bananas in a country that grows them!

That year Miss World was a statuesque Indian medical student. Beautiful and articulate, she sat on the edge of the stage in her gorgeous sari, maintaining a gracious composure while quietly talking to those young men. It was a touching moment, which gave way to raucous cheering when the sexy dancing of Joey Heatherton took over.

I laughed and I cried. It was such an extraordinary experience.

At the end of the show, while we were trying to get out of the jostling crowd, someone asked for the team that had received the Chinook casualties to report backstage: Bob Hope had asked to see them so that he could thank them. He knew the soldiers had been flown out to see his show. Though I had no business there, Mike dragged me along with him but I hung back when the team were meeting the star. Bob Hope hugged each member of the team and spoke with them, then asked who I was and beckoned me forward.

I was introduced and, for some reason, I started to cry. He was so kind to everyone and was himself upset at the accident. Everyone's emotions were raw. He was rather taken with this 'little English gal' and was interested to hear about the Centre for wounded Vietnamese children. I told him about the wedding rings, and how distraught I had felt.

He hugged me to his chest and said, 'Try not to feel sad. Be happy that you saw the show. They had been told on board that they were coming, and I'd like to think they died looking forward to a good time. They could have died alone, terrified in a ditch somewhere as many have, and will again before this is over.'

Bob Hope held me as I wept. He was kind, understanding, fatherly. When he died in the summer of 2003, at the age of a hundred, I was transported back to that moment and then, in my mind's eye, I saw ten wedding rings twinkling on a tray.

20

SANCTUARY

I had spent four tumultuous months coming to terms with the horror of illness, injury and death on a scale that would have been unimaginable to me in what now felt like another life. I had learned to live with the constant uncertainty and chaos that the war brought to our doorstep; to cope with teeming refugees, fear, danger, poverty – a deadly cocktail laced with the oppressive, sapping heat of this place. But there were huge rewards in knowing that one's skills and compassion and love were making a difference to children whose lives had been decimated.

And life, otherwise, was not all unrelieved gloom and doom. Colleagues were supportive and became friends; and other friends were made, too, among the many wonderful people we encountered in our work, and in our rationed but always enjoyable social gatherings.

There were unexpected treats, such as the visits of Mary Wilkinson, the British Ambassador's wife from Saigon. Mary became a surrogate mother to us British nurses in Qui Nhon. She would turn up from time to time bearing a large basket of home-made marmalade and jams and, best of all, British magazines and three-day-old English newspapers. As one of only three British girls outside of Saigon, these visits, bringing us a touch of home, were to be treasured, and treasure them we did – particularly as we were well aware of the risks that Mary took by making the journey up north.

The mind, I was beginning to realise, adapts to circumstance and attunes itself to finding flashes of light within the darkness; to accept that there are aspects of life which brighten the soul even in the darkest corners.

Around the bay from the Children's Centre was a landscape of exquisite beauty, where palms fringed the turquoise waters that lapped against a white sandy beach. At this beach was a building, a leprosarium as it was known, for this place of beauty was a leper colony, complete with its own hospital, six kilometres north of Qui Nhon.

The fear and stigma of leprosy was still prevalent in the 1960s. Its cause was little understood and it was considered chronic, incurable, progressive and highly contagious. Now called Hansen's disease, it is indeed chronic, but very slow growing and not highly contagious. It is caused by the bacterium *mycobacterium leprae* and primarily affects the peripheral nerves and mucous membranes of the respiratory tract. The most obvious external symptoms are the skin lesions, which affect fingers, toes and, in the latter stages, the nasal area. Left untreated, Hansen's disease can and does cause permanent damage to skin, nerves, limbs and eyes.

Historically, this disease has affected humanity since at least 300 BC, and was well recognised in the civilisations of ancient China, Egypt and India. In 1995, the World Health Organisation estimated that between two and three million people were permanently disabled due to Hansen's disease.

I knew little of this in 1967, and the leprosarium was my first contact with an illness I knew only from biblical references and my teenage admiration for Albert Schweitzer, who so famously and tirelessly worked with African lepers in the Gabon, at his ramshackle hospital in Lambarene. In and around Qui Nhon in 1967, anyone found to be suffering from Hansen's disease was immediately segregated, together with their immediate family members, and brought to the colony, where they lived for the rest of their days.

The discovery of the Qui Nhon leprosarium was, strangely, that it was a place of tranquillity, respite and natural beauty. This special refuge was staffed by French nuns who, like religious sisters the world over, radiated inner calm, serenity and good humour that put others at ease.

Surgeons from the 85th, and later the 67th, evacuation hospitals regularly donated their skills and precious time to holding clinics at the leprosarium. Not just so they could study this ancient disease, but so they could enjoy a more tranquil aspect of this stupid war. The French sisters always put on a wonderful lunch for the American physicians and surgeons, who took such a warm-hearted and civilised approach to the health problems of these people hidden away in this beautiful valley – and usually so ostracised and feared. Also, time for a swim and a sunbathe in the sparkling South China Sea added to the attraction for the hot, tired and overworked doctors.

With the US army nurses often restricted to base, and the leprosarium considered off limits for security reasons, we civilian nurses in the area often volunteered to assist. Bumping our way along the unpaved, potholed road leading down to the isolated bay to offer help and support to the welcoming French nuns remains a happy memory, shared by all who knew this special place.

As leprosy attacks the nerve endings of the extremities, fingers and toes become numbed and register little or no sensation. If the trauma remains untreated, sufferers end up stubbing or burning themselves, with little awareness of encroaching gangrene. In such cases, the surgeons amputated infected areas, or nibbled and trimmed affected bones, easing the plight of the sufferer. For the nurses, there were plenty of messy dressings to be changed, mothers to be encouraged, and children to cuddle and play with.

The male patients spent much of their time fishing off the rocky promontories at either end of the bay. Their skill in handling rods and nets, despite often being without fingers, or even hands, was impressive. Many of the men were left with ragged stumps ending just below the elbow or just above the wrist, yet they adapted fishing rods to fit their stumps by fixing a tin can at the base around which they would wind the fishing line. Their stump, fitted snugly into the can, could be slowly turned, pulling in the plentiful supply of plump, glistening fish. I used to marvel at their self-sufficient adaptability and total lack of self-pity.

We used to joke that if the 'effluent really hit the fan' and the town was invaded by NVA or Vietcong, we would seek refuge at the leprosarium. As most people gave it a wide berth, it would hands down be the safest place to be!

Joking aside, those of us privileged enough to have experienced the hospitality of the French sisters and to have known the stigmatised families living at the leprosarium in Qui Nhon would remember it with love and gratitude. The inhabitants of the leprosarium taught us a valuable lesson: grab life and live it, no matter what cards you are dealt.

21

THE YELLOW RIBBON

The life lessons of the leprosarium were not, unfortunately, available to the traumatised children who came our way. Helicopter gunships take no prisoners – a bitter truth that eight-year-old Hue learned when multiple shards of shrapnel tore into the right side of her face and peppered her leg. Her shattered bones left no option but amputation just below the knee.

The death of her parents and little brother on that same sunny afternoon had left the child timid, withdrawn and given to tearful bouts. At the Centre, she often went off alone with a broom to sweep the long veranda, an occupation that seemed to give her a small measure of comfort. Perhaps sweeping was one of the chores she had helped her mother with before her world was destroyed.

In a sad attempt to hide from the world the ugly scarring that puckered her soft cheek, Hue insisted on wearing her thick, glossy black hair combed forward onto her face. She never played or conversed much with the other children, and could generally be found sitting on a wooden bench, face turned to the wall.

The laughter and trust of young children can be a powerful healer. The American and Australian soldiers who regularly visited the Children's Centre – drawn perhaps by its reputation as a place of good humour and hope and a semblance of normality amid the insanity of conflict – would bring gifts of sweets for the children, and a touching willingness to help us with chores. It was the voluntary help offered by the military that enabled humanitarian teams such as ours to function as well as we did.

One afternoon a US army general arrived to learn about our project and to see how his men could help. I noticed his driver, a young man barely out of his teens, sitting alone, shoulders hunched, head down, clearly a damaged soul. It was not an uncommon sight.

We offered him a soft drink. 'No thank you, ma'am,' he stuttered, looking up briefly and with enormous effort. It was always the eyes that told the story: haunted, unable to focus on anything. The thousand-yard stare.

Over the next few weeks, the general and his driver visited regularly, and we became aware that a special friendship was gradually developing between the physically damaged, withdrawn little girl, Hue, and the traumatised soldier.

Visit by visit, little by little, hesitantly and cautiously, he began to alight from the jeep, raise his head, look around nervously for Hue. She, in turn, began to notice the strange young man who spoke to no one, and we could tell that she would look out for the visits.

As the weeks went by, a transformation took place between these two damaged people. First, a tentative smile was exchanged between them, then another – and another. Slowly, he gained her confidence, and one day a little miracle took root. He sat down in the dirt, removed his boots and started cutting them up. He fashioned a crude sling out of the canvas boots and painstakingly fitted it to the ragged stump which had once been her leg, visibly agonised over getting it right.

It took several visits, much concentration and the addition of buckles, straps and laces. Then a piece of aluminium pipe appeared, and was cut down to size. The protective rubber tip on the end of the pipe was carved from the heel of his boot. Hue co-operated and became increasingly excited as her new leg took shape.

Then, slowly, he taught her to walk. Back straight, head up, no limping. Well . . . not much.

And finally, the *pièce de résistance*. He went to the local market and bought a small mirror, a comb, a length of yellow ribbon and a piece of elastic. I lent him a needle and thread and painstakingly he stitched until, with a beaming smile, he was able to present Hue with an Alice band. Gently coaxing the curtain of hair from her scarred face, he slipped the yellow ribbon over her head. Tilting her chin upwards, he smiled down at the child, took her hand and together they walked the length of the compound. Hesitantly at first, then gaining confidence, Hue held up her head, laughing into his anxious face and limping awkwardly but happily on her new leg.

No more long silences, no more staring at the ground. The soldier began to smile, began to talk. He told us his name was Dave and that he was from Philadelphia. He spoke of his mother, of his father who was a builder, and of his eight-year-old sister whom he loved so much. He hadn't dared hope that he might live to see his family again. Until he saw Hue. Hue had given him the spark, had reawakened his crushed spirit and made him embrace the possibility that he might actually survive this hellish place and make it back to his world. It had seemed an eternity since he and his two best friends from school had joined up proudly to serve their country, and to buy themselves a coveted place at college – the reward for service in a combat zone.

Now his buddies were both dead and where, he asked, was

the sense that their efforts were of benefit to their country, or anyone's country?

Dave from Philadelphia was back. And so was Hue. He had made her feel the way a pretty little girl should. Each had broken through the paralysis caused by the horrors they'd experienced. Here were two souls who made a connection and allowed themselves to heal.

I have often wondered whether Dave got back to his family, have prayed that he did – and with a medal.

Such extraordinary connections were infinite; some had happier outcomes than others, all pointed to the amazing reserves of courage and compassion to be found among the tragic and innocent victims – soldiers and civilians, adults and children alike – of this truly dreadful war.

Ten-year-old Ba was travelling to market with her mother when the rackety, makeshift Lambretta bus hit the mine. Wooden seating was reduced in split seconds into thousands of splintered matchsticks; fragments of twisted metal mixed with human limbs and spilled vegetables; a few downy feathers floating in the hot breeze all that remained of the crate of plump ducks . . . Just another everyday occurrence in South Vietnam's peasant community.

Ba was the only survivor of the carnage. Passers-by spotted the flickering signs of life in the half-dead child and took her to the local hospital in Qui Nhon, where the team of New Zealand surgeons were based. Blood transfusion was unfamiliar and culturally unacceptable among the local people, and blood couldn't easily be stored because of the erratic electricity supply. So, as often happened in cases of dire need, blood was donated on the spot by nurses, doctors and soldiers to improve the child's chances.

It was several days before Ba realised she had lost both of her legs at the buttocks. Her shattered life could be salvaged only by the surgeons carrying out bilateral hindquarter amputations, as they had done with many before her. A few days later she was transferred to our convalescent centre for post-operative nursing and as much tender loving care as was humanly possible.

How do you heal a child who has lost everything? Father, mother, brother, sisters, legs. All gone in an instant, just like that.

As days turned to weeks, this little girl's character and personality began to emerge. Even with the pain and shock, she couldn't suppress a mischievous nature that kept us all on our toes and, as her wounds healed and her condition became more bearable, she became the leader of a gang of pranksters.

Most of the children were assigned chores. Each evening, four of the older boys gathered to scrub the rubber-thonged flip-flops which all the children wore. Then four of the girls, giggling and chattering, would deliver the sandals to the foot of each bed or sleeping mat, ready for morning. Many of the children had only one foot, or no feet. If a left-footed sandal was left for a child with only a right foot, there was loss of face all round.

Ba quickly established that she was to have a pair left at her sleeping mat, and they were to be red. She protested vigorously until this was done to her exact wishes. The flip-flops were for her hands, with which she propelled herself at speed around the corridors and compound. She was always busy with something: marshalling children into the classroom, helping to feed the younger ones, guiding those who were blind. Wherever she was there was laughter and movement. One morning we found all the babies in their cribs had acquired moustaches, and the chubbier infants had beards. Ba had organised the prank, arming a bunch of kids with indelible pens for the purpose.

At that time, there was only one limb-fitting centre in the whole of South Vietnam. It was based in Saigon, but facilities were basic and the staff inundated, largely with maimed servicemen. In 1970 the Canadians would send a team of physiotherapists and limb-fitters to Qui Nhon to set up a rehabilitation centre, but for now there was only Saigon to pin our hopes on.

Somehow the miraculous Bridget Stevenson got an appointment in Saigon for Ba. Several trips were made – no easy task in itself. The 360-kilometre journey south was accomplished by hitching rides on military aircraft. Often it took several stages in C130s or helicopters, hopping from Qui Nhon to Nha Trang, and on to Saigon. The military authorities always did their best to accommodate civilian personnel involved in humanitarian work, but military matters took precedence and you could be – and often were – bumped off flights at any time.

After her final fitting, Ba and I travelled back to Qui Nhon. Her new legs were ugly, heavy, cumbersome contraptions, kept in place by buckling thick, leather straps, criss-cross fashion, over her chest. The legs were wooden with a hinged knee joint. A swift nudge at the back of the knee made the leg bend – maybe.

Ba hated them and flatly refused to wear them, so we travelled with them strapped to the side of my weekend bag while I, as usual, carried the child perched on my hip. Her pretty dress was always arranged carefully to conceal the fact that she had only half a body.

We careered to Tan Son Nhut military airport in a local taxi and began the long wait to hitch a ride back to Qui Nhon.

On this occasion I tangled with the efficient young soldier behind the ramshackle counter when I tried to check in. When he noticed Ba had no lower limbs, he denied us entry to the C130, explaining that if the plane came down, everyone on board had to be physically capable of getting themselves clear.

'Listen,' I argued. 'If the damned plane goes down, no one is going to be worrying about a ten-year-old Vietnamese kid with no legs. Let me worry about that.'

I was tired and hot, and felt the prickling of tears of frustration. Ba stroked my face and started singing the song she often sang to the younger children, but there was no shifting the corporal. He was following the rulebook, and it was difficult to argue with that.

Ba and I curled up on the hard floor alongside dozens of soldiers who were hugging their weapons close and using bulky kit bags as pillows and foot rests. Many of the GIs were also hitching rides and, as always, were kind. Ba always accepted their offers of gum or peanut brittle to squirrel away in her hoard of treats which she always shared with other children.

We slept fitfully through the tropical night and were eventually called and given a seat on a US Air Force hospital plane that was transporting wounded men to Clark air base in the Philippines, from where they would eventually be sent home. I had been told about these planes and their tragic loads – so many young men in their prime, now horribly wounded – by army nurses in Qui Nhon. I didn't envy the air force nurses working on those flights.

This particular plane, half filled with wounded men, was scheduled to stop at Qui Nhon and take on more casualties from the 67th Evac. I strapped myself in, Ba on my knee as always, her dress carefully arranged. I watched the nurses with professional admiration as they quickly and efficiently tended the soldiers with a ready smile, a quip or two, and compassion in their eyes.

Our seat was right alongside a litter on which lay a very badly injured soldier. His name and date of birth were on a label tied to a button on his blue hospital shirt. His eyes, sunken in his ashen face, seemed decades older than his twenty-one years. I watched the blood drip slowly through the tubing inserted into his neck and saw that his right arm ended abruptly in a bloodied, bandaged stump just below his elbow.

His left hand was heavily bandaged and consisted of a lobster claw: the pincer-like thumb and forefinger only.

He was shivering, and focusing hard on trying to pick up a cigarette that lay on the blanket that covered his chest. Ba watched him carefully, seeming instinctively to realise the importance of allowing him the dignity of trying to pick it up himself. She smiled at him. There was no way you could ignore Ba's smile. The soldier tried to smile back, and Ba picked up the cigarette, lit it, expertly took a couple of puffs, and placed it gently between his lips. The look of peace and contentment that came with his first draw made me wonder why I had never taken up the habit. It looked so good and gave him such comfort.

The senior air force nurse told us off. Several of the wounded had oxygen masks in place, a few litres of oxygen running into their lungs. Naked flames can, of course, ignite oxygen, but there was no danger; I could see that the men were well away from where we were. Nonetheless, the nurse was right to draw my attention to it, but I was very glad she hadn't until a few puffs had transported him momentarily to a better place.

A few minutes later, his cigarette gently removed, he turned his head slowly and spoke to Ba. 'Hi, kid. Speak English?'

Ba nodded, and asked, 'You sick?'

He sighed. 'No, tired. I'm going home.' He looked at me with a puzzled expression. I explained I was a British nurse caring for wounded children in Qui Nhon.

'Can I hold her, ma'am? Please? Hey, kid, you're just like my little sister, you know that?'

I panicked for a second. I didn't want him to know about her legs. I wasn't sure how he would react; maybe he was too ill to notice. This was ridiculous, I then thought, and placed the little girl gently on his thighs, hoping he wouldn't notice how abnormally light she was. It was then, in a moment of blinding pain and anger, which I feel again as I write this, that I realised he had no thighs. He too had lost his legs. His blanket had hidden from view what I should have seen.

The breath stopped in my throat. Ba knew. I felt her torso stiffen, but her expression didn't change. She smiled and stroked his face, and he spoke to her softly of his folks, his brothers and his sister back home in Oklahoma. How he would see them soon. He spoke of his girl and how he wished he had had time to buy her a gift. His face bloodless, his breath ragged, his eyes dulled with pain. His light was slowly fading. Ba just kept smiling, and softly, sweetly, sang her song for him.

I couldn't utter a word. I was possessed by a complicated mixture of anger, compassion and grief. Here, right before my eyes, was the essence of war and what it does to people. Diamond-sharp and permanent, that moment has never left me.

A healthy boy soldier, fighting for a little-understood cause and now for his life; an idealistic young nurse, raised in the beauty and tranquillity of North Wales, who wanted nothing more than to help ease some of the pain, and a ten-year-old Vietnamese child who had been on her way to market with her mother, full of life and laughter.

Three characters brought together in a macabre drama, written by politicians in a comfortable universe somewhere far, far away.

22

OSCAR AND THE SEABEES

It's almost impossible to describe, and certainly impossible to explain, the many contradictions that were thrown up in the Vietnam War. One was constantly confounded by the unexpected in human nature as well as events, and struck by how quaint and curious certain aspects were or, more often, how moving or disturbing. And, in certain instances, all of these things at once.

Sometimes, villages where the inhabitants were suspected of harbouring Vietcong were torched by American and South Vietnamese troops in an effort to smoke out the enemy. On occasion, such villages were fired on by helicopter gunships, with bamboo and thatch huts quickly burned to the ground. No matter the reason for what happened, often soldiers would grab babies and little children, scoop them up, and hurry them randomly into helicopters. They were whirled away from danger, but also from what was left of their homes and loved ones. The soldiers on board the helicopters quickly tagged each child by tying a buff-coloured military label to an ankle or wrist and naming the casualties in sequence, using the phonetic alphabet. Thus, the children who came in – frightened, confused, injured, but safe – had names such as Foxtrot, Hotel, Tango and Victor. There was no time for niceties amid the chaos and noise.

The children would be taken into the 67th Evac.'s casualty clearing station for rapid assessment, surgery, or other appropriate treatment, then the medics would say, 'OK, send them over to the Oasis. They'll know what to do.' Later, young soldiers from places like Little Rock, Arkansas, and Birmingham, Alabama, would call in regularly to check that 'their kids' were doing OK.

Many times the makeshift names the kids had been given stuck to them. The first Montagnard I ever met was a girl named 'Oscar'. The Montagnards were members of the hill tribes in the central highlands of Vietnam, Cambodia and Laos. Oscar was a beautiful little girl of nine or ten, who had been operated on at the hospital and kept there for a couple of weeks while her abdominal and eye injuries healed. I suspected that the nurses there fell in love with her, though eventually, of course, she had to be moved and was transferred to our Centre.

We found out later through an interpreter that her real name was Thuy, but she refused to answer to that. 'No!' she would say very forcefully. 'I am Oscar.'

Two years later, during my second tour of duty – this time at Pat Smith's hospital in Kontum – I found the village where Oscar was rumoured to have been resettled. I had photographs of her and showed them around the place, asking for Thuy. Someone recognised her and took me to her, but they all called her Oscar, still the only name she would answer to.

I remember, too, a little boy tagged Bravo, who had 65 per cent full-thickness burns to his torso and one leg. He loved his name, and it suited him well, for he handled his pain and skin grafts with quiet stoicism. He eventually overcame his injuries. Bravo was a terrific name for him.

We often thought longingly of having more trained staff, another nurse, perhaps, or a physiotherapist, but we knew it was just wishful thinking. Then, suddenly, help arrived briefly but in abundance when forty United States Navy Seabees descended on us, offering their services for two days. While their ship was anchored in the bay, half had been assigned the Save the Children Fund Centre as a project for the forty-eight-hour period. The other half descended on one of the orphanages in town.

To say we were nonplussed is an understatement. When they arrived, we had no idea who or what the Seabees were or what they did. When they left two days later, we'd more than learned all about them.

Seabees are the construction workers of the US Navy. What these guys cannot do can be written on the back of a postage stamp with room to spare!

In a whirlwind of hammering nails, sawing wood, mixing concrete and painting white anything that stood still and didn't salute back, they transformed the Centre. The children were goggle-eyed as they were coaxed to join in by these caring men, and they soon did so with gusto. OK, so a few thumbs got hit, there was a cut or two, but mostly it was fun.

As if by magic, the compound was landscaped. A white picket fence sprang up around sections of newly planted saplings and flowering bushes. Cu happily watered everything in sight at regular intervals. A square, concrete paddling pool was built and filled with two feet of water – and that was just the first day!

We had time to think about what we'd like them to do during the second day. In the classroom, the children sat on straw mats on the floor. Not after the Seabees were done! These incredible craftsmen made twenty-four desks and chairs, painted white. Just like that. The children, and their Vietnamese teacher, were thrilled.

Unbelievably, in between all this activity, the men actually found time to play with the children; sing songs accompanied by harmonica and guitars, barbecue steaks and drink root beer.

Then they left. But first they tidied up. How many men do that? It was like being caught in the aftermath of a hurricane. You would almost think you had imagined it all but for the incredible legacy they left behind: a super classroom, a paddling pool, a pretty landscaped garden . . . and the children talked about them for months.

I salute you, Seabees. You did, and still do, a terrific job.

23

EBB AND FLOW

The 67th Evac. consisted of a cluster of Quonset huts huddled together at one end of the airstrip, just over the back wall of our children's rehabilitation centre. These huts housed the broken young men of America, wounded in body and spirit. The casualty receiving area looked out onto the tarmac where choppers landed with sickening regularity to disgorge their bloodied payloads. Teams of medics, men and women, hunched over to avoid the spinning rotor blades, ran out trundling gurneys between them and unloaded the men. I stood in awe of those courageous Huey 'dust-off' pilots who went in so often under fire to rescue the wounded; and I so admired and felt for those nurses and doctors working in such circumstances. To see your own men so horribly injured, many beyond repair, day in and day out, must have been devastating.

For the female nurses life was particularly restrictive. It was difficult and unwise for them to leave their bases because of the unstable security situation, and most times they were too exhausted anyway. Working at such a pace in emotionally draining conditions over a period of time meant that the effort to go out was often just too great. Inside those ugly barbed-wire perimeters, life shrank to nothing but a blur of work, sleep whenever possible, a rushed meal, and back to working in the face of death. These nurses counted the months, the weeks, the days – and, finally, the hours – until that blessed moment of leave for R & R or, better yet, boarding the freedom bird for home.

But some did seek a little change of scene by visiting our Centre. It is infinitely sad to see innocent children orphaned, traumatised and displaced by war; at the same time, children are resilient and, with the right support, can bounce back. Most people respond to the shy smile or giggle of a child, and adults instinctively reach out to comfort a child who is frightened or in pain. So the nurses who came round changed dressings, cuddled toddlers, and fed and burped babies. They were rewarded with affection and hugs, and a welcome reminder that they were still capable of feeling.

I felt that we, as civilians caring for children, were perhaps more fortunate. And, as British citizens, at least we did not have to deal on a daily basis with seeing our own young men being blown to smithereens. But sadness and despair at witnessing the relentless carnage built up nevertheless. It was only years later that I became aware of the reservoir of pain that had nowhere to go. Most doctors and, particularly, nurses, carry this same reservoir of pain, wherever they apply their skills. It's all too easy to recall the memories, images seared into the brain, crystal clear and immovable. One such memory that haunts me is of the letter.

Just as we encouraged the American army nurses to have a change of scene by coming over to spend time with the children, they suggested we come over to their hospital and do a bit of volunteering. It might do us good to lend a helping hand with those small things no one had time for, like reading mail to the men, sharing a joke, or holding someone's

Above: Me, aged one year old, with my father

Left: Captain Arthur Frederick Watts

Below: Village party to celebrate VE Day, 8 May 1945. I'm in nurse's uniform, front row, second from right

Village School, Pentrefelin, 1948. I'm third from left in second row. Hugh is at the end of the same row

Family portrait circa 1955. Left to right: Joan, Susan, my father, me, Hugh and Paul (seated)

Me (left) and Pat Ashe, Holy Family Hospital, Qui Nhon, 1967

The Children's Centre, Qui Nhon, Christmas Day, 1967. American soldiers helping out

Above: Ruby, Pat and Me receiving flowers from military chief of South Vietnam Army at Qui Nhon, 1968

Left: Ken Shapiro, journalist for the 'Stars and Stripes', Qui Nhon, 1967

Below: US Navy 'Seabee' after building swimming pool at the children's centre

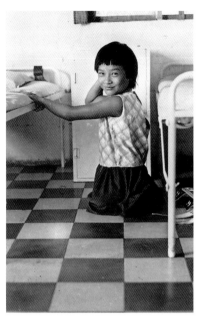

Ba. I will never forget her.

Hue, wearing her yellow ribbon

Oscar, who loved her new name

The US Navy 'SeaBees' built desks for the children …

… and fences and swings

Lily, Jean Ringe and me, leaving Qui Nhon in tears

Montagnard people of Kontum, the Central Highlands of Vietnam

Drinking rice wine, New Year's Day, Kontum, 1970

Catching up with young friends, Kontum, 1969

Sisters Gabrielle and Caliste, who nursed me when I had malaria

hand when they were frightened. Just being there, not having to rush off some place, was (and still is) such an important part of caring; and patients were (and still are) often short-changed because of the time, effort and energy that went into saving lives.

The first time I went over to the 67th I was sent to the surgical unit to sit with a badly wounded soldier, hooked up to blood and saline drips. I could see only one of his eyes through his heavy bandaging – and that eye looked abnormally bright and not focusing well. A chest drain protruded from the blood-ied bandages round his torso; the fluid level barely moved, so shallow was the swing up, down, up, down in the glass tube, marking his laboured breathing. Nothing was draining into the bottle of his urinary catheter. Not a drop. It was not a good sign.

I sat down quietly beside his cot and took his hand with a gentle squeeze. That eye swivelled in my direction, and he slowly, softly, returned the squeeze.

I was twenty-seven years old; this lad was twenty-one. I had a brother of eighteen at home. What the hell were we doing in the middle of this appalling mess? I thanked God it was not my brother lying in that bed.

He wanted something. 'Water?' I asked.

The eye blinked and he gave my hand another soft squeeze. There was a disposable waxed cup on the locker, but he was unable to suck on the straw that was in it. I managed to find some cotton-ball swabs and a kidney basin of ice cubes. I damped the swabs on the ice and brushed them across the soldier's lips. His colourless tongue peeped out, and I kept on squeezing little drops of fluid onto his dry and bloodless lips. Every now and again there was a slight pressure on my hand, almost imperceptible but definitely there.

Somebody stopped at the bedside, and I looked up to see Mike standing there. He was Jeff's surgeon. Our eyes met and held for a moment, then he crouched down, put his hand under the pillow beneath the mortally wounded head and brought out a letter. 'Jeff, there's a letter for you . . . would you like to hear it? Is it OK for Anne to read your letter to you?' Jeff squeezed my hand. Mike handed me the crumpled letter and moved off to another young man fighting for his life.

I opened the sealed letter and slowly began reading it out loud. It was a letter from a wife to her husband. Her love for him lifted off the page, and I felt embarrassed voicing the intimate words meant only for him. I don't suppose I recall the letter exactly word for word, but this is near enough what she had written:

Dearest Jeff
My love for you grows day by day, hour by hour. I have some wonderful news for you, honey. I wanted to wait until we are together, when I can look into your eyes, but the happiness is more than I can bear alone, and I have to tell you now, my darling. When we met in Hawaii, I thanked God for allowing us to be together again. I will never, ever forget that special time. Now I have part of you growing inside me. I am carrying our child. Please come home soon. Know that I love you and pray for the day we can be together. Be strong, my darling. Be safe. We are both waiting for you, your Jeanie.

It wasn't a long letter and I sensed that she, bursting with the joy of new life and with that sixth sense that women have, somehow knew what he was facing. She was willing her husband to survive. I felt embarrassed and privileged and heartbroken all at the same time to be the messenger. Jeff squeezed my hand when I said his wife's name, Jeanie. I was chirpy to begin with. 'It's a letter from Jeanie.' Gradually, as my voice wavered and thickened with emotion, his eye dimmed and closed. I read on, willing myself not to break down.

I reached the end of the letter, 'We are both waiting for you, your Jeanie,' but the touch of his hand had faded and the fluid level in the chest drain sat silent and still.

Jeff had gone, quietly slipped away.

Nurses are expected to maintain a strong, cheerful demeanour at all times, keep their own emotions buttoned down. I was pretty good at that, especially as I learned as a child to keep my true feelings hidden. In training we were taught how to conceal distaste or pity from patients, and I suppose my father's oft-repeated blandishments about keeping a stiff upper lip and getting on with life, though seemingly harsh, stood me in good stead.

But somehow, at the moment of folding the letter into its envelope and tucking it carefully between Jeff's fingers, the tender words of a wife had made this particular death just one too many. And I wasn't managing it well. Perhaps I was just tired, but as I sat alongside Jeff's body I felt lost, as if with his last breath something had gone out of me too.

It must have shown on my face because when Mike appeared, he looked at me hard and said, 'You're not OK.' He quickly called for an orderly to take care of Jeff's body, signed off the clinical chart, and said, 'Come on. I've time for a quick drink.'

In the small area set aside for personnel who had no time to go for a meal, one could get a cool drink, a sandwich, sit down for a little while, maybe smoke a cigarette. Mike fetched us iced tea from a large urn. I hated iced tea, but it didn't seem to matter right now. He put in some sugar and stirred.

'I don't take sugar,' I said.

'Right now you are having some sugar. Drink it.'

'He was going to be a father,' I said quietly.

Mike's handsome face was drawn with fatigue but his bright, intelligent eyes were alert and expressive. In them, I read frustration and compassion. I picked up the waxy disposable cup of horrible tea and drank from it, noticing a spray of tiny blood spots on the shirt of Mike's scrubs, the pattern almost beautiful . . .

In the silence that hung between us, Mike looked at his watch. 'I've got two more surgeries lined up, but I'll be through by six,' he said. 'Why don't we go get a bowl of hepatitis soup at the hooch round the corner from you? We need to talk – *you* need to talk.'

I was beginning to feel better. Who'd have guessed a simple iced tea, laced in more ways than one with sweetness, had the power to recover my recently mislaid sunny disposition? I nodded my agreement to his suggestion.

'Good,' he said. 'I'll pick you up at the Centre.'

We sat opposite each other at the small battered Formica table in the beaten-up little restaurant, which looked God-awful but where the noodle soups were delicious. I don't think anyone ever got sick from eating there, but the soldiers called their favourite choice hepatitis soup and the name stuck.

The general surgeon from Pueblo County, Colorado, and the nurse from Wales looked at each other over the large steaming bowls.

'I suppose it's some comfort to know he had a hand to hold at the end,' I said. 'But I can't stop thinking about that baby who'll never know its father, and that poor wife raising the child all alone. It's the waste, Mike, the terrible, mindless waste. I just don't get it.'

Mike looked at me intently. 'Let me tell you a story,' he said. 'When I was ten, my aunt's husband died of a massive heart attack. They were still young, you know – she was my mom's kid sister – and they hadn't been married long, and all of a sudden he was gone. She really loved that guy and she was totally shattered.'

He stopped to devour some more soup then went on with his story. 'My aunt was one of the first women law students in her college and she'd fought tooth and nail to get on that course. Now, a month after Ed's death, she discovers she's pregnant. It's a disaster for her dream of becoming a lawyer, so what to do? There were a lot of long, whispered discussions went on in the lounge room at night, and I used to eavesdrop from my bedroom door. As a farm boy in Colorado, I already knew about the birds and the bees, but listening to these debates about the baby, I learned a lot more.'

Mike gave me a wry smile and signalled for a couple of beers.

'What my parents and aunt were busy discussing was whether or not Margie should have an abortion. That was a really sinful thing even to think about in our small Baptist community, but she could easily go off to Denver and nobody would be any the wiser. But if she kept the baby, could she face raising it on her own, and what about her law degree . . .

'Margie really agonised for a while, but the love she had felt for her husband and the knowledge that this was his child too helped her decide. There was no way she was going to lose Ed's baby as well as Ed.

'My family would have understood if she'd decided the other way, but she chose life. I've always respected her decision, especially because that baby turned out to be my cousin Randy. He's an ophthalmic surgeon and a great guy. So you see, Anne, Jeff's wife's situation is not a lot different from my Aunt Margie's. She's got the same choices.'

I took a gulp of cold beer and slowly twirled some noodles

around my chopsticks. I was aware of tension and a sense of urgency in Mike.

'I keep telling myself that life at any cost is precious,' he said. 'I have to try and believe that in order to stay sane when I'm struggling to save those guys on that operating table. And you know . . . sometimes in this war I'm not so sure that saving a life is always doing anyone a favour. Some of these men will live, sure, but they'll be so disabled they might wish they had died. Many do die, and then their families will be thinking they would give anything to have them come home alive, even if they were brain damaged or paralysed or basket cases – just so long as they have their loved one back. I guess a lot of bargaining with God goes on, but if they live, what will be their quality of life? I feel those who don't make it are sometimes better off, but I still feel depressed when I can't save them.'

He toyed with his soup, looked at me with anguish in his expression, then said quietly, 'Anne, I lost four today.'

Instinctively I reached out to him. He took my hand, and held my gaze for a few moments before taking a deep breath and continuing.

'Two went quickly. There wasn't much to save when they brought them in. The third one was a surgical nightmare and I wasn't sure he'd pull through. He died about two hours after he was wheeled out of the OR. The fourth was Jeff.'

Silence.

'I tell myself I can't be God, and if I'm to remain human I have to believe in life. But they're dying all around me, Anne, and like you I'm finding it hard to deal with the senseless waste of young guys in their prime.'

My heart went out to Mike, and to all of us caught up in this maelstrom of poor political decision-making that allowed the military juggernaut to crush innocents in its path.

'You know, the children at your Centre are the lucky ones,'

he said. 'Most of them will survive – maimed, yes, but they're full of life and fun. I wonder where they'll be five, ten, twenty years from now. Many don't know if their families have survived or where they are, and I worry about who will care for them once we've all gone. It seems so unjust that I don't really want to think about their situation at all. So, try and take it one day at a time, and I hope that being around people who give them love and care instead of bullets and hate, will help them deal with the life ahead of them. I guess that's all any of us can do.'

I thought of Jeff and Jeanie, and of the children; he thought of the countless others he couldn't save and of those with whom he'd succeeded. It was comforting to know that we felt the same way about things, and that we had each other to share the heartache with.

Mike stood, held out his hand.

'Come on, girl,' he said. 'Time to go.'

That night, the mutual respect and friendship between Mike and me, fuelled by the raw emotions of the day and the threat of danger around us later on, exploded into a full-blown, deeply passionate liaison.

We left the café and walked the short distance back to the Centre. The night was sultry beneath the velvet Vietnamese sky, but it was very dark as we slowly picked our way back to the compound. We could hear the oscillating murmur of voices floating on either side of the dirt road where candles flickered here and there, makeshift kerosene stoves sputtered into action, and the smell of food, smoke and sewage wafted across the night air. The roadside was home to countless dispossessed people fleeing the destruction of their villages, and their hidden presence made for a ghostly atmosphere.

The unmistakable sound of rifles being cocked by unseen men as we passed by was nerve-wracking: they could have been anyone, friend or enemy, but how could we know? I was not only very conscious of Mike's physical presence but, in those few minutes, very grateful for it. Time had flown by and we were now, stupidly, breaking the curfew.

Safely back at the compound living quarters, I left Mike in the lounge area while I went off to my room to fetch the book he wanted to borrow. With James Michener's *The Source* in my hand, I turned to go and saw, in the soft light thrown by the oil lamp on my bedside table, Mike standing in the doorway.

For a moment it really did feel as though the world stopped spinning, holding its breath for one long, intense moment. We stood reeling with the powerful attraction so far denied.

Caught up in emotions that were challenged daily in an arena where the normal parameters of our world had been blown apart, we made love that night until all those emotions – tears and joy both – were spent, and then we slept in each other's arms.

Our passion was an expression of need as much as of desire: a need to affirm life in the middle of so much death and destruction; a reminder that love existed, that it was still possible to have feelings. That we were not dead yet.

A few days later, Mike quietly told me he was married.

It was not that he had deliberately hidden the fact or that I had wilfully refused to read the signs – the subject just never came up. Aside from the cold water I felt being poured on my growing feelings for him, my rule about married men, which I had never before broken, was – and is – that they were strictly off limits. I believe that the emotional havoc caused by my father's infidelity to my mother shaped my own morality; I had always known that I would never, ever allow myself to be the cause of such pain in others, so the news came as a shock.

Mike loved his wife and family. An honourable man, he

made no attempt to minimise or gloss over what they meant to him, and I saw how tormented he was over our situation. We had been drawn together in the most excoriating of times: love and solace were in short supply, and I think we both realised that our relationship would not have been allowed to develop in more normal circumstances.

I was determined that when his tour of duty ended, there would be no further contact between us.

For the remainder of his posting at 67th Evac. Mike and I remained close, always good friends. In a war zone, finding time alone is almost impossible, which was probably just as well, and frequent mortar attacks, or ammo dumps being blown sky high, gave a whole new meaning to 'Did the earth move for you . . . ?'

But we were able to steal odd moments: share special times reading poetry to each other on the beach; laughing together at a show put on for the troops; enjoying T-bone steaks and get-togethers with a group of friends who, like us, were trying to make the best of this bloody war.

The day Mike Samuels left Vietnam, the pain I felt was indescribable. I imagine that undergoing an amputation without the benefit of anaesthetic would feel as I did that day.

But I had drawn a line. Neither of us were bad people, and I was not my father. It was over.

It didn't work out exactly as I'd determined it would. I do believe it's possible to love more than one person, and I've had other meaningful relationships since those long-ago times but, over the years, one way and another, Mike and I have remained in touch. Despite several long periods, even years, without contact between us, he always tracked me down.

Our friendship has survived the years, but it has never held me back, never influenced my personal decisions, or troubled me. There are still times when I see a striking sunset, read a good book, hear a wonderful piece of music and think: Mike would enjoy this.

It has never felt like cheating.

24

A GIFT FOR SANTA

My first tropical Christmas: hot, humid, dusty; incoming mortars and sweating soldiers. But we were not going to allow such minor details to interfere with celebrations.

As a way of thanking the local US military personnel for the magnificent help they offered in their spare time, the Vietnamese staff wanted to invite them to spend Christmas Day with us at the Centre. Christmas is about children after all, and we certainly had plenty of them.

The soldiers were very enthusiastic and set about planning the day with gusto. Many had young children back home, and maybe this might lessen their homesickness a little. It was terribly important to them to make this Christmas happen, and preparations became their obsession. The Centre was a hive of activity for several days beforehand. Some of the army nurses taught the children how to make brightly coloured paper chains and the soldiers shared Christmas cards from back home with the children.

Soon the wards were festooned with home-made decorations: drawings of Bambi and various Disney characters, little angels with sparkly halos. A few young men were detailed to go to market and bring back girl gifts and boy gifts which they then wrapped. The children were goggle-eyed at all of this, not too sure what was going on but having the best time fixing up the place.

Not to be outdone by the soldiers, the airmen appeared with what looked like a real Christmas tree. They had flown up to Dalat, lopped off the tops of a few fir trees, and presented us with one of them. The rest were for the wards at the military hospital.

Now all we needed was a Santa Claus.

Bill was a crusty old sergeant who sometimes drifted into the Centre. A veteran of the Korean War and a heavy drinker, he was trying to keep body and soul together till the freedom bird took him back to home and retirement. On his best days he looked like W. C. Fields on a bad day. Bill was a man of few words, who kept himself to himself, but he used to come round and visit the kids in his own quiet way.

He was thrilled when we approached him to be our Santa Claus. We found some bright red, shiny material in the local market and, with great solemnity, we measured Bill for his costume. Xuong, one of the nurse aides who was a whiz at tailoring, excitedly ran up a suit for Santa. Great discussions took place about the whiskers, and eventually John, a helicopter pilot from Evansville, Illinois, decided his creative skills could stretch to producing a fluffy white beard on the day.

The plan was that Santa would arrive in the back of an army jeep, carrying a sackful of gifts. Due to security restrictions, time was short because our guests had to be back at their bases by early afternoon. So, nothing for it, we would have our Christmas get-together at the hottest part of the day.

As our guests arrived, each was 'issued' with either a baby or a child to look after for the day. They took care of nappies, food and so on for the period they were there. There is something indescribably touching about a teenage soldier bottle-feeding a baby, or feeding a blind child. All we had to do was tend the more seriously ill children, and keep an eye on the episodes of sheer panic as young men from Honolulu, Flagstaff or Missoula grappled with full nappies and regurgitating babies!

Cold drinks and even some turkey had been provided by the military, and Tinh, our trusty cook, produced colourful platters of stir-fried vegetables and grilled fish caught by local fishermen. With the meal ready, soldiers, nuns, nurses and children waited for Santa to arrive. And waited. The allotted time came – and went.

Disappointment was setting in when we were disturbed by the noise of a chopper coming ever nearer and louder. Within minutes it was hovering about fifteen feet above the compound. Little ones were petrified and ran for cover under beds and tables laden with fruit, food and drink. They knew from experience that choppers could mean trouble. Dust choked us. Flowers were blasted out of the dry earth, sapling trees bowed to the ground. Cu lost his pith helmet in the downdraught, and was deeply miffed.

Then, from the chopper a rope ladder snaked its way to the ground. Santa's rear end appeared and, slowly, the swaying, inebriated man slid down the ladder. His beard, a riot of cotton balls and paste, completely obliterated most of his face. In the middle of a lusty 'Ho ho ho', Bill slipped and crashed to the ground. I remember thinking, oh my God, we've killed Santa Claus.

GIs carried the now inert figure into one of the dorms and laid him across two of the small beds, where he slept off the effects of responsibility with many pairs of young eyes anxiously watching over him.

The sack of scattered parcels was rescued, the gifts were opened, and the hilarity continued. The array of pretty combs, mirrors and ribbons, the crayons, paints and exercise books were brilliant. The bags of rubber bands, from which the boys made all sorts of extraordinary things, were a stroke of genius. Peanut brittle, a staple of the soldier's care package, was supplied in great tooth-rotting slabs.

Later, Santa enjoyed copious amounts of good, strong black coffee prepared by Tinh, and then opened his own gift, shyly handed to him by one of the children in the quiet room where he was recovering. I think he could cope better in the quiet of a room alone, rather than in the middle of the more raucous, crowded celebrations, the fear of which had maybe scared this lonely man in the first place. He was absolutely thrilled with his gift, a neck chain from which hung a bamboo carving.

The twenty-fifth of December, 1967, had certainly turned out to be one of those special Christmases that nobody there would ever forget!

25

VACATION IN PARADISE

We four British nurses, Jean, Ruby, Pat and I, taking care of babies, toddlers and children, were often emotionally and physically drained, but Save the Children Fund generously ensured we had breaks from duty. As we were so few, it was impossible for more than one of us at a time to take leave; it would have been unfair to the others and to the Vietnamese nurses, so we took turns to go away individually and alone.

During the Tet Offensive, there had been widespread fighting in Danang, Hue, Qui Nhon and Nha Trang, and the civilian airport in Saigon was closed more often than it was open. Because of the unstable situation, I was unable to get away when my leave came up, which caused a backlog for the others. We were growing more fatigued and depleted by the day, when one of our regular visiting generals dropped in and saw how exhausted we were.

'You girls can't go on like this,' he said, 'No, it's not right. I'll get you the necessary papers and you can go out on one of our R and R flights.'

'Where do they go?' we all asked at once.

'Well, you can go to Hawaii or Australia, and Hong Kong, Singapore, Penang . . .'

I thought, hey, this is great. He came back later that same afternoon, gave all of us the token rank of captain, and presented us with military travel orders allowing us R&R privileges.

'Right. Now: where would you like to go?'

'I'd love to go to Hawaii,' I said.

'No, all the seats to Hawaii are taken up. The married men get priority to meet their wives in Hawaii so there are no seats on those flights. Where else would you like to go?'

'Australia?'

'Nope, sorry, all the seats to Australia are taken up. The single guys like Australian leave.'

'Well, General, you tell me where I can go.'

'Right now there's only Penang.'

'OK, I'll go to Penang.' I thought: where the hell is Penang?

Within a short time I was off to Tan Son Nhut airport, courtesy of the US military authorities, where I was processed along with a hundred and fifty soldiers and junior officers. GI was understood to mean 'government issue', and I certainly understood the term during that experience. I was a number, just like everyone else. There was no flexibility, only the tunnel vision of official rules and regulations. I recalled soldiers referring to the army as the 'green machine', young men fed into one end of the machine, broken down and rebuilt at boot camp, then spat out at the other end, all wearing green, all numbered, and looking and sounding exactly the same. I was processed efficiently, exactly as though I *was* a GI – which, rather obviously, I was not. They were determined to make this round peg fit into a square hole.

I was the only female on board and everyone was terribly polite – 'After you, ma'am' – and so I was always ahead of the crowd. First in line, first on the plane, first off. I was tired, way beyond excited, and could hardly wait to get somewhere where people weren't killing each other, where no helicopters clattered night and day and, especially, where there were no

wounded or dying children. Penang, it turned out, is a beautiful island off the coast of Malaysia, a jewel in the sparkling
Strait of Malacca.

On the plane the American stewardesses were a bit surprised
to see me but I was treated kindly and well. It wasn't a long
flight, and when we arrived at Butterworth Air Base I, needless
to say, was ushered off the plane first. 'After you, ma'am, after
you.' I really wanted a strong man, preferably Mike, to take
control, lead me down the steps and whisk me away from all
this. No chance. As I hit the baking tarmac I saw a waiting line
of gorgeous Malaysian girls in tight-fitting dresses waiting to
welcome the boys. They were a bit nonplussed to see me
coming down the steps. For each soldier they had a colourful
garland of flowers to place round the neck, a big kiss on the lips
and a cold beer. So I got the garland round the neck, a cold
Tiger beer pressed into my hand – and a quick peck on the
cheek. I think the men were kissed rather more enthusiastically!

A clearly startled sergeant said, 'Welcome to Penang, ma'am,'
and waved me across to a large, temporary-looking building,
with rows of chairs facing a screen on a wooden stage. Behind
the screen were red satin curtains which had seen better days.
Maybe it was the insufferable heat – there was no air conditioning – that made everything look faded and dowdy. All I
wanted was to get the hell out of there to a comfortable hotel,
a cold shower and a clean bed. From the look of things, that
wasn't going to happen any time soon, but at least I could sit
unobtrusively at the back – I thought. Naturally, I was ushered
along to the centre of the front row for what was obviously
going to be a briefing of some sort. Most of the men were looking at me quizzically, and there was some whispering and
laughing among the rowdier soldiers, but the young officers on
either side of me seemed kind.

An officer entered and took the stage. He looked hard at me,
hesitated, then said, 'Ma'am, and gentlemen,' and launched

into a lecture on venereal diseases. No detail was spared, and each point was fully illustrated with slides, the likes of which I have never seen before or since. Never have I stared so hard at a rip in a curtain! The lecturer identified all the local strains of venereal disease and how to recognise them; where to get treatment, what would happen if you ignored symptoms, which parts of town to avoid at all costs, etc. On and on it went. I just wanted to go – anywhere, as long as it wasn't there. It felt like a hundred and fifty pairs of male eyes were watching my reactions and, as with so many surreal situations, I kept thinking: how the hell did I end up here!

When it was over, the officer who had given the lecture came up to me. He smiled kindly, took me by the elbow and said, 'Come with me, ma'am. I'll show you what's next.'

I said, 'If it's anything like this, I'm not interested!'

He laughed and said, 'No, we'll get you out of here.'

We all filed out, me first of course, into the blazing sunshine. My cotton dress was plastered to my body with the sweat of heat and embarrassment. Now what? Six beautiful girls were standing in line, one behind the other, a few feet apart. Each girl held a huge placard, bearing a capital letter: A, B, C, D, E, F. Each placard bore a huge photograph and details of amenities provided by Hotel A, Hotel B, Hotel C, and so on. You were to walk past, read about each hotel, study the photo, and then tell an officer which hotel you wished to stay at. I didn't care; I was just desperate to get out of there. The last one, F, was a pretty hacienda on a white beach, with bougainvillea blossoms tumbling over the whitewashed walls. I thought it looked welcoming and simple. I said, 'Hotel F, please.' On the tarmac a few hundred yards away stood six buses marked A, B, C, D, E, F.

'Get onto bus F, ma'am – if you're quite sure,' he said, hesitantly.

I got onto bus F and sat in the front seat. The bus started

filling up with the more raucous of the soldiers, but I switched off. I just wanted to get to the hotel.

When the bus was full, a very serious-looking young officer got on, reached up to the rack for my canvas bag, then took me by the arm saying, 'Come with me, ma'am.'

I said, 'No. I want to get to the hotel.'

He more or less lifted me out of the seat and said, 'Ma'am, you are coming with me, trust me on this one.' Before I knew it I was off the bus and, embarrassingly, started to cry. Behind me the soldiers on the bus were shouting, 'Enjoy your holiday, ma'am. You have a good vacation now, ma'am, we'll see you on the trip back.' And some of them began clapping. I just had not got a clue as to what was going on.

A car had driven onto the tarmac. The officer opened the rear door and pushed me into the back seat. The car was icily air-conditioned – thank God.

'I'm taking you to the European and Oriental Hotel, ma'am. Hotel F is no place for a lady.'

Naturally, I found out later, the buses were shunting all the guys off to brothels, and Hotel F – my personal choice – was one of the wildest. The European and Oriental, by contrast, was a traditional, colonial-style hotel, which was perfect – and which I knew I couldn't afford.

'Absolutely do not worry, ma'am. All this is taken care of, courtesy of the United States military. Now, ma'am, you have a good vacation, and if you need any help, here are my details.'

In a daze I was taken to my beautiful room. I locked the door, put the security chain on, undressed, and stood under a cold shower for what seemed like hours. I then lay on the bed and did what I had dreamed of doing for so long: stared at the ceiling, basking in the silence, and drifted off into a deep sleep.

I could have wished Mike were with me, but I nevertheless had a wonderful five days. It took me a while to sleep off the exhaustion; to stop seeing images of children with no legs or no arms or no sight; images of young soldiers losing their limbs, their minds, their lives. It takes energy to block out all that stuff, but then I suppose that's what we did: tuck it all away and tell ourselves we were coping.

But the rest was pure, revitalising luxury – AND I got to be an expert on venereal diseases caught in downtown Penang in 1968.

Another of the welcome breaks I took was to Cambodia, that mysterious, brooding neighbour lying to the west of Vietnam's jungles and home of the ancient and magnificent Angkor Wat temples of which my old geography teacher, Mr Pritchard, had spoken so eloquently.

As a schoolgirl, I dreamed of visiting this magical place one day, and that day came when I saw an opportunity and grabbed it with both sweaty hands. Despite B52 bombing strikes, scary checkpoints where flint-eyed, heavily armed soldiers eyed me up and down, and two back-breaking crowded bus journeys that bounced me along the highway from Saigon to Phnom Penh, and then north to Siem Reap, I got there in one piece.

It was beginning, though, to seem I was destined to find myself dogged by eccentric circumstances and odd experiences when I took vacations in Southeast Asia. This time I went straight to my hotel, appropriately named the Angkor Wat, a grand establishment in the French colonial style, fitted with highly polished teak and where the ceiling fans set high in the rafters creaked reassuringly. The omnipresent orchid arrangements that seemed to be a feature of such hotels were particularly in evidence in the dining room, where large, round tables, generously draped with stiffly starched, snow-white tablecloths, were set for what appeared to be a banquet. Yet, for the whole five days of my visit, I was the only guest!

Thank heavens the staff made it their mission to take care of me and the local people were kind and welcoming.

Nonetheless, I felt rather strange, and tempted to move on. On one shoulder sat the spirit of Mr Pritchard, whispering words of encouragement, while on the other sat my father, saying, 'What the hell are you doing? Come home. Now.'

I smiled at both apparitions, and continued on my way. If Buddhist monks and French explorers could do it, then so could I . . .

The sheer drama and spectacle was overwhelming, indescribable, and like nothing I'd ever seen. The first time I gazed at the giant faces, representing Buddha, carved into the Bayon temple in the Angkor Thom complex, I was stunned by the scale of the exquisite workmanship, lost in wonderment at how much beauty had been created by ancient peoples of whom we knew so little.

One of the waiters at the hotel had a brother who owned a few horses. One day they escorted me around some of the temples, on horseback. We trotted amiably around the timeless monuments with only the sound of crickets, the occasional chatter of a monkey or the haughty snort of one of the horses to break the serene silence. That day is a cherished memory. Most other days, the hotel arranged a car and driver to take me to a particular temple, where the driver would snooze in his car while I roamed alone to my heart's content, lost in the peace and beauty. The tensions of nursing in a war zone melted away.

Ta Prohm is one of the temple complexes where giant tree roots grow over and through the ancient boulders, splitting them asunder and looking as though gigantic celestial candles have floated down from heaven and slowly dripped all over the ancient structures. There, I was able to get right up close to one of the beautiful, carved faces. I knew little then of meditation, but when I placed my hand carefully on his cheek, silently promising myself that one day I would return, I experienced an extraordinary inner peace that surely was spiritual.

Another day, roaming about, lost in a daydream, I became

aware of a disturbing sound: heavy breathing, then sporadic grunts. Oh my God . . . The driver was quite a distance away, and I was suddenly aware of the vulnerability of my situation. I was in a long, narrow stone corridor, a Buddha face filling the opening at one end and staring implacably at my growing nervousness. Halfway down the corridor was an opening in the stonework. My heart thumped painfully in my chest and I felt myself going from blazing hot to icy cold.

This was not the time to be girlie and faint, I told myself, and slowly took the few steps forward to reach the opening. Gingerly looking through, I laughed out loud, slightly hysterical with relief. It was a young cow, tugging at the lush green grass, snorting and breathing heavily as cows will do while munching. It was stranger than it might appear as I had not seen anything like a cow or a goat in the area until that moment.

A teenage youth, wearing the traditional black cotton pyjamas of the Cambodians, suddenly appeared, startling us both. It turned out he was tending a small herd of cows and we quickly realised that neither of us was a threat to the other. He smiled shyly and I attempted some conversation. My French was no help, neither, it seemed, was my basic Vietnamese, and my mastery of Cambodian didn't extend beyond hello. So we just kept smiling.

I held up my camera and mimed taking a picture. He looked slightly bemused, but I took his picture. I spent the next twenty minutes or so encouraging him to take mine. This involved my running backwards and forwards to a tree, against which I draped myself in what I thought was an alluring pose. The reality was I got hot and sweaty, while my teenage friend snapped the sky, the ground, his chest or his feet, before walking me back to the car. He must have thought I was an escaped lunatic, but we parted friends.

Later, when I developed the film, there was one photograph

of me, leaning against this amazing tree and looking remarkably OK – given the circumstances.

The hotel manager insisted there was a very special temple that I must not miss, and escorted me there on my last day. The history, the scale and the beauty of what I had already seen had left me totally stunned. What on earth, I wondered, could he possibly show me that would outstrip the rest?

We parked the car and walked through the noonday heat to the entrance of one of the smaller temples. As we started down a flight of steep stone steps, I was immediately brought up short by the jarring sight of a metal handrail recently cemented into one side of the staircase.

The manager pointed proudly at the rail and said, 'This is very important for you to see, madam. This rail was put here for Jackie Kennedy.'

'This is what you wanted me to see?'

'Yes, madam. Jackie Kennedy was the wife of the American president, you know. She came here to visit our temples with Lord Harlech. This rail was put here for her safety.'

He stroked the rail reverently, smiling at me for approval.

'Thank you for showing it to me.' I didn't have the heart to crush his enthusiasm, but I was both taken aback and depressed by it.

In the midst of this astonishing place, this wonder of the world, to a local man who had grown up taking the magnificence for granted, Jackie Kennedy and her handrail was the talking point.

Do people who live cheek by jowl with the pyramids, or the Temples of Luxor, or Machu Pichu, end up immune to these flagships of long lost cultures?

26

TURNING POINTS

The five months from October 1967 to March 1968 was a stretch that I always think of as my settling-in period in Vietnam. It included the Tet Offensive at the end of January 1968. That particular Chinese Lunar New Year, when coastal towns throughout South Vietnam were attacked by North Vietnamese Army troops and Vietcong in well-planned, synchronised waves, was a pivotal point in the war. Radio stations were seized and enemy broadcasts urged the population to help drive out the foreign troops now that the country was under the control of Ho Chi Minh. One group of Vietcong actually breached the perimeter of the American Embassy in Saigon, and a few marines were killed before the NVA was stopped from getting into the embassy itself. It was a dangerous and sobering time, which clearly exposed the vulnerability and inaccuracies of military intelligence.

At the Children's Centre on the eve of the Chinese New Year, we spent the whole of the day making traditional paper lanterns with the excited children, while Tinh baked cookies and prepared enough food for a multitude. At the stroke of midnight, the New Year is seen in with firecrackers being set off by just about everyone. The noise they make scares off evil spirits and welcomes in the New Year. This was to be my first Chinese Lunar New Year, called Tet in Vietnam. It was the Year of the Monkey and I was every bit as excited as the children.

From eleven-thirty p.m. onwards, we all sat out on the concrete terrace, ready to light the candles inside the little lanterns, with our strings of firecrackers hanging at the ready. We'd been warned repeatedly to expect lots of noise, but not to be scared by it. So we weren't.

At the stroke of midnight, all hell was let loose. Anyone in town who had a gun, be it a pistol or a machine gun, fired it into the night sky, and firecrackers exploded in their characteristic riff of staccato bursts. The children cheered, their little faces shining with excitement in the candle-glow of their paper lanterns. Suddenly an almighty explosion shook the ground, lighting up the entire area somewhere towards the beach, and I remember thinking: Wow, these people really know how to throw a party!

But the older children grew quiet, sensing something was wrong. Slowly we drifted back inside and tried to settle the younger ones. The next day the military police told us not to leave the compound, and to stay inside the buildings. The huge explosion we had heard the night before was the vast ammunition dump down at the harbour being blown up. Later, we learned that a suicide squad of Vietcong, with some thirty civilian hostages, had taken control of the radio station. They managed to broadcast for a short while, until South Korean troops of the First Tiger Division blew the station apart, killing everyone inside. Up and down the coastline, key towns experienced similar activity, but the city of Hue, on the Perfumed River north of Qui Nhon, suffered most. Fierce battles took place in a siege that lasted thirty-two days, with much loss of both American and North Vietnamese lives.

After March 1968, it gradually became obvious to those of us not in the military, and to the local Vietnamese people, that there was a shift in the mood of the military. There was noticeable and increasing friction between black and white GIs, and between enlisted men and officers, which led to incidents of breakdown in discipline.

There were distressing incidents of 'fragging', as they were called, where Claymore mines were turned around the wrong way so that instead of showering shrapnel outward towards the enemy on the perimeter, they fired inwards and injured their own officers. Air-conditioners were booby-trapped with hand grenades, and explosive devices were rigged to hurt their own men. The racist aspect of this was very disturbing and upsetting. Later, when I thought about that awful time, it seemed to me that three significant events in 1968 triggered the shift of simmering black anger and frustration into insubordination and militancy. The mood was especially ugly among the infantrymen, the guys at the sharp end of the fighting.

What was obvious to those of us who were there is now well documented: a high percentage of young black men from America's deprived inner-city areas were drafted into the infantry to be sent to the front lines. The three events I think of as sparking black anger were, first, the assassination of the great Civil Rights leader and Nobel Peace Prize winner, Martin Luther King, on 4 April 1968. This devastating event was a terrible shock to everybody, not just to black soldiers in Vietnam. It was Dr King who, in 1965, had led the campaign to register black people to vote. In the same year the US Congress passed the voting rights act.

Years later, in January 2009, sitting alone in a little cottage in Devon, I watched the inauguration of Barack Obama on TV. When not weeping, I was applauding – and remembering the faces of those young black soldiers. Fifty-eight thousand Americans died in that war. Many more died later of their wounds, both physical and mental, back in their home states.

Others rotted in poorly staffed and underfunded veterans' hospitals, forsaken by the government that used them up, then spat them out. Places, languages, uniforms change, but not much else.

Why is that, exactly?

The second turning point for blacks was the tragic assassination of presidential candidate Robert Kennedy on 6 June 1968. The younger brother of John F. Kennedy, the New York Senator was committed to civil rights, racial equality and justice for all.

Then, in August, following these terrible events, came the historic black power salute given by Tommie Smith and John Carlos, two black athletes, at the Mexico City Olympic Games. The photographs of the two black American sprinters on the podium, with heads bowed and fists raised, came to represent one of the most memorable moments in Olympic history and was certainly a milestone in America's Civil Rights Movement. Their action was intended to bring attention to the fact that civil rights had not gone far enough in eliminating the injustices faced by black Americans.

Smith, the gold-medal winner, later explained that he raised his right, black-gloved fist in the air to represent black power in America. Carlos, the bronze-medallist, raised his left, black-gloved fist to represent unity in black America. The black scarf round Smith's neck stood for black pride, and the men's black socks – no shoes, just black socks – represented black poverty in their country.

No one had seen anything like this before, and it reverberated around the world. To me it seemed obvious that these events spurred on the many black soldiers in Vietnam to express their resentment and anger at their treatment – sadly, not always choosing methods that were likely to gain them sympathy. I was told that many were locked up in the military stockade of Long Binh Jail, LBJ as it was known, somewhere

down in the Saigon area, prior to being shipped back to the
States for disciplinary action.

A couple of incidents typical of the changing mood affected me
directly. One day, I was taking some books back to exchange at
the library we were welcome to use in a small military compound. I often took advantage of this; escaping into the pages
of a good book was one way of relaxing and forgetting about
the war for a while.

It was the middle of a burning hot day, and I strolled along,
happily lost in my own thoughts, which included wondering
briefly why the streets were so quiet. Clear and quiet streets
were sometimes a sign of possible trouble, though we were
usually notified of an alert – orange status meant caution, stand
by, and red meant 'Get out of the way, it's about to hit the fan.'

Suddenly a military jeep screamed to a stop alongside me
and the driver, a young white officer, shouted out, 'Ma'am,
what in hell are you doing out here?'

'Going to the library to change some books,' I replied.

He looked at me like I had taken leave of my senses. 'Ma'am,
just get in the vehicle. Now. Don't you know we're on orange
alert, about to go into a red?'

I gulped and managed to say, 'Oh! I did think it was a bit
quiet.'

I tell you, we lived on another planet from the military.

I climbed into the jeep and as we drove round the next bend,
we came upon a makeshift barricade of wooden crates and
tyres strewn across the road forcing us to stop. The driver, a
first lieutenant, tensed up, and I saw three or four black soldiers
slowly approaching us. They were not behaving quite as
you would expect members of the US Army to behave. They
appeared to be sort of half in and half out of uniform and either
drunk or drugged. The lieutenant quietly said to me, 'Don't say
a word. Stay where you are.' That scared me. Then, turning to

the group, he said, 'Are you guys aware that we're about to go into a red alert?'

The soldier who looked like the ringleader was by now standing on my side of the jeep, with an aggressive, menacing air. He slowly took a knife from his belt. I looked at the floor. I sat there, barely breathing, and kept looking at the floor. Then, very slowly, very deliberately, he drew his knife through the canvas roof, slicing it almost in two. I could hear the sound of it close to my head. I also heard the lewd sexual comments aimed at me and the abusive language he used to the lieutenant. I had never experienced anything like this and I was terrified. There was no reasoning with these men. It obviously meant nothing that they were speaking to an officer.

'I think you guys should report back to base, now,' said the officer, gunning the jeep as he spoke. We shot forward through the crates and debris in the road, and drove very quickly away from them. I never spoke a word; he never spoke a word. He just drove us into the heavily armed compound housing the library. Turning to me he said, 'Ma'am, you *do not* – are you clear? – You *do not* walk back to your Children's Centre. You choose your books and I'll arrange for transport to take you back.' He spoke rapidly with another officer, and almost immediately two vehicles carrying military police left the compound. When I was driven back a short time afterwards, there was no sign of the men who had stopped us.

That was the first time I witnessed an act of gross insubordination and a breakdown in discipline. In the days following, several incidents were hushed up. There were stories of soldiers stripping off their uniforms in the street, placing an American flag on top of it, urinating on the flag then dousing the pile in petrol and setting it alight. These men were quickly dealt with and it was rumoured that they'd been taken off to military stockades, but our staff told us stories of distressing scenes they witnessed on their way to and from work. They were confused, and asked us why the Americans were fighting each other. It was unnerving to see soldiers taking the laces from their boots and braiding them together into black wristbands, or chokers to wear round their necks. You could see what was happening: they were deliberately downgrading their military uniform. Some of them took to wearing a black glove on either their left or right hand . . .

Things were going from bad to worse.

We had a number of sick Amerasian babies and toddlers, fathered by American and Korean soldiers, in our care. One day, I took a beautiful baby boy, fathered by an American, to the X-ray department at the 67th Evac. About ten months old, he was found to have pneumonia affecting both lungs, and he was very ill.

While I waited in the little makeshift X-ray unit, alongside soldiers in their hospital-issue blue pyjamas, I cradled the child in my arms and administered oxygen as he struggled for breath. A handsome black soldier was sitting opposite me, watching this. Suddenly he leaned forward, leered at me and nodded meaningfully towards the child. 'Cute little bastard, isn't he?' he said.

That's when something snapped. In that moment my exhaustion, my compassion for the child, and the sheer frustration and anger I felt towards this silly, leering man, rose to the surface in an explosion of fury. 'You know, one thing this country does not need is people like you, leaving behind innocent little babies like this.' I said. I felt like handing him the child and saying, 'Here, you take care of him for the next eighteen years.'

But he just looked at me and laughed. 'You know, honey,' he said. 'While there are people like you in countries like this, the kids of people like me will always have someone to take care of them, so why should I worry?'

Luckily they called me into X-ray at that very moment, or who knows what I might have said or done next. At the very least I probably would have slapped his face. Here was yet another example of tragedy and waste, and, worse, the corrupting, dehumanising effect of war on the human spirit.

And who *was* going to look after this little child until he was able to look after himself?

I was so bloody mad because I knew that soldier was right.

27

CULTURE SHOCK

I left Qui Nhon to go home for Christmas in 1968. We were not allowed to stay in a war zone for longer than our twelve-month contracts, but somehow I'd managed to stretch my stint to almost fifteen months. What I hadn't realised – and didn't until I was back home – was the full extent of the toll taken on me, emotionally and physically, by the demands of the children and stresses of the environment.

Nevertheless, saying goodbye was heart-wrenching. I coped fairly well with the afternoon before I left, when there was a party, with lots of food – and speeches. Then, much later, when I'd packed my few belongings and the children were in bed, I quietly walked, on my own, through the rows of cots, taking time to look at the face of each sleeping baby. On to the next room, where the toddlers lay on their straw mats or beds, some face down, knees drawn up, bottoms in the air as little ones do. Others were encased in casts, bulky bandaging, or lay with intravenous tubes silently infusing fluids into their little veins. I said my silent farewells and went to the bigger children. A few were awake, and their eyes followed me as I walked around, trying not to let the tightness in my throat get the better of me. Ba and Hue were fast asleep, their dark silky hair tumbling across their pillows; Hue's home-made leg and Ba's pair of red flip-flops for her hands were present and correct.

I turned and left the room. I was ready to go.

At the airport the following morning, Jean, Lily Ho and Mr Bom were with me. I felt in control now, prepared for the long trip ahead. All around us was the usual cacophony of noise and crush of men. Suddenly, some soldiers nearby began gesturing and shouting: 'Hey! Look at this . . . What's going on . . .?'

We turned, and to my horror we saw an army bus bursting with children and nurses trundling towards us. Little arms waved out of the windows and voices, in between shrieks of laughter, were calling, 'Co Anne, Co Anne,' (Miss Anne, Miss Anne). Someone had had the bright idea of staging an impromptu send-off.

That was the end of any shred of composure. It ended in a tangle of kisses and hugs and everyone – especially me – in tears, until a helpful soldier grabbed my bags while another took my arm. 'They're calling your flight, ma'am. Let's go.'

I allowed them to lead me to one of the several C130s lined up on the tarmac. All engines were roaring, the noise was deafening, and I seemed completely incapable of stemming the flood of tears. Somehow I was propelled on board and strapped into a seat up front with the flight crew.

In a daze, I simply gave in and allowed the soldiers to look after me. Once airborne, a worried-looking young officer kept giving me some horrible-tasting water to drink. Poor guys, they did their best for me, sensibly not trying to speak. Eventually I recovered enough to ask what time we'd be in Saigon. The men looked at each other then stared at me, until one brave young man broke the silence: 'Ma'am, this flight is for Danang. We get there at 1400 hours!' That's when I started laughing, and suddenly I felt OK. It took me another twenty-four hours to hitch a ride on another military flight from Danang to Saigon. I must have looked a wreck, but who cared. God, I wondered, would I ever be free from this madness!

Yet another twenty-four hours, and I finally arrived at Heathrow where I was met by a favourite aunt and a couple of good friends. That's when the culture shock began.

London in December 1968 was as far removed from Saigon as anything could be. First, the bitter cold hit me like a ten-ton truck and robbed me of my voice for a few days, and I felt oppressed by the dull, largely sunless December skies. What I really needed and wanted was to catch up on sleep and to give my throat a complete rest, but instead I was treated to a whirl of restaurants, shopping and even a West End show. I was being thoroughly spoiled, but I found it difficult to relate to anything that was going on around me.

I realised, though, that the new fashions were great. Girls wore shiny, colourful plastic raincoats over their Mary Quant hot pants. Impossibly high boots reached well above the knee, laced up the entire length of the leg. Skinny-rib sweaters and geometric hairstyles were all the rage. It was the height of Twiggy mania. It all seemed very strange.

On the morning of the third day, I took a train to North Wales and home. The hotel was fully booked for the Christmas holidays and my father, after welcoming me with a rushed, tearful greeting and a couple of warm hugs, asked if I could help in the kitchen! No change there then. My sister Joan, who had started her nurse training in the Royal Air Force, and was home on leave, was already in the kitchen, up to her ears in slicing and chopping. It was wonderful to see her; we kept each other going and enjoyed doing the chores together.

After Christmas, a few journalists who knew where I'd been came to interview me. Most of their questions were pretty daft: 'How did you cope with the heat? All those handsome young soldiers – did you have a boyfriend?' I suggested that they might like to know about the orphaned children, the desperate injuries, the wasted lives and endless carnage. 'Oh, yes.' Then there were the photos. The *Daily Mirror* reporter asked me to sit on the garden wall, and to please hitch my skirt up a little higher. I remember leaping off the wall and delivering a stinging opinion of his attitude.

London might have been swinging; North Wales was anything but. It was, however, reassuringly familiar and safe. Over the next couple of weeks, as my voice returned, my sleep improved and I found my appetite, I tried to settle in. I needed to keep busy and was happy to help around the hotel. I made beds, waited on tables, polished and cleaned – after all, I'd grown up with domestic activity. But, when taking my turn to wash dishes in the back kitchen, I found myself observing food being scraped into the swill bins as though from afar.

I listened as a pompous guest complained to my father that his Chablis was not chilled to quite the right temperature, and fought to contain my rage and frustration. Did these people have no idea what was happening just a plane ride away? What the hell did the temperature of the wine matter when young men were drowning in their own blood and for no good reason? That was the day I said 'fuck' out loud for the first time ever, shocking even myself, and all around me.

I began watching news on television. This was the first war to be so extensively covered by cameras. Families in the States had a steady diet of this, watching every evening, worrying about fathers and sons, husbands and brothers, and dreading the knock on the door.

The anti-war movement in America was growing, and becoming more vocal on the streets of major cities. Draft dodgers were going north to seek refuge in Canada, where the government turned a blind eye. Protests had erupted abroad; a demonstration outside the American Embassy in London's

Grosvenor Square had turned into a bloody riot, and governments were beginning to realise that their involvement in Southeast Asian affairs was being questioned. Just what in hell was going on over there? According to General Westmoreland – commander of US troops in Vietnam – everything was just fine.

No. It was not.

I knew I would return to Vietnam for another tour of duty. I wasn't ready to turn my back on a place where so many nurses were badly needed. My father extracted a promise that I would wait a couple of months. Then, if I still wanted to go, I would go with his blessing. My stepmother remained aloof, cold and ill-tempered in her kitchen domain. No advice or support there.

At times I felt tearful and angry. It was so good to have Joan. She and I walked for miles along the local beaches, wrapped up against the cold while I tried to share my thoughts and feelings, to explain how things had been in Qui Nhon as far as I could. Joan worried about me, quietly listened as I agonised, and was always there for me. She too had the strong heart of a nurse – like our mother. She understood the need to go where help was most needed.

I needed to get away for a while, to think about the wisdom of returning to Southeast Asia. My father, my sisters and our family friends were worried about me going back. I needed to escape the pressure of their reactions when I spoke of the children at Qui Nhon, or showed them the photographs. I needed a clear head before I could make any firm decisions.

And so it was that I decided to visit our relatives in Canada again.

28

FACING REALITY

As soon as I arrived in Vancouver in early February 1969, I was aware of a different mood in the country. It felt more urgent. There was much more talk about events in Vietnam and what the war was doing to Canada's neighbour. There was a lot of television coverage, and many people were expressing grave doubts about this conflict. Soldiers appeared on TV, openly denouncing their government; one young officer publicly ripped off his uniform patches, his medals and his shirt and burned them. I was shocked, but I understood his anger and recognised the courage of his action.

I was asked to do some public speaking to help raise funds for the Vancouver branch of the Save the Children Fund. By now rested and reinvigorated, and having seen up close how public donations were spent – sparingly but effectively – I was happy to help. Another Bridget, the Vancouver SCF director Mrs Bridget Dewhurst, took me under her wing, and I gave several well-attended talks, illustrated with photographs I had taken myself. The only downside was my discomfort at some of the probing questions I was asked. People really wanted to know a lot more than I could, or should tell them.

There was some local press coverage about my experiences, and I agreed to appear on a morning television magazine programme for women, only to discover it would be a live broadcast. Since I'd never so much as seen the inside of a television studio, I was terrified at the prospect.

On the day, escorted by Bridget Dewhurst and my cousin Hilary, I arrived at the studios, my nervousness not helped when a man wearing headphones and a frantic look said, 'Ah . . . Watts. Are you the dog trainer?' Mrs Dewhurst stepped forward. 'No, children's nurse back from Vietnam.' The man checked his clipboard. OK. Got you. Come with me.' I was whisked off down a tiny passage behind some flimsy screens that appeared to be made of plywood stuck together with tape. On the other side I could see rolls and lines of electric cable, a battery of overhead lamps, and more frantic-looking men wheeling cameras around.

Mrs Dewhurst had disappeared, and I ended up in a tiny room with two young women who began daubing orange make-up on my face and neck and plastering violet eye shadow on my lids. When I blinked, my eyes looked like garage doors opening and closing! I was then handed over to someone who quickly explained how a countdown worked. He also demonstrated how a circular movement meant 'finish your sentence' and a finger drawn across the throat meant 'stop'.

This was definitely back in surreal territory.

At last, my mouth dry with fright, I was led onto the set as a man wearing the same orange make-up as I was walking off it, looking a bit shell-shocked too. He had just been interviewed about his stamp collection! The place was a hive of activity as camera angles were changed and lights adjusted – in fact, the lights were the brightest I'd seen since the ammo dump blew up in Qui Nhon!

The presenter, a heavily made-up woman with hair piled up

into a kind of beehive arrangement, sat in a tiny corner that had evidently been decorated – very badly – to look like a rose arbour. There were two small white wicker chairs and a matching table on which sat two glasses and a carafe of water. Unsmiling, the presenter stared at me and asked, 'Are you the flower arranger?' Someone behind me said, 'Watts. Kids' nurse. Vietnam.'

What was wrong with these people? Were they all working from different clipboards for God's sake? I was quickly seated in one of the little white chairs and, with barely a minute to go, the presenter rapidly briefed me: she would ask me to describe my work in Vietnam, then some clips would be shown from a newsreel film I'd provided that showed footage of the Children's Centre in Qui Nhon. While she spoke, a young man hooked me up for sound, which involved threading the cord of a small microphone *under* my skirt . . .

Suddenly we were on air and the difference in the presenter was immediate and astounding. She beamed at the camera, flashed me a warm smile, and gushingly introduced me with the words, 'You will love my next guest, Anne Watts, as I do. Just back from Vietnam . . .' etc. etc. I was so astonished that my nervousness disappeared, replaced by determination to get the story of the children across. It was all over quickly and I walked off, past the next hapless guest looking terrified in the wings. When they played back the tape for me, I appeared quite normal. So did the interviewer. How was that engineered? I was reunited with Hilary and Mrs Dewhurst and we got the hell out of there.

We went to lunch, where they told me what a natural I was in front of the cameras!

A day or two after my baptism of fire at the TV studio, I was invited to talk about doing another interview, this time for a current affairs programme for the Canadian Broadcasting Corporation.

I had lunch with the interviewer, who told me he'd seen my morning appearance, and would like to do something similar. The programme wouldn't go out live, so there was no need to be nervous – anything I wasn't happy with, we could stop and do it again, or edit out later. His name was Al, and he was very easy to talk to, and seemed really interested and sympathetic. He said the interview with me would be an interesting take on the Vietnam War. He also asked if he could use some of the film I had, from which clips had been shown on the morning programme. The film, which had won an award, had been made for a current affairs programme in Britain called *24 Hours*. In it, I was interviewed by the noted British broadcaster Julian Pettifer, and it clearly showed life at the Children's Centre in Qui Nhon. I was still nervous, but less so than the first time, and Al was very good at putting me at my ease, so I agreed to go ahead with the interview.

The next morning we met at the CBC studios. That same awful orange make-up was daubed all over my face and, to my amusement, over Al's face too. This time I was taken to a large room, bare but for two comfortable green chairs and a coffee table. Al and I sat opposite each other, knees almost touching. Somewhere to my left was a glass panel where I assumed the cameras were, but I couldn't see anything. The whole set-up felt quite relaxed and we began talking. We talked for a good hour, possibly longer, and then we went for lunch, and that was that. Quite painless.

How very naive I was.

A few days later Al called. 'Tonight. Eight p.m. Enjoy,' he said. With my cousin Hilary, his wife Iris and some of their friends, we settled down with some excitement to watch this great event but, within moments of the programme starting, I felt the stirrings of unease. For a whole hour I was transfixed, and I learned an invaluable and unpleasant lesson about what can be done with editing.

The programme was vitriolic in its denunciation of what American troops were allegedly being asked to do in Vietnam. Soldiers who had gone AWOL; those burning uniforms and medals; it was all there. Then I came on. I appeared to be sitting in front of a large screen showing newsreel footage of US soldiers torching villages and laughing at their brutalised Vietcong captives. It appeared that I was fully aware of these things that were going on behind me, and I had to listen to myself saying things that had been taken wildly out of context. I was shocked and disturbed by the whole business.

The phones rang with several requests for more interviews, but I was no longer interested. I felt like I had been used, and I wanted no part of political games played out in the media. I was a children's nurse, nothing more, nothing less. However, when the dust had settled and I had time to think about everything, I realised that having a nurse speak of the children who were maimed and orphaned by this war added weight to the argument for getting the hell out of there. The way I was suckered into the whole scenario was such a sobering lesson. I had been wrenched back from the day-to-day practicalities of dealing with the consequences of war and deposited willy-nilly into the middle of a bitter debate where the rationale for fighting this war at all was being seriously and justifiably questioned.

My straightforward, factual and truthful account of the children's lives, their deprivations and their injuries, had been used as part of a political argument in which I was well and truly out of my depth. In my innocence, I had allowed myself – and the children – to be used as a political football. I felt betrayed and somehow sullied.

*

Towards the end of February, with my father's blessing, I left for the Central Highlands of Vietnam to work with a doctor called Patricia Smith.

29

PAT SMITH

Kontum, a hilltop town in the beautiful Central Highlands, was French colonial, quiet and serene – very different in landscape and atmosphere from the busy coastal town of Qui Nhon, teeming with refugees and surrounded by military bases. Architecturally, the town was dominated by a sprawling and very lovely French seminary. In time I would learn that the hills, the jungle landscape and the town itself harboured Vietcong and North Vietnamese soldiers to an extent that proved significant to their winning of the war.

There were fewer American and other allied troops in the area than there had been at Qui Nhon, and the indigenous people were not Vietnamese but an ethnic minority of hill tribespeople who inhabited the mountain areas of Burma, Thailand and Cambodia as well as Vietnam. Treated as a political pawn by all sides in the conflict, all the Montagnards themselves wished for was independent rule.

I had only previously met one Montagnard; the girl named Thuy but called Oscar. I would come to love the purity and simplicity of the Montagnard people and their way of life, but first I had to get through some more culture shock: these nut-brown people were very different from the Vietnamese as I'd come to know them.

The Montagnard men wore loincloths and hunted wild boar with crossbows. The women went bare-breasted, carrying their babies slung low on their backs. Toddlers tugged at their mothers' long, black skirts, decorated with a band of bright colours woven into the hemline. The four largest Montagnard tribes were the Bahnar, Jarai, Rhade and Koho. Those in the Kontum area were Jarai, with a few Rhade.

The Americans used the Montagnards as trackers. No one knew the mountains as well as they did, neither did they much care for the communists. The Vietnamese regarded the Montagnards as *moi* (savages). There was little love lost between the two cultural groups.

The only soldiers around in 1969 were American and ARVN Special Forces, with a few Australian Special Forces, and the 57th assault helicopter unit.

The nearest military staging post was at Pleiku, a flight of some twenty minutes to the southeast of Kontum, or a very scary, fast ninety-minute drive on an unsafe road. If there was no alternative but to drive to Pleiku you needed to negotiate it in the middle of the day, sitting bang in the centre of a military convoy of tanks, preferably with air cover! Between dusk and morning, nobody ventured near this no-man's-land. That is when the area belonged to Charlie.

The conflict in the highlands was more of a guerrilla war. The Americans joked that in these parts they didn't call the Vietcong Charlie, they called him Chuck – because the relationship was so much closer! Humour always exists alongside stress – I saw a road sign that read 'Caution. Charlie crossing.' Special Forces soldiers stitched together Vietcong flags, staining them with chicken or boar's blood and stamping them into the dusty ground to 'age' them. These 'captured VC flags' were sold down in Saigon at an astronomical profit to the

REMFs (rear echelon mother fuckers) and assorted adventurers and souvenir hunters.

Dr Patricia Smith was a champion of the Montagnards. She loved them and taught herself the Jarai dialect, and they loved and revered her. They gave her the respectful title of *ya thi* – grandmother. She was an incredible woman: tough as old boots but with a heart of pure gold. When she went to Kontum, she was the first Western woman the Montagnards had seen. Pat told me how some of the women would sit and stroke her arms in amazement – they had never seen anyone with hair on their arms before. She was so moved by these people and their circumstances that she dedicated her professional skills to helping them, eventually adopting two little boys and taking them back to the States.

Patricia Smith travelled back and forth to the States in the early years to raise money to fund a hospital for the Montagnards, which was built on the outskirts of Kontum. She made it a rule to take only Western-trained nursing staff who had already completed a tour of duty in Vietnam, or the culture shock might have been too great. But those who had already spent a year or two in the country were halfway to understanding the problems, and their nerves were no longer so raw.

When I first travelled up country to be interviewed for the job, Dr Smith was no longer in the original hospital buildings, but had been moved into temporary premises lent to her by priests at the Seminary. Unfortunately, that was where her hospital remained for several years until the deteriorating situation in the country finally forced her to leave. The supposedly temporary move had come about when Dr Smith was strongly advised by the military brass to evacuate her hospital because tunnelling had been discovered beneath the walls, which threatened the building with subsidence.

All of this was explained to me when I first arrived at the Minh Quy Mission Hospital, but the significance of tunnelling rang no bells at all for me. It wasn't until years later, in 1990, when I first returned to visit Vietnam and toured the tunnels of Cu Chi that the penny dropped.

On that visit, I bumped into a couple of American veterans in Saigon who invited me to go with them to visit Cu Chi, where both had served with the infantry. At first I declined. 'No, I'm not interested, that wasn't my war. I'm trying to get up to Kontum.' But as it happened, local officials wouldn't allow me to travel to either Kontum or Qui Nhon, so I did go to Cu Chi, and was very glad I did. It put into perspective the fundamental differences between the warring sides and just how inadequate military intelligence must have been.

The tunnels in Cu Chi were part of a complex 340 kilometres long. In many places they were dug four deep, with a series of staggered trapdoors. The Vietcong and North Vietnamese Army soldiers (NVA) lived in these tunnels, sometimes for years at a time. When American bombers dropped their Agent Orange, and other defoliants and noxious sprays, the NVA were able to escape by crawling into the tunnels and dropping down through the trap doors to the much lower levels, thus surviving the bombardments of the B52s. The reason the Americans were unable to find the Ho Chi Minh trail is because most of the trail was underground. No amount of defoliating would have exposed large sections of it.

At Cu Chi, we stood with a retired NVA officer, looking at the map of the tunnels on a wall. He told us he had lived underground for six years, and explained how food and weapons were hidden there; how wounded Vietcong and NVA men were operated on underground. At night, like a ghostly army of silent assassins, men rose up from underground, killed their unsuspecting enemy, only to sink from sight below the leafy forest floor. The old soldier also walked us through several booby-trapped areas, deadly and invisible, to demonstrate how this was done. The North Vietnamese had been fighting a completely different type of war; one which, ultimately, defeated the aerial bombardments.

That day, these revelations wrenched my memory forcibly back to the tunnels beneath Pat Smith's hospital. Just how extensive had they been? If we had known then what I had just learned twenty years later, surely none of us would have remained at Kontum.

Sometimes ignorance truly is bliss.

I arrived at the Minh Quy Mission Hospital to take up my duties in late February, 1969. I was disorientated, sweaty and desperate for an air-conditioned ladies' room. What I got was a force-ten-gale hairdo, courtesy of the US Army's Hueys, chloroquine-resistant malaria-carrying mosquitoes, and sweat running into my eyes and down my legs.

Dr Patricia Smith had been a young intern in Seattle, Washington, when she volunteered to go with a Catholic charity to what was then called French Indochina. Interested in gaining experience in tropical medicine, she had had little idea what lay before her, or how her decision would change her life. She had agreed to go for a year; by the time I went to work there she had served the Montagnard population for eighteen years.

The hospital staff when I was there consisted of a wonderful senior nurse called Jean Platz, who had been with Dr Smith for many years and was her right-hand person. A team of four nurses, of whom I was now one, worked under Jean, and the military supplied an army doctor who would be exchanged every two months on a rotating system. Administration was in the capable and courageous hands of the amazing Gloria – a volunteer of whom more later – and the nursing team was often supplemented by an extra pair of hands that would come for a limited term. An excellent German male nurse named Gunther coincided with my first months.

As for Jean's team of four, apart from me there was shy, quiet English Barbara, British–Chinese nurse/midwife Shirley Chu from Hong Kong, and Sister Marie Clare, a nursing nun from New York. While still a schoolgirl, Shirley Chu had been inspired to take up nursing by a talk from Dr Tom Dooley at her high school. Dooley, an American naval doctor appalled by conditions in the camps in 1955 Haiphong, went on to write and speak extensively about his experiences, and to found clinics in various countries in Southeast Asia under the auspices of MEDICO (the Medical International Cooperation Organisation). His example led President Kennedy to establish the Peace Corps. Marie Clare, copper-haired and with sparkling blue eyes that reflected her bubbly sense of humour, was very attractive. Many broken-hearted admirers had been forced to accept that she was committed only to God and her work. One of the modern breed of nuns, she didn't wear a habit, but a simple white blouse, black skirt and a gold crucifix. She was great fun, and we became good friends.

I settled in, pleased to be back, but with a lot to learn and take in.

30

THE SHOW MUST GO ON

My first week at Kontum turned out to be rather unpleasantly eventful, thanks to an invitation to a show being held at one of the Special Forces bases in the area. Apparently, the content alone of most of these shows, involving strippers and general wild behaviour, was not for the faint-hearted and generally off limits for us. In addition, the security situation after nightfall not only made travelling to these bases very risky, but it was dangerous to be in a military compound at night when it was more likely to be targeted by the Vietcong. Consequently, permission from Pat Smith to enjoy an evening out was rare and, since the hospital couldn't be stripped of its entire nursing staff at once, not everyone could go.

On this occasion, the show was being put on by a group of travelling South Korean entertainers – it's amazing what can seem like reasonable entertainment out in the boondocks of a war zone! – and I was chosen to go along with Marie Clare. The military base was just over the river, but after dark it was considered unsafe to do anything other than fly and so a helicopter arrived at the back of our quarters at seven o'clock. We were whisked away over the river and set down close to a cluster of bamboo and thatch huts. Nearby, a sinuous bend of murky water slid by. This was my first glimpse of the Dac Bla River.

When civilians were invited to a military base, a young officer would always be assigned to each guest. As Marie Clare and I ran crouching from the chopper, two junior officers moved forward to meet and greet us, and escorted us to the hall where the show was about to begin.

The hall held about a hundred men, already seated, who stared at us all the way to our seats in the centre of the front row. On stage, alongside a four-piece band, a Korean version of Connie Francis and an Elvis lookalike were limbering up.

The music struck up and I immediately forgot about the jungle pressing in on all sides. Now my world was reverberating to a bizarre Southeast Asian imitation of Tony Bennett leaving his heart in San Francisco and, let's face it, anything by Elvis made the madness fade a bit. But about ten minutes into the show there was a sudden commotion at the back of the hall and the music came to an untidy halt.

At that moment my nice, attentive lieutenant clapped his left hand very firmly over my nose and mouth, gripped the back of my neck and forced my head down with his right, and shouted, 'Run!' Marie Clare was getting the same treatment from her escort. It was pandemonium as we ran, semi-crouched, for the exit. When we reached what passed for fresh air, my eyes were streaming and stinging. Then the commanding officer appeared and started yelling that this was exactly what the enemy would have wanted us to do – run out where we could be picked off one by one. Only he didn't put it that politely.

However, it turned out that it wasn't the enemy who'd caused this disruption. The South Vietnamese troops on base, resentful that they'd not been allowed to attend the show, had shown their feelings by lobbing some CS-gas grenades through an opening at the rear of the flimsily constructed hall.

A huge fan was set up; Marie Clare and I were instructed to

stand in front of it and let the blast of air rid us of as much of the gas as possible, before we washed our faces. It was all very unpleasant but we were unharmed, and our lieutenants took us to their officers' mess for a much-needed drink. They were attentive and pleasant, behaving as though everything was normal, while Marie Clare and I pretended that being gassed was perfectly routine and looking like the irrepressible comedienne Phyllis Diller was something to which we had aspired.

During drinks, a shaven-headed but very handsome major came and joined us. He was clearly out to impress the ladies, but we listened to his tales of derring-do without moving a muscle, barely taking in what he said but trying to appear polite. We were reacting to the fact that there was something sinister about his cold grey-blue eyes, which drilled into us and seemed to see things that we didn't. We both picked up that this was a damaged man, trying to socialise normally but long since severed from anything close to normal. We were drinking Martinis, but it was we who were shaken and stirred, and I thought again of the thousand-yard stare, of which this seemed to be a variation.

In the middle of the major's monologue, in sauntered a tall, lanky black sergeant smoking a huge cigar. Without taking his eyes off us, he walked nonchalantly up behind the major, drawing deeply on the cigar until the end glowed bright red then, very deliberately, he ground it out on the major's bald head. We held our breath, fearful of what might happen next, but the major simply continued his tale without a flicker. The flesh on his scalp began to bubble and blister, and the smell was nauseating. The black sergeant continued staring at us. This place was not a normal place to be, and these war-damaged men were like ticking time-bombs, waiting for the tiniest signal to set them off.

When his tale finally came to an end, the major said, 'Excuse me one moment, ladies, please,' stood up, slowly turned and, with one swift punch to the chin, knocked the sergeant clear across the room with such force that, cartoon-like, he went straight through the flimsy rear wall.

You don't see that every day.

In one smooth-as-silk movement our lieutenants, ever the perfect hosts, picked up our drinks and guided us firmly by the elbow into another mess hut next door. There, they refreshed our drinks and once again carried on as though nothing untoward had happened, despite the unmistakable sounds of fist fights coming from next door. At one point a body came crashing through the thatch wall and landed a few feet from us. Eventually, and incredibly, we were told that the hall was cleared of gas and we could go back in. The show went on, just like nothing had happened.

After more Connie Francis and Elvis, we were with our hosts in the bar, waiting for the chopper that would take us back, when my lieutenant started talking about dogs and how he knew the British were great dog lovers. I told him about Bronwen, the beautiful collie who was our family dog, and how I missed her. He told me that he was a dog handler and loved his German Shepherd. Would I like to see him?

He took me to his hooch, another bamboo and thatch construction nearby, and opened the door with a 'you first, ma'am'. But as he reached over my shoulder to flick on the light switch, a huge, black Alsatian dog, fangs bared, ears flattened, streaked through the air and came straight at me. I stepped backwards, terrified, but the dog's fangs ripped the front of my dress, and the force of its charge knocked me to the ground, winding me completely.

The lieutenant drew his gun and shot the dog in the head. I was left kneeling, clutching the front of my dress where blood seeped through my fingertips, and staring at the dead dog, its brains sprayed all over the room.

Men came running. The CO yelled. I was carried to the first-aid area, where I was given some oxygen, and four sutures took care of the thankfully small laceration in my abdomen. Then we were taken home by helicopter.

I learned later that these animals were used to sniff out enemy soldiers, but that night the attack was meant for its handler: someone who wished him ill had slipped the chain off the dog. Pat Smith gave everyone in sight a royal chewing out for allowing the dog to be shot. In order to establish whether there was a serious risk of rabies, it would have been useful to keep the animal alive and under observation so, as a precaution, I had to have a course of fourteen anti-rabies shots. I have had better nights out.

31

THINGS THAT GO BUMP
IN THE NIGHT

One moonless night, the air was humid and the incessant buzzing of hungry mosquitoes trying to find a way through the tightly tucked mosquito netting made me nervy and irritable.

My toes scraped reassuringly against the canvas boots that lay under the sheet with me. You quickly learned to do that in this part of the world where, otherwise, stepping out of bed in the middle of the night and sliding your feet into your boots, you might feel the wriggling of an insect, possibly a scorpion, or even a snake against your toes.

I tried to ignore the hard lump under what passed for a pillow. The safety catch was on, so I should be OK.

Pat Smith had a firm rule that no weapons were to be kept by anyone at the hospital. The military authorities in the area all knew her and the wonderful work she had been doing for the past eighteen years in the highlands. She was highly respected by all the Allied forces in the area, who were deeply concerned at all times about our security. The Vietcong and North Vietnamese Army were active in the vicinity and the

American military simply couldn't understand how we could cope without weapons or armed guards.

One of the commanding officers in the area was so worried about us, that he eventually prevailed upon me to keep a .38 calibre revolver for use in an emergency. He showed me how to load it, secure it and use it, and also gave me a box of CS-gas grenades. I hid the grenades in a cupboard in my room, and kept the gun secreted under my pillow.

Another of Pat Smith's rules, and one that was strictly enforced, was that none of the Western nursing and administrative staff were permitted to spend a night at the hospital. We lived in a compound, up a gently sloping hill and about a kilometre away from the hospital.

This arrangement was the result of a horrifying incident two years earlier when a German nurse called Renate Kuhnen had stayed at the hospital to watch over a particularly sick child, when Vietcong guerrillas broke into the wards looking for Pat Smith. They interrogated and killed several patients, then found Renate and forcibly abducted her. She was held prisoner for a whole year, and paraded on Hanoi television, although she had in fact been kept in various North Vietnamese camps, always on the move, but never too far from the Kontum area. She was eventually released on condition she left the country, and under threat of death should she ever return. Since that time, Dr Smith was adamant that we work only from sunrise to sunset, leaving Montagnard personnel to take care of things at night.

We lived in the compound up the hill, entered through a door made of light trelliswork, which we solemnly padlocked once we were all in. Actually, any one of us could have brought the door down with a firm shove, but it felt more comforting to padlock it at night. Our living quarters, basic but large, airy and comfortable, were housed in two buildings about a hundred yards apart. The open-plan living-dining room in one building was a haven of peace and relaxation at the end of a back-breaking day: the comfy rattan sofas and chairs reminded me of the chairs my father had brought from Singapore all those years ago; the generous selection of paperback novels and magazines were brought by American military personnel and other visitors from Saigon. As at Qui Nhon, a generator provided sporadic electricity; otherwise we used kerosene lamps.

Along with the shower rooms and a small kitchen, sleeping quarters were in the second, single-storey building, reached by a narrow concrete path edged with scarlet and pink bougainvillea and tropical shrubbery. Eight of us – two to a room – shared the four large bedrooms, sparsely furnished with army cots. This building was surrounded by a low wall, about four feet high, topped by a three-foot-high trellis covered in more bougainvillea and climbing plants.

My roommate was Barbara, the other English nurse, who had been in Vietnam far longer than I. Her nerves were absolutely shredded and she needed to go home. Meanwhile, she took sedatives to sleep. Barbara was a gentle and efficient nurse, but I never got to know her well. So, my best friend and confidante was not my roommate but Gloria, the indispensable American administrator.

Gloria, from Oshkosh, Wisconsin, was larger than life, and one of life's great characters. She was large, and somewhat plain, but blessed with a magnificent soprano voice that had been operatically trained. She also possessed the most infectious, roaring laugh I have ever heard. On Sundays, Gloria regularly sang at the church service held in a tent by the army padre, and soldiers came from miles around to hear her. I found the sight of these young men, many still in their teens, listening to her soaring, sublime voice singing the soprano arias from *Madame Butterfly* intensely moving. I saw that, in those few shining moments, they were part of something magical, transported for a moment from the fear and violence and bloodshed.

Gloria's voice – and her laugh – had that effect on people.

On that humid night in question, I lay musing for what seemed hours over the circumstances and surroundings in which I now lived and worked. I must eventually have drifted off to sleep, because I was woken by a gentle shaking. There was Gloria, her fingers held to her lips in a silent 'shush', and clearly scared. She was shining a dim flashlight onto a large piece of paper on which she'd written, 'I hear something outside.'

I quickly slipped my feet into my boots and, as I had told Gloria (and only Gloria) about the gun, I took it from under my pillow and disentangled myself from the mosquito net. Barbara, fast asleep, didn't stir, and Gloria and I moved silently into the corridor. There was definitely some movement outside. My heart thudded painfully and I had trouble breathing. Gloria was behind me, hanging on to the tail of my flimsy cotton nightshirt. I held the gun out in front, both hands gripping the butt and sweat pouring into my eyes and down my chest. We must have made quite a sight as we slowly crept – terror mounting – round the entire building, following the stealthy sound we could hear outside.

Outside the kitchen area we had a US military field telephone to use if help was needed. Everyone else was still asleep, and we thought that two terrified women seemed a better option than eight terrified women. So, instead of waking the others, we decided to use the emergency phone. I followed the official procedure: do not speak, crank the handle, and press the button that would alert the nearby base to our need for urgent attention. A red light blinked three times, acknowledging that they had received our message.

With no moon, the velvet blackness was suffocating, and all the time we could sense something outside. The wait for help seemed interminable, and I honestly thought my heart might give out before help came. My hands were so slippery with sweat I could barely keep hold of the gun.

At last we heard the rhythmic sound of feet, softly but swiftly coming towards our dwelling. A patrol of men was on its way. Suddenly, a flare split the darkness, and an American voice yelled, 'Holy shit! Look at that. Get down, get down.' This was quickly followed by bursts of M16 machine-gun fire. I didn't just get down; I tried to dig a hole in the cement floor! Gloria started praying, which did not help calm my screaming nerves as the gun slipped from my sweaty grip and clattered away from me. Everyone else, now awake, came running from their rooms. More American voices called, 'It's OK, it's OK. You can come out. Holy shit, take a look at this.'

My shaking hands were incapable of opening the padlock. Someone had vomited. I think it was me. Gloria was still hugging the ground; the others were half asleep and confused. All Pat Smith wanted to know was who in hell was responsible for the gun.

Somebody unlocked the padlock, opened the door. There, just outside the doorway, lay the body of a full-grown tiger. I could not believe my eyes. Its head was massive, its teeth enormous. This magnificent jungle creature could have swatted down the door to our quarters with one swipe of its paw. And there was I with a .38 revolver?! At best, I could have clipped its ear, only annoying the hell out of it.

In the morning the soldiers winched the glorious beast onto a truck and took it to their base. They told us it weighed exactly nine hundred and forty-six pounds and asked us if we wanted the skin. No, we did not. I have a photograph of it, though. I never touched a gun again and, boy, did I get a roasting from Pat Smith for having that revolver in the first place.

The tiger in these parts is the Indochinese tiger. Smaller and darker than the Bengal tiger, they feed on wild boar, water buffalo and, occasionally, monkeys and fish. The adult tigers are territorial and fiercely defensive, preferring dense vegetation for which their camouflage is ideally suited and where a single predator – as opposed to a pride – is not at a disadvantage. Among the big cats, only tigers and jaguars are strong swimmers, and are often found bathing in, or in the vicinity of, rivers and lakes.

During the war, the bombing and the slash-and-burn creation of fire-breaks in both forests and open scrub forced the tigers away from their normal habitats, and their feeding patterns were severely disrupted. Increasingly, Montagnards had been reporting disappearances of people. When tribespeople walked the mountain trails, they did so in long lines, one behind the other. Now there were often reports that the person last in line would simply vanish. Sometimes a trail of fresh blood was found; often there was no trace. They knew that this was the work of tigers looking for food. Before the bombing and disruption, tigers had rarely been known to be man-eaters. But things can change, and they surely and tragically did in that particular area.

32

HEY, JUDE

Minh Quy Hospital was surrounded by thatched huts, with the thick jungle foliage pressing in on all sides. Dusky, bare-breasted women, their chubby babies slung low on their backs, waited quietly in the shade to be seen at one of our busy clinics. The men, clad in loincloths, crossbows for hunting wild boar over their shoulders, carried the sick and wounded on home-made litters. We walked slowly and carefully up and down the lines of patiently waiting people, identifying the most urgent cases. No one ever tried to push themselves forward or jump the queue, and we frequently found seriously ill patients lying some way down the line.

Among the soldiers who would come to volunteer help in any way they could, Denny was a regular visitor. He was a chilled-out individual attached to the nearby helicopter base, and never took the army too seriously. When asked what he did, he replied he was in graves registration, somehow making it sound like he was in real estate. His job was to identify the American dead, place them in body bags, and record their names. Like many of the soldiers, Denny was shy around Western women – the war was such a surreal, painful experience that to be confronted unexpectedly by women who perhaps reminded you of your sister, mother, wife or girlfriend back home was unnerving. We understood that.

Denny's guitar was his best friend. He loved it, and played it well, and he had a sweet voice. To see him ambling up the pathway to the hospital, his guitar on his back, was always a welcome sight. Denny was from Evansville, Illinois. His parents had a potato farm. I guess coming to Vietnam was the most exciting thing that had ever happened to him.

It was also the last thing that happened to him.

Denny was one of life's fixers. You told him your problem, he'd give it some thought, then, without any fanfare, he made it go away. Some people do that in life.

Courtesy of the US Army, a fifteen-kilowatt generator provided electricity for a few hours a day. This powered the X-ray machine, so essential in a war zone, where it was too dangerous to operate on those with multiple shrapnel wounds unless you knew exactly where the shards had penetrated and lodged.

One night the generator was demolished by a direct hit from a mortar. Apart from scaring ten years off the lives of everyone inside the hospital at the time, we were unable to take essential X-rays, a serious setback. We put the word out: what would it take to get another generator? The answer came back: four AK47s. American and Australian soldiers liked to get their hands on these weapons as souvenirs, so we casually dropped hints to our Montagnard personnel.

Two mornings later, lying on the office desk were four AK47s.

We gave them to Denny, and next day an army truck trundled in with a generator – the old 'redistribution of army goods, ma'am', – all part of the wheeling and dealing that goes on in any war zone. It was installed, and everything continued as normal. Whenever Pat Smith's hospital badly needed something, wonderful things happened, all for the greater good. Quite a contrast from the world I had come from, where everything was done by committee and signed in triplicate, often with no result at all. This would have come as a mystery to the locals of Kontum, where real need brought instant help.

Denny would always politely ask for permission to enter the hospital, where he would stuff his cap in his back pocket and make his way between the overcrowded straw mats and old iron bedsteads, with a ready smile for the patients lying on them. Many were paraplegic or amputees. Some were blinded, others had burns, malaria cases were frequent. The human cost of war lay all around. Denny was special and they looked forward to his visits.

He would squeeze himself into a space, settle down and start gently singing, first to himself, his blond head down, and then to everyone, head up, sharing folk songs and popular songs of the day. The people of the mountains lay there, quietly listening to the soldier with the sweet voice and an air of calm serenity. Often they started humming, trying to learn the songs, young men tapping fingers on their paralysed legs. One time, one of them crawled slowly to our treatment room and commandeered a plastic bucket. It made a great drum.

Hiao was one of several young tribesmen who owed their lives to Dr Pat Smith, and were now employed at the hospital. He was the joker in the pack, full of fun and a joy to be around. As a teenager, Hiao's leg was shredded by a landmine and had to be amputated from mid-calf. Pat had operated, saving his knee joint, and his life. She fixed him up with a rudimentary prosthesis and trained him to work in the laboratory, where he was responsible for grouping and cross-matching blood when needed for a transfusion. We had no proper refrigeration for storing blood safely, so we had a register of people we could call when blood was required, and often gave it ourselves.

When a child needed blood, as long as its group matched hers, Pat was usually first to volunteer. When she gave an order, it was not to be questioned. All she asked was that, while her blood was being drawn, she be brought a can of Budweiser! She would only allow her staff to give blood on the spot if it was literally a matter of life and death. It often was.

The military themselves, particularly the American and Australian Special Forces, were a ready and generous source of donors. If a call went out for six units of A-positive, those not scheduled for a mission within the next twenty-four hours would quickly appear from their base across the river, sleeves rolled up at the ready. Their reward was a lukewarm Budweiser, a smile from a pretty nurse, and the knowledge that their blood saved many lives.

Hiao and Denny became good friends over time. While Denny played and sang, Hiao would take him a drink, and a snack of sticky rice wrapped up in a banana leaf. Then he'd sit at the soldier's feet, listening intently, his eyes fixed on the guitar. He especially enjoyed 'Hey Jude', which was Denny's favourite too. Hiao was shy; he never tried to strum the guitar when invited to do so and was content just to listen, a big grin on his trusting face.

I was unlucky enough to contract chloroquine-resistant falciparum malaria while at this hospital. I was very ill for a while, and Denny came to visit me. I remember him standing awkwardly by my bed, shuffling his feet from side to side. I noticed that he didn't remove his cap this time, even though it was standard courtesy, but as soon as his commanding officer left the room, Denny gingerly removed his cap and solemnly handed me four eggs which he'd commandeered from the base camp kitchen and smuggled out. Good eggs were hard to come by, and were badly needed for my diet. I was so touched by that, and will never forget him.

Denny was killed in action.

One of his friends came to the hospital to tell us. He brought

Denny's guitar with him and gave it to Hiao. He also gave him a small cassette player, a handful of batteries and some music tapes. One was a Beatles tape. We didn't see Hiao for a while. He went off, alone, walking in the mountains, grieving at his own pace for his friend.

The rest of us grieved for Denny too, but work had to go on. The tide of sick and wounded did not, alas, slow down for the death of the kind young man with the sweet voice.

When Hiao was ready, he returned to his duties. The battered little tape recorder was always near him, always on. He played that Beatles tape many times, and 'Hey Jude' over and over again.

Then one day he picked up the guitar. Over the weeks he painstakingly taught himself to play this magical song. Whenever he had a spare moment, he sat with the recorder clutched to his ear, learning the words parrot fashion, concentrating hard on getting them right.

He walked to and from work along the mountain tracks singing 'Hey Jude' for several weeks and eventually became word perfect and chord perfect. We had a hell of a time keeping him in batteries. Whenever soldiers went on their five-day R&R breaks to Hong Kong, Penang, Australia or Hawaii and asked what they could bring back, the answer was always the same – batteries! After a few months, Hiao's mastery of this song was astonishing. He could play nothing else, but boy, could he play 'Hey Jude'!

Now, whenever I hear this beautiful melody, my thoughts soar towards those mountains in South east Asia and Hiao, a Montagnard with a ready grin and a limping gait, singing the song he so loved in tribute to his friend.

33

A NUN, A NURSE
AND A TRUCK

Sister Marie Clare had an adventurous spirit to match my own. We were a good mix or a bad mix, depending on your point of view, and I know we gave Pat Smith some headaches. All Dr Smith's staff were categorically forbidden to go to the original hospital under any circumstances, because of the subsidence which had caused it to be closed in the first place.

We occasionally had to drive down to the American evacuation hospital in Pleiku to refill our oxygen tanks. On one occasion we were running dangerously low on oxygen, but heightened enemy activity in the area ruled out any kind of trip to Pleiku.

However, we'd been tipped off by some junior military that there were still some full oxygen tanks in storage at the old hospital. So, Marie Clare and I decided together to ignore the rules. All we thought about was the patients' need for oxygen, and if it was there, well, we could go get it. And the less anybody knew about where we got it, the better. So, of course, we couldn't tell anyone. We just did it. I figured we'd be OK; after all, Marie Clare had a hotline to God . . .

We drove off in an old pickup truck that had been donated to the hospital, me at the wheel. The road to the old hospital was a jungle path that was little more than a dirt track, which had deteriorated into a series of potholes because of the constant stream of heavy military traffic. Somehow I managed to get us there, but it was a hell of a drive, and scary too.

God knows how we, two young women, loaded the four enormous oxygen cylinders that we found there into the back of the truck, but we did. There was not a soul around, just jungle noises, crickets and the prr-prr sounds of hidden creatures. It was really eerie; in this hot, steamy, mysterious place, the deserted hospital felt like the medical equivalent of the *Mary Celeste*.

On the way back Sister Marie Clare drove. She had to be the world's worst driver. As we clattered and banged along, I kept up a running commentary. 'For God's sake, be careful . . . this is oxygen we're carrying . . . you nearly went into that pothole . . . watch out!' Then the front tyre hit a rock and we bounced up, slowly, into the air, the truck seeming to leave the road in a graceful arc.

Marie Clare steered us into the bank. We rolled over – I think once, who knows – ending upside down with the cab crushed on my side. How we weren't killed by the rolling oxygen tanks, I don't know.

There we were, Welsh nurse and New York nun, crumpled upside down in a crushed pickup. When the wheels stopped spinning and the sputtering and banging noises quietened down, we gradually became aware of our surroundings. We were dazed but conscious, and I remember tentatively moving my arms, then my legs, which were wedged above my head.

'Are you all right, Marie Clare, are you all right?'

'Yes, I think so . . . are you all right?'

And then we started to laugh, giggling insanely and uncontrollably, two young women, upside down in a beaten-up old truck, on a jungle track in the mountain area of a war zone. We were so thrilled that we were alive, able to move our limbs and to speak. Then Marie Clare got busy praying and thanking Mary, Jesus and Joseph, while I tried to figure out how the hell we were going to get out of there. The roof on my side of the cab was badly caved in, and we could smell petrol.

'I can't get out this side, you have to try and get out your side,' I said, and at that moment we heard the sound of an approaching vehicle, which grew noisier as it got closer. We were in the middle of nowhere and nobody, but nobody, knew where we were. We were just asking for trouble, and terrified we were about to get it. We were in too much of a state to figure out that neither the Vietcong nor the NVA soldiers would be driving around in a noisy vehicle. Then the vehicle stopped and we heard the chilling, unmistakable metal-on-metal click of weapons being cocked. I tried to manoeuvre my head so I could see who these people were. Marie Clare was praying again.

Then I heard the familiar exclamation, 'Holy shit!' and saw a pair of army boots cautiously approaching my side of the cab. Americans. Thank God for that! Then a startled face appeared upside down and briefly at what remained of the pickup's window. He disappeared, and I heard him say, 'There are two round-eyes in there.'

'No shit?' said another voice.

Then two pairs of boots walked our way and two faces appeared, one on either side of the truck. One of the faces said, very politely, 'Hi, ma'am, where are you folks from?'

Marie Clare said, quite calmly I thought, 'I'm from New York. Could you get us out of here please?'

'Jesus, ma'am, begging your pardon! I left New York to get away from woman drivers! How come you're here, ma'am?'

The soldiers dragged us out and, despite being shocked, battered, bruised and upside down, I couldn't stop laughing. The vehicle didn't blow up the way it does in movies, but it looked a terrible mess and the smell of gasoline was terrifying. It was much more frightening when we got out and looked at the wreck than it had been when we were in it. Boy, did we get a tongue-lashing when we got back for putting ourselves in graver danger than we knew.

But we did turn up with four full oxygen cylinders, which were put to immediate and effective use.

We never, ever went back to the old hospital.

34

THE PRESIDENT
REQUESTS . . .

On 20 July 1969 man first landed on the moon. In the mountains of Vietnam and Cambodia there was no access to telephones or television and mail from home was sporadic, delivered courtesy of the Army Postal Services via San Francisco. News was gleaned from the wonderful *Life* magazines donated by Pat Smith's visitors from Saigon, or had to wait till we were on leave. The day we first saw the breathtaking photographs, taken from space, of Earth rising and Neil Armstrong stepping on lunar dust was truly astonishing.

We showed them to our Montagnard colleagues and tried to explain. Though the pictures, in all their beauty and clarity, showed the momentous events, the explanation that these were men walking on the moon was met with puzzled looks and some unease. The news was difficult enough for us to digest; how could our tribesmen colleagues possibly grasp the enormity of this 'giant leap for mankind'?

The following morning no one turned up for work. Strange. The explanation was not long in coming. Two of the local village elders came to the hospital to see Pat and, from their solemn demeanour, we could tell this was an official delegation arriving to discuss serious matters. They warned us not to fill their young men's heads with wild stories of men walking on the moon, otherwise they could not permit them to return to the hospital.

In the developed world, technology races ahead relentlessly but not always comfortably for the human spirit. Thinking of how long it took for my 'soul to catch up with my body' when I first arrived in Vietnam, I could certainly understand that we all need to allow time for our souls to catch up with events. These tribesmen, living close to nature and respecting it, cherishing the world around them, as we all once did, related to the moon with their whole being. They were, and are, wise in the ways of the natural world in a way that we in the developed West seem to have lost.

How we marvelled at man shooting into space, landing on the moon, stepping out of his spacecraft and taking a few dusty steps to gaze across at empty craters. Here in Kontum were tribesmen who respected the power of the moon – and the wind, the sun and the rain. It doesn't hurt to be reminded at intervals from whence we came. It seems to me that the more technically advanced and sophisticated we've become, the more we've begun to lose our basic survival and observational skills. I will always remember the effect our moon-landing stories and photographs had on the pristine minds and souls of those Montagnards who worked for Pat Smith in Kontum.

Soon after these events, a jeep arrived at the hospital carrying two officers, escorted by a second jeep carrying two military policemen. They jumped out, came up to the busy outpatient clinic where I was assisting Pat, stood to attention, and saluted.

'Doctor Patricia Smith?' asked one of the officers.

'Yes, just wait a moment, I'm busy,' she said, and carried on examining her patient. Eventually she turned to the nonplussed officer and said, somewhat abruptly, 'Yes, what is it?'

'Ma'am, the President of the United States, Richard Milhous Nixon, issues the following invitation, ma'am.'

Pat, who was reading a patient's notes and smoking a cigarette, which she did constantly, barely looked up at this, but they certainly had my attention! Pat was being summoned to the White House – it was more of an order than a request – on such and such a date and time, at such and such an entrance, to receive the medal for Women of Valour.

God! I was so excited for her. But she just sat there, reading the patient's notes and puffing on her cigarette, then gave me an order concerning a change in medication.

'Did you hear what he said, Dr Smith?' I asked.

At that, she squinted at me through the cigarette smoke, then looked at the officer, still standing stiffly to attention.

'Listen to me, fella, and listen good,' she said. 'If that horse's ass wants to see me, he can come over here. If he leaves the White House for three days, nobody's gonna miss him. If I leave the hospital to go over to Washington for a few days, who's gonna care for the people here? Who's gonna care about these kids? Nobody. So if that horse's ass wants to see me, you tell him to come over here.'

I was aghast. So was the officer delivering the message. He sort of spluttered, saluted, and then seemed at a loss as to what else to do. Pat took a long draw on her cigarette and turned her attention back to her patient.

'Tell him that, from me,' she added, and we continued with the endless round of sick and wounded.

The two bemused officers clicked their heels, saluted, turned to the right and marched in unison to their jeep. Off they went, and that was that, never to be mentioned again.

At a later date the valour of this selfless, fearless American woman, Dr Patricia Smith M.D., was recognised. On 24 November, 1970, between 1:04p.m. and 1:09p.m., President Nixon met Dr Pat Smith in the Oval Office. He gave four minutes of his time to this remarkable woman, who gave so much of her life to others. She lives on in the hearts and minds of all who knew her.

35

STRUCK DOWN

For some time I had been ignoring the fact that I felt unwell: it went with the territory. We all worked very hard, but had learned to live with a level of fatigue, both physical and emotional.

Then, one day, while I was completing patient rounds with an American army doctor who was seconded to the hospital for a couple of weeks, I felt strangely distant from what was going on and found myself clinging for support to the metal trolley holding the patient files. My fingers were swollen, very white and quite numb, I couldn't feel my feet touching the ground, and everything took on a dreamlike, disconnected quality. The earnest young physician said to me, 'When we finish here, Anne, I want to examine you. You are a terrible colour and not at all well.' That's the last thing I remember.

I woke up in a bed, three days later. As I opened my eyes, trying to orientate myself, I could see Dr Smith standing at the foot of my bed, with the army doctor. It seemed ages before I could focus clearly. They appeared to be moving and speaking in slow motion, yet their voices seemed terribly loud to my ears. Pat Smith boomed, 'She's the first member of my team to have contracted this in all the years I've been here.' I thought: 'Oh God. I've got bubonic plague.'

Recently there had been two outbreaks of plague, and I'd been shocked to learn that this medieval disease still existed. Caused by a bite from the fleas on infected rats, it spreads like wildfire. Death from septicaemia ensues within a few hours unless diagnosis and treatment commences in the earliest stage. In Vietnam in 1969/70, as soon as the disease was suspected and identified, the entire family/village/community was urged to leave rapidly, abandoning all their belongings. With all people moved out, the area was immediately torched, the fire efficiently destroying everything, including the fleas and, hopefully, the rats. The whole area was then sprinkled liberally with DDT powder, as was the inside and outside of the hospital.

The medications of choice were the antibiotic tetracycline and intramuscular streptomycin, both highly effective if the plague was diagnosed early enough – and the main difficulty with plague lies in early diagnosis. Once bitten by the infected flea general sepsis spreads quickly, and death ensues within a few hours of the appearance of the buboes (hence the name 'bubonic') – a collection of infected pustules that pop up over the lymphatic glands in the groin or armpit. In each of the outbreaks I witnessed, we all continued to work while popping our tetracycline tablets and with the whole area doused in DDT powder, giving the hospital and everyone in it a ghostly air. We must have been breathing in pure DDT powder, but we all survived to tell the tale.

Now, lying there convinced I was dying, I just wanted to be put out of my misery.

It was not plague, of course, but falciparum malaria. The resistant strain was becoming increasingly common in the highlands and, despite swallowing the large and horrible pink chloroquine tablet each week, I had been unlucky. Falciparum is the more serious form of malaria, and can be fatal. My haemoglobin had dropped to an incredible three and a half grams; my blood must have been almost straw-coloured. I was physically very weak and could barely raise my head off the pillow. I remember being startled by a frighteningly loud noise, like the sound of an old train releasing its steam right next to me. It was deafening, blotting out everything, completely numbing the senses. It took me a while to realise it was the sound of my own breathing.

This is where I learned the full meaning of cerebral irritation. It is no bad thing for doctors and nurses to endure some of these diseases. It gives valuable insight into what patients in your care are experiencing. When people complain of being unable to tolerate light, or are hypersensitive to sound, unless you've experienced it yourself you can't possibly know what that really means. I remember hearing a very loud 'shushing' sound. It took an age for me to realise it was the movement of my hands against the sheets. It was quite a few days before I was oriented to time and place, or knew who was around me and just exactly what was going on.

I was in a little screened-off area in Pat's hospital, and I was looked after well. The Montagnards brought me bunches of hibiscus blossoms every day and put them on my bamboo bed-side table. This was the time when Denny visited and brought me those four precious eggs.

The Minh Quy was a Catholic mission hospital. Every Sunday a priest from the Seminary held a Communion service, and at Christmas we had a nativity play. Joseph wore a loincloth and had a crossbow at his side; Mary was dressed in the distinctive ankle-length black skirt, bare-breasted and with her baby Jesus in a sling across her chest.

Though I've never been very religious, I was raised to attend our village church every Sunday morning with one of my parents, and to go to Sunday school in the afternoon. It was characteristic of the disciplined 1950s, an integral part of my growing up, and did me no harm. I acknowledge the presence of God and have been thankful for His presence on several occasions – never more so than one particular Sunday when, still strictly confined to bed, I lay listening to the Communion service going on in the ward, behind the screens that separated me from the other patients.

The beautiful chanting and singing of the Montagnard congregation was calming and comforting, except that my bladder was almost bursting with the need for the bedpan. With everyone otherwise occupied, I thought it would be a good time for me to use the large old-fashioned commode, standing like an imposing wooden throne at the side of my bed. I heaved myself up to a sitting position, but it took me forever to swing myself round. My ankles were very swollen, and my fingers and toes were still snow white and pudgy like rows of sausages. Yikes! Surely they couldn't be mine! I sat on the edge of the bed for what seemed like an age, staring at my fat, alien toes and swollen legs. These were signs of the gross anaemia and attendant heart problems I was suffering from as the malarial parasites ravaged my system. I was thirty years of age and weighed one hundred and twelve pounds. I felt breathless, helpless, and old beyond my years.

I finally got myself onto the commode with difficulty. Having relieved myself I tried, and failed, to get back into bed, and the effort left me breathless, sweating and shaky. I had never been ill before, and this was a humdinger. I simply couldn't move and all I could think about was that Dr Smith would kill me if she found I had been out of bed against her orders.

I was exhausted and trying to figure out what to do when the screens were moved aside suddenly and in walked the French priest. Behind him were two Montagnard nuns, Gabriel and Caliste, gently moving incense burners back and forth. The priest had come to give me Communion, and I was sitting on the commode! I just remained there, frozen. I hadn't the energy to do anything else. I placed one palm over the other. Speaking in Jarai, the priest gave me the host. Then he offered a sip of wine from the chalice handed to him by one of the servers. How I prayed – mainly that Pat Smith was not behind him, and for the strength not to pass out.

The screens were drawn again when the priest withdrew, and I wondered if I was hallucinating. I simply could not get back into bed unaided but, to my great good fortune, Sister Gabriel and Sister Caliste had immediately got the picture. They quietly left the service and came back to rescue me. They got me back into bed, firmly telling me off but unable quite to hide the big grins they were trying to suppress. A few days later I was moved to our living quarters. I couldn't get myself up the short corridor to the toilet, so they brought that bloody commode up to the house. I was happy to use it.

At the Minh Quy Mission hospital we all just got on with the job in hand, until it was decided it was no longer safe to do so.

The infamous My Lai massacre had occurred in 1968, when more than five hundred civilians were murdered in cold blood, fuelling Vietcong hatred of US troops. It was in 1968 that Sister Renate Kuhnen, the German nurse working with Dr Smith, had been captured by the NVA. Though we didn't dwell on the thought, we knew our situation at Minh Quy Hospital could become untenable at any time. During 1969, fighting escalated and the flow of body bags carrying dead American soldiers back to their loved ones for burial was relentless. Despite Nixon's reductions in ground troops, and ongoing diplomatic meetings in Paris between Nixon's envoy, Dr Henry Kissinger, and the Vietnamese government, the war would go on for another five years. I, however, would no longer be there to witness the slow deterioration in morale, or the appalling bloodshed that didn't seem to diminish.

Towards the end of 1970, it became clear that I couldn't

continue at Minh Quy Hospital or, indeed, remain in Vietnam. The malaria had left me weak and exhausted and, although it broke my heart to leave these people, jeopardising my health would benefit no one.

Although the situation in Vietnam was steadily deteriorating, Pat Smith stayed on, continuing to rebuild her hospital, with new labs, a kitchen and a laundry. Her energy was amazing. She was almost ready to move out of the borrowed schoolhouse and back into the original hospital when, in 1972, the Vietcong and NVA launched a massive offensive, known now as the Battle for Kontum. Villages in the area were overrun, bringing tragedy to their inhabitants. A boy was shot in the stomach while fishing; two girls bathing in a stream were killed and another wounded; after Mass one Sunday, a mortar shell exploded near the church, wounding a number of children. Life was changing. It did not look good.

At this particular time, I had travelled overland from England to Singapore, intending to return to Dr Smith's staff, when I was informed by American Embassy officials that it would be wisest to cancel my plans. The security situation was rapidly worsening, and at any moment they would be advising Pat and her entire team of foreign staff to vacate the hospital and leave Kontum. I was heartbroken, but friends I was travelling with made me see sense until I finally faced the sad fact that I would not be returning to Vietnam.

In the following days, roads north of Kontum were cut and the airport came under constant shelling. The Montagnards hid Pat to protect her from the bombardments, but it came to the point where the last French bishop in Vietnam told Pat she had to go. If she stayed, she would be killed. She had no choice but to leave, taking along her two adopted Montagnard sons, Det, whose mother had been killed by Vietcong, and Wir, who had been abandoned in a burned-out village.

I can only imagine how devastated Dr Smith and her loyal staff must have felt. For Pat Smith, to abandon the Montagnard people she loved so much and to whom she had dedicated so much of her life must have been profoundly painful.

I never saw her again after leaving Vietnam and we didn't keep in touch, but I knew from press reports that she and her adopted sons returned to Seattle when South Vietnam fell. She settled in the area of Bellevue, east of Seattle, and worked as a doctor for a Group Health Co-operative for a further twenty years, retiring in 1997. She then moved to Lake Cushman, halfway between Seattle and the Pacific Ocean. Det eventually became a Navy dentist and Wir a musician. She died on 26 December 2004, at the age of seventy-eight.

Everything I learned from Dr Patricia Smith and her dedicated staff has served as a template for the rest of my life. The power of one is powerful indeed. For anyone looking at what seem like overwhelming problems in life, prompting thoughts of, 'I am only one person, I can do nothing,' the most important lesson I have learned is that each and every one of us can, and does, make a difference.

Part Three

DISPLACEMENT

January 1979. Pol Pot's four-year killing spree in Cambodia ends when his Khmer Rouge forces are overthrown by the Vietnamese. Hundreds of thousands of brutalised, sick and destitute Cambodian victims of Pol Pot's regime flee westward to the ill-defined and disputed border with Thailand. Tensions build as the Thai authorities attempt to protect their borders against illegal entry, illicit trade, smuggling, and foraging raids by the remnants of the Khmer Rouge.

July 1979. Representatives of fifty nations gather in Geneva to express their concerns. Additional aid is pledged, and increased numbers of refugees will be given permanent asylum. Thailand revises its refugee policy in October: although still considered illegal entrants, Cambodians will no longer be stopped and turned back at the border, but given every possible assistance, as a matter of compassion.

October 1979. A humanitarian disaster is building up on the Thai-Cambodia border. Several large holding camps are erected on or close to this border, and within two months house one hundred and fifty-six thousand refugees. The Thai military has assumed responsibility for another one hundred and forty-nine thousand Cambodians; and a further one hundred and thirteen thousand are accommodated at Khao-I-Dang and Sa Keao.

Sa Keao is situated in Thailand itself, approximately sixty kilometres from the border, and holds about forty thousand refugees who are the most severely in need of medical care. Thus, doctors, nurses and necessary supplies are concentrated in Sa Keao, and international medical teams are sent there. The Save the Children Fund sends a medical team.

After nine years working away from Southeast Asia's war zones, I am on my way back once again.

36

SENSORY OVERLOAD

After leaving Minh Quy Hospital towards the end of 1970 I had little idea of what I would do or where, other than holding on to the notion that, eventually, I would go back to work for Dr Smith in Kontum.

Meanwhile, I resumed nursing in a very different environment from the one I'd left: the emergency room at St Stephen's Hospital in Fulham, London. Two years there taught me what drug abuse does to people right across the social spectrum; there were those brought in dead or half dead from amid the detritus of the city streets; others, from the media, entertainment and business worlds, several of them public figures, had been able to hide their addiction until the money ran out and they ended up in the same place as the less privileged. It was a sorry sight.

The stint at St Stephen's was my first in a variety of different settings that allowed me to broaden my experience and hone my skills. The wanderlust kicked in again and I travelled overland to Singapore with a boyfriend, a wonderful adventure and one that I intended to end with a return to Kontum. When this proved impossible, I carried on to Australia and spent four amazing and happy years discovering life in the outback.

That ended when an opportunity came along to crew on a fifty-foot ketch. I'd always wanted to learn how to sail, and I grabbed the chance with both hands. This learning curve took me to the Pacific Ocean and the Caribbean Sea, exploring Central and South American coastlines and some of the Caribbean islands for ten magical months. Never one to run from extremes, in 1978 I went from the sunny climes of the West Indies to nurse in a traditional Inuit settlement in the Canadian Arctic.

I returned home only because my father became ill, and I stayed with him until he recovered his health. Then, before I had time to choose another far-flung adventure, I was once again approached by SCF and the choice was made for me.

Sitting in the London office of Save the Children, the assignment I was about to accept (working with Cambodians in Thailand) seemed clearly defined and perfectly straightforward. Our team of five nurses and two doctors was briefed to identify vulnerable mothers with children under the age of five, and to set up clinics from where they would be provided with medical and supplementary feeding support.

However, the sight that met me on my first day of work in early October 1979 stunned me almost into paralysis. As I stood there in my loose-fitting white cotton uniform, Manchester Royal Infirmary penny pinned carefully to my chest, it took quite some moments and an effort of will to gather my wits and attempt to process what I was looking at. I'd approached the area on foot, walking across the scrubby field from the main road where the SCF vehicle had dropped me, but all I could see stretching ahead of me to infinity was a mass of blackness on the ground. Army vehicles and various trucks trundled along the only access road, a narrow dirt road, kicking up clouds of dust which hovered in the heat haze above the blackness.

As my senses adjusted, I realised with horror that the mass of blackness was people. Thousands of people. They lay there, on the ground, clad in ragged, black pyjama-like outfits. Occasionally an arm was slowly raised in silent supplication, only to fall back weakly. That was all there was to identify the mass as human. What struck me then, and stays with me now, was the silence. There was no sound of talk or of laughter; no babies cried, no one coughed or wept. And the stench was overpowering.

My first instinct was to turn and run from the scene, go home. What could I possibly do to help something on this scale . . .

Most of the displaced Khmer people were housed in a number of camps strung out along the border area, but a percentage of this tide of human misery appeared more debilitated than most. Many had survived torture and imprisonment in addition to the general famine, and the decision had been made to bring those most urgently in need of attention to the holding camp, placed in the middle of otherwise deserted scrubland, that became known as Sa Keao.

Ideally, a displaced persons camp is assembled before thousands of people flood into it. Quite aside from the shelter needed to protect people from the elements, latrines have to be dug and safe drinking water has to be sourced, transported and distributed. Food – rice, flour, oil and high-protein biscuits – must be delivered and securely stored, ready for fair distribution. A hospital area needs to be set up, supplied and equipped to take in the sick, wounded and traumatised, with additional clinics to support the mothers and children suffering from those illnesses common in the dispossessed. To organise this monumental task and make it happen quickly and effectively takes a lot of efficient manpower, and usually involves military personnel.

I had never seen anything like this before. Tears pricked my eyes and anger flared at the human degradation which had resulted from a man-made catastrophe. As I gazed helplessly at the scene, I wondered what action Mike would take were he here beside me. Then my nurse training kicked in. I became very calm and got myself a jeep ride with a Thai soldier who deposited me outside a tent, where a sign pinned to the canvas announced: MEDICAL DIRECTOR UNHCR. REPORT HERE.

A harassed-looking man, red-faced and uncomfortable in the heat, emerged from the tent clutching some lists. He greeted me enthusiastically in German, which I do not speak, but I perfectly understood he was desperate for doctors, nurses and nutritionists. I explained I was the first member of the London SCF team to arrive; the others would be coming over the next few days. He was the co-ordinator of the international medical teams arriving daily. I did not envy him his task, but over the coming days I learned much about the logistics of planning for the delivery of effective aid to large numbers of displaced people. The UNHCR (United Nations High Commission for Refugees) and the Red Cross are vastly experienced in this field and I was privileged to see first-hand how they work to restore order from chaos. I came to wonder often why people of this calibre never seem to go into politics. If they did, it might prevent such humanitarian disasters from occurring in the first place.

I had reported for duty on only the second day of Sa Keao's existence. Conditions were bad. The co-ordinator assigned me temporarily to work with the Médecins sans Frontières team, and pointed to two nearby tents. A handful of French doctors and nurses were battling to stabilise skeletal and shocked children, many in the throes of cerebral malaria, their little bodies contorted with the seizures caused by the malarial parasites attacking their brain. Nearby was one of several tents that were being used as temporary morgues. It was emptied several times a day, the bodies removed for burial in mass graves.

Though my school French was inadequate, these medics

were so organised and experienced that I quickly cottoned on to what they wanted me to do, and I was hugely impressed with their speed, efficiency and dedication. MSF has always had an excellent reputation for getting things done, and remaining independent of any political, religious or economic affiliations. They have no time for bureaucracy and are usually the first group to reach the scene of a disaster. I saw up close just how they work, and learned so much from them in the three days I was seconded to their team. It left me with a deep respect for this particular charity. Formed in 1971 by a group of French doctors following their experiences in Biafra, their belief is simply that the needs of people supersede respect for international borders. Amen to that.

In 1999 Médecins sans Frontières won the Nobel Peace Prize.

Over the next few days, as the scale of this catastrophe became clearer, medical teams arrived from many countries. Convoys of trucks constantly moved between Bangkok international airport and the camps, ferrying supplies donated from all over the globe. Water was trucked in from an area forty kilometres away and stored in large metal tanks. Vast rolls of blue plastic were distributed for shelter from the sun, the heat from which was further dehydrating people who were suffering from dysenteries and under the threat of cholera. The Thai army cleared roads and erected fences to demarcate and secure the vast area. The levels of logistical planning and co-ordination required were extraordinary.

On the fourth day, one of the MSF team took me to the border area to see where and how the casualties were being found. There we watched, stricken, as teams of volunteers armed with long sticks searched in the long grasses. They found small groups of terrified Cambodians huddled in the undergrowth, often not yet aware that they had already reached the safe haven of Thailand. Hundreds were being transported to Sa Keao in Red Cross vehicles, Thai military trucks and even farm carts pulled by oxen. One of the volunteers carrying out the back-breaking work that day taught me a lesson I will never forget.

37

THE BELGIAN WOMAN

The situation in the camp was slowly, steadily improving, but it remained a scene of degradation and the blistering heat only added to our despondency.

Yet it was here that we met an extraordinary woman. It was one of those fleeting encounters that occur throughout a lifetime and generally fade from memory, but those of us there that afternoon would never forget her or the words she spoke.

It was on my brief visit to the border that I first saw the woman. In her mid-fifties, blonde and physically strong, she worked tirelessly under the hot sun. Back and forth she went, carrying in her arms, or on her back, emaciated children, and young women too weak to walk further. She held them tenderly, ignoring the vomit and leaking bodily fluids that soiled her clothes, and placed them gently in the waiting Red Cross and military vehicles. Her fiercely determined demeanour, together with her kind smile and words of comfort for each precious bundle in her arms, singled her out from the many who were helping on that border.

Some days before, one of the supply trucks travelling from Bangkok had been driven off the main highway. It was later found in a side road, abandoned and ransacked. The following day it was reported that the precious medical and pharmaceutical contents were being sold in one of the teeming city markets. Unfortunately, a few days later this featured prominently in the international press, fuelling the cynical view that most aid fails to reach its intended destination. This can have a seriously frustrating and depressing effect on field workers, donors and charities.

I was sitting in the shade, taking a break with a small group of doctors and nurses who constituted a mini league of nations. We came from France, Holland, Japan, Australia, New Zealand and Britain. Sweaty, exhausted and disheartened, we sipped warm Coca-Cola and discussed the effect of this report, wondering why good news is never deemed to *be* news. What was the point of all our efforts if only negative stories were reported? The press always appears ready to print bad news. Doctors, nurses, nutritionists, healers and carers of every description see good things happening daily in their work. Small miracles of healing and resolution bring smiles and comfort to those in sickness and pain, wherever in the world that is, yet random acts of kindness go unnoticed, while random acts of hatred and violence are dramatised and highlighted. Why is that?

Into our group stepped that blonde woman I had noticed at the border days earlier. Speaking quietly but firmly she told us the following story:

You are wrong to think like this. I have been listening to you all, it is your exhaustion speaking. Listen to me. I live in Belgium. I am not a nurse or a doctor, I'm a mother and a grandmother. As a child I was raised happily with my family in Poland. My father was a watchmaker. I was the eldest of five brothers and sisters, and when I was eighteen my whole family were arrested and taken to the Treblinka concentration camp because my father had sold a watch to a Jewish doctor. We were all accused of associating and doing business with Jews. My mother and I, and my two sisters were immediately and brutally separated from my father and brothers. We never saw them again, and my mother was taken from us within a few days. Over the coming months my sisters died of disease and exhaustion. I lost all hope and knew death would be my friend. I lived in a foul-smelling hut with two hundred and forty other women and girls. Every day there were rapes, beatings, suicides . . . each day new prisoners arrived.

One day, some Red Cross parcels appeared. The contents were pathetically inadequate for our needs, but they delivered a powerful message that was far more important. These parcels told us there were people outside this place who knew of our existence and cared; that we should not lose hope but somehow hold on till help came. We were not alone.

Hope is the most powerful gift you can give people who have lost everything. I saw how those parcels offered the women a spark of hope, and I vowed then that if I survived that hellish place, I would carry that same message with me always; that I would spread it far and wide whenever I could, to the best of my ability. I know that many of those Red Cross parcels were stolen or went astray and ended up in the wrong hands during World War Two, but I don't care about that. What matters is that a few of them did reach us in that hut, and no words can describe the message of love and hope those parcels held.

Do not waste your energy on that one truck that didn't make it. Think of the many that do, and what their contents allow you to accomplish here. Now, go back to your work, hold your heads up high and give these people that message. Can you not see how they need it?

With that she turned and walked away. I never saw her again, and I never knew her name, but will always remember her.

38

BROTHER AND SISTER

Björn Larsson was a Norwegian press photographer with an unusually gentle, sensitive and compassionate approach to his subjects. They say a picture can speak a thousand words, and I have such a picture, taken by Larsson.

It shows a teenage boy, maybe fifteen years old, staring lovingly at a girl of about eight. They are brother and sister. Anyone who has seen the film *The Killing Fields* will know the story of Dith Pran and the hellish journey he took over difficult terrain from the Killing Fields of Cambodia, avoiding Khmer Rouge patrols, until he saw the border camps and knew he had reached the safety of Thailand.

This boy and his sister, the only members of their family left alive, had (like so many others) undertaken a similar journey. Carrying his sick little sister all the way on his back, the boy had somehow just kept going, following the rumours of a place of safety where foreign people would help his sister. They would have been among those found in the long grasses on the border area. I like to think it was the woman from Belgium who found them.

By the time he got to Sa Keao his sister had a dangerously high fever and convulsions. What her brother didn't yet know was that she was dying of cerebral malaria; we brought the convulsions under control, but the damage was done. I first met the pair in our bamboo and thatch children's ward, where there were many, many cases such as this. Most of them died. The boy sat quietly at his sister's side, day and night, sometimes talking quietly to her, sometimes singing softly, wiping the sweat from her face and moistening her clenched lips with a bit of cloth soaked in a little of the water I had given him to drink.

When she died I prepared to remove the intravenous infusion from her arm, but he gently pushed my hand away and took the swab and the band-aid from me. He carefully eased the needle out, and tenderly wiped the spot on her arm where it had been before placing the band-aid on it. I gave him some water in a tin and he washed her face and wracked body, wrapped her in his blue-and-white checked scarf and picked her up in his arms. I led him out to one of the blue tents used as a temporary morgue, where he laid her gently next to the other bodies already there and disappeared.

A short while later he came back with two hibiscus blossoms and asked if he could go back to the tent, which was guarded by a Thai soldier. I went with him and stood waiting at the entrance to the tent. Already several more bodies had been placed next to his sister's in the short time we had been gone. He tucked the blossoms into a fold of her scarf, murmuring to her the whole time. At last he turned from her, and we left.

I lost track of the boy for a couple of days, but then he turned up at my clinic and, with the help of an interpreter, told us he wanted to learn to be a doctor. Could we help, please? He said there were so many people in Cambodia with the same illness as his sister. He knew that, as foreigners, we could not go over the border. The Khmer Rouge would kill us and him, but if we could teach him what to do and give him medicines, he could go back there and treat people.

We explained that you had to study for many years to be a doctor, but he could help the doctors in our team here in the camp. We would give him extra food and make sure he didn't get sick. I gave him an exercise book and a couple of pencils, and told him to write in it the names of the medicines we were giving to people and note the illnesses they had. Mark, one of our doctors, took him under his wing and helped him with this. He thrived on it, and became a great help around the camp.

With his obvious thirst to learn, I'd like to think he survived, and that he made it safely to a country where he became a doctor. Otherwise, he stood no chance.

A disaster of such magnitude as that of the displaced Cambodians needed manpower. Lots of it. In the early days, the UNHCR appealed on local radio and television stations in Bangkok for fit, strong volunteers to report to various collection points in the city where clearly identified coaches would transport them to the camp. They were instructed to wear loose-fitting, comfortable old clothes and advised that they would need strong stomachs in order to do whatever was asked of them. No cameras were allowed, and they had to provide their own food and water. A day's work would last as long as daylight allowed.

It was hardly the most attractive proposition, yet the response was immediate and impressive. People from all walks of life – businessmen, housewives, students, travellers – horrified by the reports from the border area, came to help. Some, for whom the stench, the degradation and the death was too much to deal with, lasted only a day; most rolled up their sleeves and got on as best they could. Without the help of these marvellous volunteers, Sa Keao would not have made the progress that it did.

39

THE POWER OF LOVE

Triage, as anyone who has had occasion to go to hospital emergency or outpatient departments will know, is a system, used worldwide, whereby triage nurses check new arrivals to identify who needs what help, and which are the most urgent cases. At the camp, while the dead had to be removed to special areas for collection and burial, those requiring immediate help had to be identified and carried to the appropriate treatment area. This was triaging on a vast scale.

Working as we were with limited resources, supplies and energy, we gave precedence to those whom we thought most likely to respond to rapid treatment; the walking wounded had to wait. The dying, together with family if they had any, were taken to a separate area where they could be afforded as much dignity as possible in the circumstances. Accepting that some people are beyond help is always hard on medical staff, and decisions not to try and stave off death are difficult.

A Norwegian team was responsible for the intensive feeding of severely dehydrated children under the age of six, whom we would find by picking our way carefully among the many children who were too weak to stand. One day I picked up a distressed little boy whose ragged, laboured breaths tore at his fever-wracked frame, and whose eyes were rolling back in his head as I quickly carried him to the treatment area.

The Norwegian medics were inundated with severely ill little patients and I was uncertain what to do with my little boy when I noticed a tall, slender, blonde woman sitting on the edge of a makeshift bed on which lay four or five sickly toddlers. She was gently stroking faces, holding hands and attempting to keep the flies away.

Assuming this woman was a Norwegian nurse, I asked her if she spoke English. 'Good Lord, yes. Who are you?'

I explained why I was there and asked where I should put the boy.

'I don't know,' she answered, and to my surprise said, 'I'm not a nurse, I'm a volunteer from Bangkok. These doctors and nurses are so busy and I don't know how to help, so I'm just sitting here with these children. I have two children of my own, so I thought, at least I can mother them. They are so alone.'

I was very moved by that and asked her name – Jennifer Stewart. A nurse then appeared and took the child off me, so I was able to chat to Jennifer a little. She was from England and married to a Glaxo executive based in Bangkok, where they lived in a comfortable villa. She'd responded to the call for volunteers and found herself in the middle of this nightmare. Initially overwhelmed, she had seen the need and placed herself among the dying children. She scribbled down her phone number on a scrap of cigarette packet. 'Next time you come to Bangkok, call me,' she said.

In the circumstances in which we lived and worked, one rarely saw the same people twice. Miraculously, I managed not to lose the phone number, and a couple of weeks later I did call. Jennifer, her husband Brian, and their two sons David and Richard 'adopted' the whole SCF team, supporting us in countless ways. They sourced various needs in local markets and collected toys, colouring books and pencils donated by friends, who they rounded up to pitch in for the children at Sa Keao. AND they mixed a mean gin and tonic on the days we travelled to Bangkok for our three-day breaks!

Those breaks surely kept us going. The contrast between our work and sharing the loving warmth and generosity of this family in their beautiful home did more for morale than perhaps they ever really knew, and they have remained my close friends ever since.

Another volunteer was an American named Margaret. She, her businessman husband and their young family lived in Malaysia where, from the comfort of her home in Kuala Lumpur, she had watched the drama in Thailand unfolding on television.

'How on earth did you get here?' I asked her.

'I'm a mother of three happy, healthy children,' she said. 'My youngest is six months old. When I saw these kids on TV, I knew I had to help. I couldn't just sit and watch that terrible suffering or flip to another channel and pretend it wasn't happening.'

Margaret's husband gave his blessing, although it couldn't have been easy for him, and she made arrangements for the care of her own children, flew to Bangkok, got herself onto a UNHCR coach, and here she was. She had no nursing or medical qualifications, neither was she a nutritionist, but she said, 'Listen, I have breast milk and these babies look as though they could use some good stuff. That's what I can give them.' Every day for two weeks she expressed her plentiful milk into bottles; her gift to those sickly little babies cannot be measured.

God bless you Margaret and Jennifer, and all the others sufficiently moved by what was happening to step unhesitatingly out of their comfort zones in order to help those in such need.

You just don't forget people like that.

40

SAVING THE CHILDREN

Many of the people we were treating and nursing in the camps died within the first few weeks or so. It was as though to have found a safe haven, where kind strangers offered a helping hand, was too much for damaged bodies and souls to cope with. Exhausted by their ordeals, often brutalised beyond healing, and their little bodies ravaged by disease, they just quietly slipped away.

But nothing stays the same, and the situation moved on. In time, while the weakest died, the survivors grew stronger, and slowly but surely the camp began to take on a life and character of its own.

Our Save the Children team was seven strong: the five nurses were Margaret from Australia, Frances and Barbara from New Zealand, Helen and me from England. Doctors Mark Reacher from London and team leader Ivan Cox from Birmingham completed the group.

Our team lived in Kabin Buri, a small Thai village lying ten kilometres from the camp where SCF rented two traditional wooden houses for us, complete with a cook. The house I lived in, typically of the area, was built on stilts over a small lake.

Conditions were basic, reminding me of my days in Vietnam. Our schedule was tough, working twenty-one days straight, then having three days off, spent at the mother house in Bangkok. Some of the other medical teams lived in Bangkok and had to travel two hours each way to get to work, thus losing a good four hours a day that would have been better spent with their patients. Experienced in these situations, SCF used our time and skills more efficiently.

There was no electricity in the camp, so teams worked from sunrise to sunset; in any event, no foreigners were allowed to stay in the camp overnight by order of the Thai military, which was responsible for the security of all. On two occasions, vehicles carrying casualties, including young men with bullet wounds, arrived at dusk just as teams were departing. Quickly, Red Cross ambulances and other vehicles were driven into a semi-circle, their headlights providing light for doctors to assess the condition of the patients. In those early days, a particularly impressive Israeli surgical team was present. These seasoned warriors dealt with such casualties in an inflatable operating theatre which they had brought with them. They were not out there for long – overall, there were few surgical emergencies.

During these early days, Rosalynn Carter, wife of President Jimmy Carter, visited the border camps. We first realised that something was up when a fleet of shiny limousines arrived at Sa Keao and a dozen or more sharp-looking guys with identical haircuts leapt out of the still-moving vehicles. All wore dark suits, crisp white shirts and aviator shades. For a split second I thought they were shooting a Clint Eastwood movie! This was the security detail arriving ahead of a helicopter carrying the First Lady.

The chopper landed right alongside the hastily erected barbed-wire fence, covering those nearest in thick, choking clouds of dust. With the scrum of international press jostling for position and closely surrounded by men apparently cloned from the first security detail, Mrs Carter was quickly ushered into the centre of the entrance, where an official gently placed a skeletal little child into her arms.

The press went berserk as batteries of cameras tried to capture every possible nuance of the moment and I felt really sorry for Rosalyn Carter. Ivan Cox and I were standing within a few feet of her, close enough to see the tiredness on her face, but also the compassion in her eyes. Then she was gone, rushed back to the chopper, which whirled away almost immediately, again covering everyone in dirt. The clones hurried out to their limos, which tore off down the road. It had all happened so fast, I wondered if my eyes had been playing tricks. We went back to work, wondering what the point of the flying visit had been, but we soon found out. Next day, the international press was full of emotive photographs of Mrs Carter and the child, and the United States government almost immediately approved a generous amount of aid for the border camps.

Over the coming few weeks, an endless stream of politicians from all sorts of countries seemed to arrive on 'fact-finding' missions. They all asked the same daft questions, and were really a bloody nuisance at such a time. They were often given short shrift by doctors and nurses trying to get on with their work!

The first stage of bringing these devastated people to the area was depressing, exhausting, challenging, but sometimes very rewarding. Looking back, it's hard to believe how jam-packed with incident the first ten or so days were; it was during that time that I encountered the amazing volunteers, witnessed the extraordinarily poignant drama of the boy and his dying sister, and became acquainted with medics from other organisations.

During this initial ten days, while we did the best we could with the acres of sick and dying lying on the ground, labourers were busily constructing the bamboo and thatch camp, designed by the UNHCR which, on the tenth day following my arrival, became Sa Keao proper. The logistical planning of the United Nations High Commission for Refugees was impressive. Thirty-eight thousand people were moved in and accommodated in blocks, each of which comprised twenty huts; a volunteer leader was chosen to represent the couple of hundred people in each block; food, water and cooking utensils were distributed; the Red Cross began registering names and logging information, enabling them to commence trying to trace relatives.

The sickest among the camp population were moved to the hospital area. Each international medical team had its own designated areas of responsibility. SCF had a paediatric ward within the ten-ward hospital complex, but our particular brief was to set up four mother-and-child clinics at various points throughout the camp. Under the cheerful and energetic leadership of Ivan Cox we made reassuringly quick progress, each of us having acquired an interpreter to work with, which effectively doubled our team to fourteen.

This was how my friendship with Solina began. When she first approached me to volunteer as an interpreter, I thought she was a teenager; in fact, she was twenty-five years old. Softly spoken, her English was halting at first, but soon improved and, hyper-vigilant as she was, Solina became my right hand as well as my good friend. She had her father and a brother with her, the remainder of her family had perished. Together, we set up my clinic, which catered to mothers and young children.

Our interpreters and helpers, who arrived severely undernourished and anaemic, worked in exchange for extra rations, and slowly but steadily their general health improved. As they regained strength, so they grew more confident and able to tell us about their experiences. I didn't question Solina but left her to talk in her own good time. I learned that she had been arrested, and taken to a Buddhist temple in Cambodia where she was subjected to more than one form of torture. Many told the same story: all over the camp, survivors of the brutal Pol Pot regime were gaining the strength to begin sharing their personal stories. Others, however, were too traumatised, and remained silent.

Solina never lost her love for her country. She often said to me, 'One day, you will come to Cambodia and I will show you my country. I will take you and show you my story.' I listened and nodded. That she had dreams and ambitions was a healthy sign.

The camp progressed, the weakest died. More international teams arrived each week. I remember in particular a US public health team from San Francisco, led by an epidemiologist. They were efficient, motivated and highly organised, but unprepared for the reality of what they now faced. Despite latrines having been dug to the rear perimeter of the camp, each morning on entering we were confronted with excrement fouling the areas between the huts. We simply couldn't understand why people continued to use these public areas at night, creating an enormous health risk for the close-packed community.

Everywhere they could be clearly seen, were illustrated charts placed by the team from San Francisco: the illustration of a stick person squatting on the ground to defecate had a large red cross drawn through, indicating that this was a no-no; a picture of a person sitting on an actual toilet, or squatting over a latrine, had a big red tick, OK, over that image. After the charts went up Solina, clearly upset, took me aside.

'Please, Anne, please tell the American public health people that we are not dirty, and we are not stupid. We know where you should go to the toilet. At night, when the younger women and girls go to use the latrines, which are far from their huts, some of the Thai soldiers grab them and rape them. Some have been sold to the brothels in Bangkok. When all the foreigners leave the camp at night to go to safety, we are left behind to face such things. This is why we women do not use the latrines at night. The men do, although even some young boys don't, but the women and young girls will not use the latrines at night.'

I passed the message on. The posters came down.

How different are the worlds we all live in.

After Solina told us what was happening, we decided, secretly at first, to take it in turns to stay overnight in the camp. There was a lot going on.

When you work in such a place, with such politically charged tensions, many field workers carry the burden of bearing witness to events that cause a crisis of conscience.

When I'd reported what was alleged to be happening, I was advised to keep quiet. The military were in charge of security, and Thailand was the host country. If this leaked, we ran the risk of deportation, and the possibility that other teams might be asked to leave. A balance had to be found between what could, or could not, be achieved for the greater good.

This was indeed utterly horrifying; unfortunately it was also the fact of the matter.

One day, a skinny fourteen-year-old named Vichuta pitched up, offering to help. Very bright and something of a tomboy, her energy and air of mischievousness were marked. She was good at scurrying round the camp, encouraging mothers who had sick children, and ferreting out problems and gossip, while generally making herself useful.

It was Vichuta who made us aware of rumours that intimidation and interrogations were being carried on in the camp, and reported certain distressing incidents that she'd witnessed. We saw evidence of this ourselves on several occasions, and it became apparent that the camp population harboured Khmer Rouge soldiers, who were still able to instil fear in their victims. Most shockingly, these fugitives were often still teenagers, both male and female.

41

SEEDS OF SURVIVAL

A few months later, how things had changed. Now when we arrived at work in the mornings we were met with the sounds of children's laughter. The youngsters were not lacking in ingenuity. Kites made from the plastic linings of rice sacks fluttered and soared high above the camp; little ones played, albeit in the dirt, with home-made toys carved from bamboo or wood, and rubber balls made from hundreds of rubber bands; older boys drew boxes on the ground with a stick and played games which resembled draughts, using differently shaped stones. Food and other supplies, now distributed three times a week, arrived from all corners: soya milk powder from New Zealand; dried fish from Norway; rice, flour and high-protein biscuits from the USA and Canada, fresh green-leaf vegetables and chillies from local markets.

A distribution programme has to be organised, controlled and fair. People must never be placed in a position of having to fight for anything they can get – a free-for-all doesn't help the smallest or the weakest, and can lead to a stampede of the hungry and desperate. And people are killed in stampedes. Things were ticking along at Sa Keao when the World Food Programme representative let it be known that food rations were to be significantly cut. How, we wondered, would we deal with this? We had a meeting with the block leaders the following day and gave them the news. Their immediate response was 'Give us seeds and we can grow our own food. We are farmers; we know what will grow in this dirt.'

I wondered why we had never thought of that, though we weren't too sure how the Thais would like what might appear to be a more permanent arrangement. The camps were, after all, only intended as a temporary measure in a crisis – but seeds would sprout quickly in this tropical climate, so we put the suggestion to officials, and to the Bangkok-based SCF team who were all Thai. Their answer was to go shopping for the appropriate seeds, which were inexpensive and, like everything bought thereabouts, supported the local economy. The seeds were distributed in small pouches to the leaders of each block, and very soon melons and various green vegetables were growing nicely in designated areas. I noticed that only half of the seeds were immediately planted; the other half were kept back in pouches, tied to the waists of the planters. They explained that if they had to flee for their lives again, at least families would have seeds to plant for food. I thought of the proverb, 'Necessity is the mother of invention.' Necessity had certainly taught these people how to survive.

For all the difficulties and misery, we had a lot of laughs at Sa Keao.

One day Solina and I were visiting each bamboo and thatch hut in our section of the camp, looking for children beneath the age of two. This was part of a measles vaccination programme. We carried our vaccines in cooler-bags padded with ice packs, and the constant stooping to enter these dwellings was crippling work in the heat.

As we moved among the huts, I heard the catchy beat of bongo drums. We found two young men, sitting cross-legged, their drums between their knees. The drums were small with fringe-like beaded decorations. I asked Solina where they got them from. They had made them.

'I love them. Would they make some for me, do you think? I'll pay them, of course.'

Isn't that just the typical Westerner: see something you like . . . right . . . I'll have one of those . . . how much? And you give no thought as to how things are made, or where the materials come from.

Solina and the boys talked animatedly and then she said, 'Yes, they are happy to make you some drums, but they don't have any cats left, so you would have to bring your own.'

I simply couldn't conceive of walking into the camp with a cat under each arm and walking out a few days later with a set of drums! So, no drums. But I still remember the sound they made. Pretty damn good.

Red Cross and immigration officials announced the quotas of refugees who would be permitted to enter those countries generously opening their doors. Then began the task of interviewing and assessing those who might be suitable candidates. Once displaced persons have their names registered and are given a number, their status changes to that of official refugee, giving them the right to apply to migrate to another country. They need to go through this process as they are not welcome to remain in the host country indefinitely. Also, until officially registered, they have no identity, leaving women, girls and young boys particularly vulnerable to rape and trafficking. Word quickly got around that young married couples were being given preference over single people, so weddings began happening all over the camp. English and French speakers, and those with a profession or a skill that was in demand, were of course given priority.

With the steady improvement in general health, helped by regular and nutritious food, women's bodies started coming back to life and functioning more normally. As host country, Thailand naturally had grave concerns about these enormous groups of people living in squalid camps along their border. It was in nobody's interests to have a semi-permanent refugee population, and the authorities were anxious for the camps to be disbanded as soon as possible. What had begun as an emergency situation was now becoming a huge social problem. If women began bearing children, the population of the camps would burgeon, adding to this ongoing and still serious humanitarian situation.

Contraception is a contentious subject in many parts of the world, and this was hardly the time to emphasise the need for family planning among a people who had survived a programme of mass extermination. However delicately and carefully the subject was raised to test out what people felt, it was met with suspicion and horror. The word genocide was even bandied about by some of the more naive religious groups. So we left it alone. It simply wasn't the time, though women in our clinics often asked about 'pills to stop babies coming'. They didn't want to risk pregnancy with their futures still so uncertain. It was rumoured that a few women strangled their babies to prevent them being returned to Cambodia and 'the hell' that awaited them there.

After a while, all medical teams noticed a rapidly increasing number of women presenting with complaints of nausea, swollen breasts and general malaise – very like the symptoms of early pregnancy, which in many cases would have been impossible. Some were single girls of thirteen, others were women approaching their sixties, still recovering from years of famine and deprivation.

The Thai military, as part of the general organisation, had rigged up a rudimentary system of loudspeakers, attached to telephone-like poles, all over the camp. Official announcements, such as information about the times of food distributions, were

regularly made, both in Thai and Khmer. We understood neither language fluently, added to which the sound was so
distorted it was virtually impossible to decipher what was being
said. Then it was learned that some of the announcements were
instructing women between the ages of twelve and sixty to
report to various points in the camp to receive injections of a
strong vitamin that would make them healthy. In fact, they were
being injected with Depo Provera, a long-term contraceptive
that was effective, but with known side-effects. The women had
been tricked, en masse, and we were very uncomfortable with
the deceit. However, the circumstances facing the Thai authorities were certainly stark, and the more I thought about it, while
I couldn't condone their decision, the more I understood it.

42

POLITICAL FOOTBALLS

In situations where large sections of a population become displaced and begin flooding over borders into another country, there is always a group classified as unaccompanied minors. These are children of all ages who appear to have no parents or extended family. Often an older sibling, themselves not yet even ten years old, might be carrying a younger child, find other wandering children along the way and team up together. But unless they actually witnessed the death of family, it cannot be assumed they are orphans. Unaccompanied children are housed in a separate area, and so it was in Sa Keao where there were approximately five hundred lone children in the early days.

One day three coaches drove into the camp, pulled up in front of the children's enclosure and were swiftly filled with about eighty children under the age of six. Word had got round that something was happening and there was consternation among French aid workers. We left our clinics to take a look. The watching Cambodians, mainly men, were strangely quiet. Some French nuns lay down in front of the wheels of the buses, defying the Thai soldiers who trained their weapons on them.

We learned that the children were to be flown to Paris, where they would be met by President Giscard d'Estaing and his wife, their press entourage, and prospective parents who had been cleared to adopt 'a Cambodian orphan'. As far as we could make out, either there had been very little preparation for this or the plan had been a very well kept secret.

It was the run-up to Christmas 1979 and French nationals in the camp were furious, describing this as a vote-winning stunt. The soldiers gave the nuns a count to five to remove themselves from obstructing the buses. Many charities, including SCF, do not advocate adoption from areas of turmoil, particularly so soon. Having seen the chaos children can be snatched from, I support that stance. It can take many months to find out and confirm whether or not the children have any living relatives. Mistakes have been made where little ones have been adopted for good reasons by good people, only for a family member to turn up with documents that prove their relationship to the child. How do you handle that, and all the angry grief that can follow?

As tension mounted, the nuns, given no choice, finally rolled out of the way of the oncoming wheels. There was dead silence as we watched the buses receding through the makeshift front gates, the little faces inside pressed up against the windows in mute bewilderment. It was difficult to comprehend what had just happened. The passion and intensity of the moment was draining.

As the buses rolled out, two or three men in black 'pyjamas' raised their arms above their heads and began to clap slowly. This was taken up by a few others, then a few more, until there were hundreds of Cambodians, hands raised above their heads, clapping. None of the aid workers joined in, we were all still quite shocked. Nobody said anything. No voices, just the clapping, which gradually speeded up. It may be that this was their way of saying goodbye, or it may be that it was a kind of mourning ritual. Hundreds of people solemnly clapping in

Military visit to assess what assistance can be offered to Pat Smith, Kontum, 1969

Hiao at Minh Quy Hospital, Kontum, 1969. He loved the song 'Hey Jude'

Sa Kaeo
Refugee Centre,
Thailand,
October 1979

Construction
of new camp

SCF ward, Sa
Kaeo, ten days
later

Save the Children ID card for Sa Kaeo,
1979/80

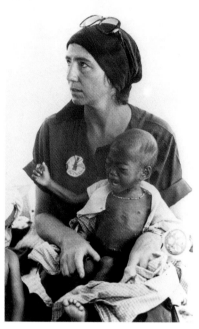

Tending to the needy
© Save the Children

Vichuta and Solina, on the left

She ain't heavy, she's my sister © Bjorn Larsson

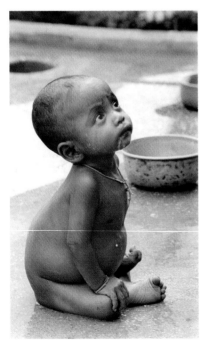

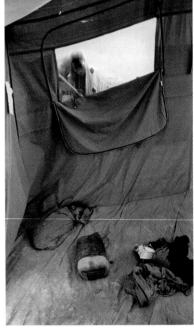

Expectation © Bjorn Larsson

The ones we couldn't save © Bjorn Larsson

Tending sick
child, Sa Keao

Enjoying
improved water
supply

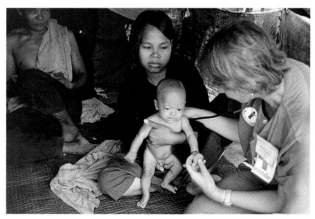

Getting Better
© Brendan Beirne

Me, Reaksa
and his wife
and son,
December 2004

Vichuta and
Solina, Jan 2005

Solina, deep in
conversation
with a
missionary
worker, 2005

Connecting with
an old patient of the
Leprosarium, 2004

In Solina's
House, 2005

View from
Solina's office,
north of
Pnomh Penh,
2005

CLARA ROSETTA WATTS
NÉE DOUGLAS
1910 - 1950
Loving wife of Arthur Frederick
Mother of Anne Patricia,
Susan Carol, Joan Rosemary.
Forever in our hearts.

Mother's resting place finally acknowledged

unison, many with tears rolling down their cheeks, men and women weeping silently. The effect was stark.

'So this is what my country has come to,' said Solina, who stood next to me with tears in her eyes. 'Taking milk from strangers and waving goodbye to our children as they disappear in front of our eyes. I am going to get out of here and I am going to train to be a nurse and then one day I will come back to my country to help my people.'

I said nothing.

It was during this period that a peace delegation arrived in Thailand. Part of their plan was to walk to the Cambodian border. Joan Baez, a lifelong peace activist, led the singing of antiwar songs.

The MP Winston Churchill – grandson of the great Winston – took time out to visit Sa Keao with his wife, in order to see first-hand the work being done there. We told him of the distressing human rights infringements we had witnessed or knew about but, given the political tensions in the region, it was difficult to do anything about these without implicating 'whistle blowers'. Mr Churchill reassured us that the situation was known and effective action was being planned. He encouraged us to visit him in London when our tours came to an end.

Soon after his visit, we arrived at the camp early one morning, as was usual, to be met by a hive of activity. At the centre of a huge crowd was a fleet of coaches into which Cambodians were being marshalled, terrified that they were being sent back to Cambodia, and certain death. In all, three thousand people were transferred out of Sa Keao that morning. Sadly, the exodus included our interpreters, who were scared out of their wits. It was difficult to reassure any of them, because none of us there knew where they were being taken, though we realised that the group being moved out were those most vulnerable to victimisation. Later we learned they had been taken to Mairut, a 'processing centre' further south.

A short time later Ivan, Margaret, Frances and I travelled down to Trat province to visit them. The camp was in a beautiful setting, close to the sea, beneath palms with fine white sand underfoot. But it was still a refugee camp and facilities, although better than at Sa Keao, were basic. It was good to see them all. Their rations were frugal, but by their standards a veritable feast was excitedly prepared in our honour. There were two tin plates heaped with large mounds of rice, on top of which sat two fried eggs. Another two platters of green vegetables completed the meal, set out on a plastic sheet on the ground. We sat cross-legged, thoroughly enjoying the chatter and the sharing. Some of the young men began singing softly, their voices blending in harmony. The mood changed as eyes filled with tears.

'They are saying goodbye to our homeland . . . The song is an old one called "Farewell Sweet Cambodia" . . . We are being processed for asylum in another country, but we do not believe it yet . . . No one dares to be hopeful. Not yet . . .'

We told them how they could get in touch with us to let us know how they were doing and said our goodbyes. It had been a very moving experience.

My tour of duty came to an end after thirteen months, in November 1980. Incredibly, the border camps remained in place in one form or another until 1995, when the last one finally closed. Those still living there at that time were repatriated to Cambodia.

In London, I did indeed visit Winston Churchill at his office in the House of Commons and was astonished at the documents he kindly shared with me. After his trip to Thailand, he had reported his findings to the Minister for Overseas Development. It was known in the corridors of power in London and

Washington that there were senior Khmer Rouge cadres inside Sa Keao and other border camps. Even the names and ranks of Pol Pot's men were known. At the 'sharp end', one can feel lonely, frustrated and impotent to help when witnessing disturbing incidents that can't be immediately or directly dealt with. I found it reassuring to know that we, and others, had been listened to after all; that information gathered at many levels led to improved conditions in the camps.

I had learned that not all politicians were useless. It was another discovery in my realisation that politics is a game of wheels within wheels. Nurses and doctors, who must constantly witness at close quarters the cruelties in a displaced persons camp, so often feel like bit players in a much larger game. And, so often, they are.

Part Four

MOVING WESTWARDS

1981. A state-of-the art private hospital on the banks of the River Nile. No rows of the dead and dying lying on the ground here; no malnutrition or malaria or sickly babies; no want of comfort, care or clinical resources. No displaced persons in bamboo huts. This hospital is for the wealthy of the Middle East and well-heeled Western expatriates, for those who live in opulence and educate their sons and daughters at the best international institutions. These people, these educated, wealthy Egyptians, are just as proud, charming and hospitable as the street sweepers, gardeners and herdsmen.

The exquisite Islamic architecture creates a dramatic and magnificent skyline in Cairo, this 'city of a thousand minarets', this cradle of civilisation, rich in history and redolent of the Old Testament. So much to marvel at, here in the desert's embrace where the pyramids at Giza and the Sphinx are nudged by encroaching suburbs. The city, too, offers a feast of antiquities in its museum, and the spices and perfumes displayed in the Khan Khalili souk make a delicious assault on the senses.

But all is not what it seems. There is no military war being waged here, but the battle for survival is being fought by the poor. Alongside the unimaginable wealth is grinding poverty. In the traffic-choked streets of the city, children scavenge in the filth, and donkeys pulling overloaded carts are seen to sink to the ground in exhaustion.

The clash of ancient and modern is not confined to objects and architecture but, more disturbingly, to social custom and ritual.

The beautiful, and exceptionally bright, twenty-three-year-old daughter of a super-rich hospital consultant is to be married. Educated in London and Paris, and a university graduate, she is fluent in several languages.

On her wedding night her mother and mother-in-law sit outside the newlyweds' bedroom door until the bride comes out and hands her mother a blood-stained sheet. The blood-stained piece is cut out and made into a little pair of cotton bootees to be worn by the couple's first-born: 'An old tradition that we still follow.'

A huge public scandal: early one morning the body of a Bedou girl is found dead outside the main doors of the discotheque attached to a fashionable hotel. The position of the girl's body indicates an honour killing. It emerges that four young socialites raped the girl after a night of drinking at the disco; the father and brothers of the girl have killed her for bringing dishonour to the family. The young men are not brought to justice. The word on the street is that they are protected by their wealth.

At the newly built hospital on the banks of the river, whose waters will take you to Aswan and to Luxor, to peace and beauty and monumental antiquities, it seems that profit can rule over principle. The Egyptian nurses here work for a shaming pittance amid the luxury, trailing home at the end of their shifts to large families desperate for the help of their hard-earned pennies.

Senior management, brought from Europe and the United States, fare rather better.

Sometimes the marriage of the new world with the old is not comfortable. I guess you can call it culture shock.

Time to move on . . .

43

FERRY-RIDE TO TROUBLE

In December 1980 I had arrived back in England from Sa Keao, a place where people had been stripped of all dignity and reduced to total dependence upon strangers for the most basic necessities of survival. In the streets of London, as brightly lit stores stuffed with consumer goods disgorged shoppers loaded with purchases, I suffered yet another bout of culture shock. The contrast was almost too much for my Gemini soul. I needed a rest.

After spending precious time with family, and doing some public speaking to fund-raise for Save the Children, I thought about my next move. Clear that I wanted to stay away from Southeast Asia and war zones, I looked for pastures new and accepted a senior post to help open and manage a large, new, private general hospital in Cairo. I faced a moral dilemma in leaving behind children in need to work with a large American health care company, catering to wealthy clients, but it was an opportunity to develop my administrative skills and widen my international experience.

After two years traversing a steep learning curve – never a bad thing – I knew I needed to move on and I accepted an offer to work in Israeli-occupied Lebanon.

*

I arrived in southern Lebanon in July 1983, one of three senior nursing officers for the soon-to-be-opened, three-hundred-bed Rafik Hariri Hospital.

Rafik Hariri was a self-made billionaire in the construction industry who was using his fortune to rebuild his beloved war-damaged home town of Sidon and, later, Beirut. Much loved and respected, he would become the prime minister of Lebanon in 1992. The first phase of his million-dollar Kfarfalous project was the construction of the hospital, a school of nursing, and accommodation blocks. The buildings dominated the skyline and had spectacular views of the beautiful surrounding countryside.

Hariri's enthusiasm, verve and sheer force of personality infused the whole project with energy and a collective determination to make the hospital a success. It had been hoped that once a ceasefire was agreed the Israeli army would withdraw to the southern border area, and a security buffer zone manned by United Nations troops would allow some normality to return to the decimated villages of southern Lebanon and the vulnerable settlements of northern Israel. Development projects would flourish, planting seeds of hope, pride and peace to counteract the politics of hatred preached daily.

Sadly, in July 1983, just as the hospital was close to opening, Israeli forces did indeed withdraw from Beirut, but not as far south as had been hoped. They stopped just half a kilometre north of Sidon, which meant both the town and the hospital community, ten kilometres up in the hills, were within the occupied zone.

Due to the conflict, Beirut International airport was closed yet again in July 1983. Together with my colleagues Cathy and Mary, I had to fly to Cyprus, where it was three days before we found a battered-looking vessel that was the last ferry boat out to Sidon – or Saida in Arabic – the ancient Phoenician fishing port in the Lebanon that was the birthplace of Rafik Hariri. The six-hour overnight crossing was uneventful and Sidon harbour was a picture postcard of turquoise waters and brightly painted fishing boats bobbing in the swells. Our pleasure at the sight was short-lived: Israeli gunboats were blockading the harbour, their guns pointed at our ferry. The ancient Crusader castle that in centuries past protected the community could do nothing against the occupiers. Disembarkation wasn't allowed until everybody's documents had been scrutinised and the boat thoroughly searched. This took another six hours. Water, and all other refreshments except beer, ran out; toilets wouldn't flush, and children were fretful in the oppressive heat.

Light-headed from dehydration, Cathy, Mary and I eventually took to the beer. At last, in the baking heat of early afternoon, wooden dinghies with outboard motors came alongside the ferry and our suitcases were unceremoniously dropped over the side into the small craft. Thanks to the beer, we weren't nearly as alarmed by everything as we might have been; which was just as well considering that we had to climb down a swaying rope ladder which stopped short a few feet above the dinghy. As we neared shore, we spotted a very British-looking gentleman in dark suit, shirt and tie, shoes and socks in one hand and trouser legs rolled up to his knees, standing calf-deep in the Mediterranean. He was waving frantically and, once we were in earshot, shouted out enthusiastically, 'Anne Watts, welcome to Lebanon.' This was the Welsh personnel officer from the hospital. He escorted us, by now helpless with laughter, to a nearby café for some much-needed strong black coffee. Such was my introduction to Lebanon.

44

CHECKPOINT

A fast ambulance trip from the hospital to Beirut should normally have taken forty-five minutes on the elegantly curved main road, bordered by the sparkling Mediterranean on one side and groves of olive trees and sweet-smelling citrus fruit on the other. Small herds of goats munched on the juiciest tufts of grass, the tinkling sound of their bells floating gently in the balmy air. Idyllic – until tank convoys burst round corners, their guns pointed threateningly at oncoming traffic. Huge, ugly concrete blocks set up across the highway just north of Sidon effectively cut off Beirut from the port and all traffic using the coastal road to and from the south. The trip to the capital became tortuous and fraught with danger.

With the main road closed to vehicular through-traffic, only pedestrians could get across, passing through a narrow walkway between rolls of razor-sharp barbed wire. At either end of the wire stood Israeli soldiers, several barely out of their teens and a few acting in an unnecessarily cruel manner which would undoubtedly have been in violation of their orders. Fluttering over their heads was the dreaded blue-on-white Star of David. These young men enlivened their boring checkpoint duty by flicking their guns beneath the *kaffiyeh*, the distinctive Arab head-dress, of old men passing through, knocking their scarves off into the dusty road; they would then erupt into laughter as the elderly gentlemen bent with difficulty to retrieve both scarves and dignity, or were sent sprawling by a well-placed boot to the behind.

Young women, carrying babies on their hips, plastic bags containing baby paraphernalia hanging from their arms, and wide-eyed toddlers clutching at their skirts, didn't escape harassment. The more crass and immature among the soldiers would dislodge the plastic bags with their gun barrels and tip the contents into the mud. If the mother dared to try and retrieve the precious items, she would be yelled at in Hebrew and prodded to keep moving.

But amid this mindlessness there were always those soldiers who showed compassion, decency and some discomfort at the behaviour of their colleagues by stepping forward with a helping hand or a kind word. Always amid cruelty there is compassion.

At this time the only route for vehicles to and from Beirut was through the Chouf Mountains. There were several checkpoints to negotiate along the way, with indeterminate waits at each; the forty-five-minute journey could now take anything from six to forty-eight hours. All vehicles had to wait in line while occupants were questioned, documents checked and each vehicle thoroughly searched. Most days, long lines of trucks laden with fresh fruit and vegetables destined for the markets of Beirut were held up for many hours, leaving the produce to rot or shrivel in the hot sun.

The main Israeli-manned checkpoint was the Batar crossing. It lay a few kilometres past the beautiful mountain town of Jezzine, which nestled between deep gorges, a white-water river and waterfalls. Application had to be made to Israeli military authorities two days in advance for each trip. Maybe permission would be given, maybe not. The decisions appeared arbitrary and capricious.

One day I was returning by taxi from Beirut. Bowling along through the spectacular scenery of the Chouf Mountains, heart-land of the Druze population, we passed uneventfully through two checkpoints protecting the strategic town of Mukhtara, home of Walid Jumblatt, leader of the Druze and a respected politician. Reaching the dreaded Batar crossing, I joined the long line of several hundred weary Lebanese travellers waiting patiently to cross: businessmen, truck drivers, students, people returning from appointments in Beirut, and families worried about loved ones in the south.

It was an August noonday, fiercely hot, and many people had been queuing since the early morning. No explanation was given for the hold-up, but this was not unusual. The soldiers sat in the shade, drinking water, eating cheese and olives, play-ing cards, chatting and laughing in full view of everyone, the young and the old, quietly waiting and wilting.

I waited three hours. Much less time than many, but still hard to cope with. A bottle of water doesn't last long in that kind of heat, and there were no drinks vendors. Not permitted. Security risk, apparently. I suppose I could have marched to the front of the line brandishing my British passport and demanded to get through, but that is not the way to observe and learn what is going on and, anyway, why should I have been treated any differently?

Eventually a soldier sauntered up to the head of the queue and yelled at the first people to advance. Slowly people rose from their haunches, dazed and lethargic from the long, hot wait. Although subjected to petty humiliations, people *were* processed and the line moved forward, and at last it was my turn. Feeling sick and dizzy from the heat, I walked up to the unsmiling young soldier and held out my British passport and travel permit. He looked startled, glanced quickly at me, then back at my passport.

'Where are you going?' He had a North American accent.

'To the Hariri Medical Centre at Kfarfalous,' I replied.

'What are you doing here?' He knew what I had seen during that wait.

'I'm a nurse there.'

He stared at me, through me, then, tilting his head in the general direction of the waiting crowd, said, 'Do you put your hands on these animals?'

I looked into his face. He was in his early twenties and handsome, but his looks were distorted by his expression of sneering disgust. I wondered what had conditioned him to hate in this way.

'I am a nurse,' I repeated.

The Uzi hung from his shoulder, its nozzle casually pointing at me. He stared at me and, without losing eye contact, slowly closed the passport and threw it to the ground.

I was aware of nervousness in the watching travellers behind me. They were used to this, but seeing a foreign nurse who worked at the hospital being treated impolitely in their traditionally hospitable country was an insult to them. An old man stepped forward to intervene. I waved him away sharply.

As I bent to retrieve my passport, I heard the soldier clear his throat; a long, deep rolling sound. The large gob of sticky phlegm hit me on the back of my neck and slid slowly down between my shoulder blades as I stood up to face him.

I looked into his grinning face, and made what I hoped was steady eye contact, trying not to focus on what was going on down my back. I wanted to slap his face, to wrest the gun from him, to ram my ballpoint pen up his nostril. I felt angry, insulted and humiliated.

But all I said was, 'Have you finished? May I go?'

He stared hard, then spat again, this time hitting my upper chest. I would like to think I did not flinch.

'Was that necessary? I have done nothing to hurt you.'

He lowered his gaze. 'Go. Get away from here,' he muttered.

I smiled, thanked him and walked silently past the other soldiers, who avoided looking at me.

When I was well past them, walking towards the waiting taxis, a young woman stepped forward and wiped my shirt, using the corner of her baby's shawl and some precious water from her bottle.

That was but a minor incident compared to what others endured. It would have been a minor incident in the early 1940s, too, when the soldiers would have been German and those questioned and humiliated would have been Jews. Today, in 2010, it is but a minor incident in Afghanistan, Chechnya, Gaza or Zimbabwe. But I remember how it made me feel, and can only wonder at how people learn to control themselves when such humiliations are constantly heaped upon them. I am a nurse, not a politician. All I see is the human detritus left in the wake of poorly conceived policies and failed diplomacy. If, as is said so often, the oppressed truly do become the oppressors, then we should all be very, very worried about the future we are leaving to our children.

45

IMAGES OF HATE

I came to respect and admire all the personnel at the hospital: doctors, nurses, lab technicians, radiologists – the A to Z of personnel it takes to run a busy acute-care facility. Professional recognition and respect have no boundaries. We all wanted this hospital to succeed, and everyone was motivated to this end. My own areas of clinical responsibility covered the emergency room, the paediatric unit and the maternity section. The three tutors at the nursing school were also British, and students under their tutelage followed the curriculum for the French baccalaureate degree. The Lebanese consultants, some of whom had dual American or British nationality, were largely top men in their fields. Most other staff were recruited locally, but many had international experience.

The younger doctors, who had transferred for a period from the ER at the American University Hospital in Beirut, were particularly impressive. They kept us transfixed with their accounts of militias storming into the Beirut hospital with their wounded and ordering staff at gunpoint to 'save him or you die'. They described how it had been necessary to sandbag key areas such as operating theatres; it was not unusual for doctors halfway through treating someone to have to dive behind sandbags when guns were fired in the department. And I had thought Saturday nights in casualty at Manchester Royal Infirmary were rough!

We, the personnel at Hariri Hospital, were a healthy mix of Sunni, Shia, Druze and Christian, and as far as we could tell we all worked together quite comfortably. In many parts of the world you wouldn't need to mention the religion of employees, but in 1983 Lebanon religious affiliations had consequences and could mean the difference between life and death. One's religion was clearly indicated on an ID card to be carried at all times. Each group tended to live in their own villages. If you came from the town of Nabatieh, then you were a Shia Muslim; Marjayoun was home to Maronite Christians; Sunnis came from Tripoli and Druze from Moukhtara. Our security department had the onerous task of constantly being alert to any trouble, both inside and outside the hospital. The guards were recruited from the surrounding area and knew what was going on.

I got to know one of the security guards and his family quite well. They wanted to improve their English and I was pleased to help and encourage them. Mohammed was well read and wrote poetry; his wife Nadia played the lute beautifully. We met once a week at the hospital for our English lesson – until the first and only time I went to their home.

Mohammed and Nadia, Shia Muslims, invited me for dinner one evening. The hospitality of Arabs is legendary, but times were strange and travel to somewhere unfamiliar could be fraught with problems, so it was unusual to be given such access to a Shia home. My hosts lived in a simple, modest stone house in a small village surrounded by olive groves. Nadia had been cooking all day, as is the custom, and delicious aromas met me as I stepped out of the car. There is no alcohol in a Muslim household, but Nadia brought a decorative tray upon which sat a generous glass of pink juice on a pretty lace doily, then returned to the kitchen where Mohammed was helping her. Like children everywhere, the three little ones peeked shyly around corners until brave enough to come a little closer and inspect me.

While alone, I looked at the several photographs – some black-and-white, some sepia – that adorned the walls. There were the children as babies, wedding photographs, grandparents, and other relatives or friends. My eyes kept coming back to one that had pride of place on the wall next to my chair. I could hardly ignore it as it was draped with fairy lights that constantly flickered on and off. I thought it was of a great-grandfather. He looked vaguely familiar, but all Muslim men have a moustache, and the old black-and-white image was rather faded. I did see that he had dark hair slicked down across his forehead.

Mohammed entered the room. 'Ah, you like this photograph?' he asked.

'I was looking at all your photographs, and wondering who this gentleman was.'

'Do you not recognise him? He is the great Mr Adolf Hitler. He killed six million Jews. He is our hero.'

The breath stalled in my lungs, and it felt like the blood stood still in my veins. Shock is a strange thing. The children were running in and out, giggling as they played tag. The little girl had been hanging on to my knee just a moment ago, looking up at me with soulful eyes as I'd wiped her runny nose. My brain was struggling to compute this domestic scene and Mohammed's words. He was smiling proudly as he gazed at the picture. I said something like, 'Why would you think that killing six million people is a good thing?'

He said, 'It is only good when they are Jews.'

'Will you teach your children this?'

'Yes, I will.'

I was not up to having a conversation about it, and in any case the English was too laboured. I needed to get out of there. I certainly couldn't eat beneath this picture. I struggled to think how Mike would handle this. Eventually, I made some kind of excuse and left, stunned and upset. This man was efficient and conscientious at work, striving to learn English. He wrote poetry about the beauty of olive groves and orange blossom. He was a good, decent family man. He had a lovely wife and three beautiful young children. How could this be? I thought: am I naive? I'm reasonably intelligent, but I just cannot take this in. I cannot deal with it.

In retrospect, I wish I could have talked more with them about that picture on the wall. But what would I have said? I had recently come from the Pol Pot experience. Were we condemned to repeat history? In all my travels I have rarely felt so uncomfortable, and I was particularly distressed to uncover this blind hatred in someone whom I had liked and helped. This was not a soldier standing at a checkpoint in the midst of conflict, but an ordinary person with nothing about him to give a clue that he harboured such sentiments.

Are we so conditioned by our group affiliations, whatever they are, that we are unable to overcome the irrational prejudices that are handed down from generation to generation? This was the same blind hatred I had glimpsed at the checkpoint. There must have been a reason why that young Israeli soldier treated me as he did. The hatred of those of his people who no longer believed that peace was possible between Jews and Arabs – who felt the only good Arab was a dead Arab – had infected him. So, too, Mohammed's children would be handed the bitter legacy of hatred and taught to believe that the only good Jew was a dead Jew.

No wonder the madness goes on. Is there no one out there with the courage to draw that line in the sand and shout 'ENOUGH'?

46

A BROTHER'S GIFT

I was due for some leave in October, but where to go and how to get there? In this particularly troubled time, all routes out of Sidon were blocked. Only the previous week, I had gone to Beirut to meet the new nursing supervisor arriving from London to join us. I stayed the night at a small hotel on Hamra Street, where I was awakened at six-fifteen a.m. by an enormous explosion. The whole room reverberated with the shock and I instinctively rolled out of the bed, and under it – a response learned and perfected in Vietnam. There was shouting in the street below, and people running, terrified by the destructive power unleashed somewhere nearby. I thought the hotel had been hit. As I crawled out from under the bed, a second explosion rocked the building. This time I threw some clothes on, ready to get the hell out of there. The phone rang. It was the night porter telling me to stay in my room, the hotel had not been hit, and breakfast would be served at the usual time. That's what I call first-class service.

The first explosion had been at the airport, where a yellow Mercedes truck packed with five and a half thousand kilos of TNT had crashed through a gate and barrelled into the headquarters of the Second Marine Division of the United States

Marine Corps. The cinder-block, four-storey building was reduced to rubble, crushing two hundred and forty-one American servicemen, the Lebanese custodian of the building, and the bomber. In an almost identical attack, the second explosion occurred two streets from my hotel at the barracks of the French Third Company of the Sixth Parachute Infantry Regiment. Fifty-eight paratroopers were killed, plus the Lebanese custodian, his wife and four children, and the bomber.

The perpetrators have never been identified.

Soon after this terrible event, the USS *New Jersey*, a fearsome battleship with a distinguished history and enormous firepower, was called into service to provide support for the marines as they departed Lebanon over ensuing weeks. I watched this huge ship lying about a mile offshore, dominating the Mediterranean horizon, its huge guns aimed at the mountains immediately behind Beirut. A flash of gunfire, clearly visible from the coast road, a second's silence, then a muffled 'boom'. Five seconds later there would be a huge, ground-shaking explosion as the missiles slammed into the mountains. Such power induced awe in all who witnessed these salvos. At night, they lit up the night skies in a hideous kind of beauty.

Travelling was fraught with stress and anxiety for all.

The coast road to Beirut was still blockaded, the airport remained closed. The Chouf Mountains were still under fire from the mighty USS *New Jersey*. The Bekaa Valley route to Damascus was strafed regularly by Israeli jets, and Israeli gunboats still blockaded the port of Sidon. The only way to get away for a few days' vacation was south, to Israel. I decided to risk it but, obviously, I had to keep this plan under my hat.

The microbiologist in charge of the hospital laboratory was a kind, gentle man whom we all respected. I will call him Yasser. Nothing was ever too much trouble for Yasser, who was first in to the hospital in the mornings and often the last to leave at the end of the day. He was the only lab man I knew who would regularly visit patients on the wards each day.

Yasser had often spoken to me of his elder brother, Tariq, who lived in Ramallah, in the occupied territories. They had not seen each other for years, since travel for them was strictly prohibited and many Palestinians refused to be subjected to the humiliations involved in applying for travel documents. Yasser had spoken of his dream of being reunited with his beloved brother one day.

I eventually plucked up the courage to tell him, and only him, of my travel plans, and offered to take a message to his brother. His joy and gratitude was very touching, though he was so astounded that at first I wondered if I was doing the right thing. It seemed so simple to me. The next day he brought me an envelope and a package, asking if I could possibly take them to Tariq at the Bir Zeit University in Ramallah, where he lectured in mathematics. I explained that I would have to see what was in both. The envelope contained a letter written in Arabic, which he translated for me; the package was a gift, a delicate, blue cashmere sweater. When I agreed to take them, the tears of gratitude in Yasser's eyes were moving but a touch embarrassing. I took several photographs of him to give Tariq.

I drove the bumpy twenty-five miles to the southern edge of Lebanon in my slightly battered but trusty Toyota Corolla. The UN peacekeepers allowed me to park the car in their heavily guarded compound, and I walked the remaining quarter-mile to the dusty border crossing into Israel. The Israeli soldiers were helpful and welcoming and showed me where I could wait for the bus to Haifa, then on to Jerusalem.

It seemed surreal that such a short distance away from Beirut life appeared to be going on as normal. Traffic stopped and started in an orderly fashion at traffic lights. Markets bustled with life and colour. Donkeys vied with sleek Mercedes to find an opening in the traffic. Where I had just come from, most vehicles had only one door; windscreens were peppered with bullet holes, and people were tense and edgy.

In Jerusalem, I checked in to the Maronite Convent, a wonderful place built into the ancient walls of the Armenian quarter of Old Jerusalem. It's a great place to stay, as proved by the presence of travellers from all over the world who fill the place. Meals are taken in the communal dining room, where the guests share long, wooden tables, tall tales and nourishing food. Conversation is warm, multinational and stimulating. Everyone is a friend. The nuns, who belong to the Order of St Therese, are helpful, informative and savvy: they keep their ears to the ground and if they say, 'Don't go there today. There may be trouble,' then you don't go. I recommend their guest house as the best place to stay.

I woke very early the next morning; kind of unavoidable in Old Jerusalem, where the muezzin calls the faithful to prayer at daybreak, followed by church bells pealing for the Christian community and echoing loudly across the rooftops. The scent of spices and fresh bread drifts in through the open windows. There is no way you would want to sleep late in this fascinating place, where vendors call to passers-by to sample their wares: beautiful blue Palestinian pottery, glassware in delicate pastel shades, brass Arabic coffee pots, scarlet camel panniers and woven rugs. All vie to catch your eye and pocket your shekel.

After a substantial and delicious breakfast of cheese, yoghurt, hard-boiled eggs, cold meat, warm pita breads and eye-watering French coffee, I wandered down to the sunny square where I secured the services of Abed, a Palestinian limousine driver. He seemed taken aback that I was headed for Bir Zeit University, but I explained where I had come from and what I was carrying in the package. He knew of Rafik Hariri and was delighted, if a little worried, to take me to Ramallah.

The roads were laden with morning rush-hour traffic, but we

eventually covered the forty kilometres to Ramallah. As we drove through a narrow side street of the dusty suburbs, young boys kicking a football stared quizzically at us – or at me – and a few began throwing stones at the car. Faces contorted with anger, they called out, 'Yahoudeah! Yahoudeah!' (Jew! Jew!) More joined in, bigger boys now, glaring at me, slowing our progress. I was frightened by the naked aggression fuelled by the obvious hatred and hurt that I saw in their young faces. I had seen that look before. The stone-throwing increased alarmingly, clattering against the bodywork of the limousine, threatening to break the dusty windscreen. Abed cautiously, and only partially, wound down his window. 'Stop,' he yelled in Arabic. 'This woman is a British nurse, not a Jew; not an Israeli. She works in Saida, for Rafik Hariri. She bears gifts for a professor at the university.'

With a suddenness that surprised me, each and every boy dropped his stones, older lads shouting at the younger ones to do so. Their demeanour changed entirely. Young faces relaxed, some even began to smile. '*Ahlan*, madam. *Ahlan was ahlan. Marhaba.*' ('Welcome, madam. Greetings.') The turnaround in mood was dramatic. They parted, waving us on, and we continued to the university with a tangle of young children running behind the vehicle, seeming to take it upon themselves to ensure we arrived safely at our destination.

Abed tried to apologise, explaining to me that many of these children had witnessed family members being forcibly taken away for questioning; some had had older brothers or fathers shot in the street or taken away and not seen again; they knew that the olive groves, their families' livelihood, were razed to the ground 'for security reasons', deliberately trampled in the madness that armed occupation anywhere in the world brings.

There was no need to apologise, I told Abed, reminding him of what I was seeing in Lebanon and telling him I understood what happens to people on both sides of any conflict.

As we drove into the campus at Bir Zeit University, I was surprised to see groups of students gathered outdoors, listening intently to their lecturers in such shade as they could find from the trees. The driver enquired for the professor and learned that he would be free in half an hour. He, Abed, would return at three o'clock; he had to be back in Jerusalem before curfew. I was shown to a shady rock where I could sit and wait.

I watched the students, intent on their lesson. The girls wore long, flowing robes, with multicoloured scarves draped and pinned securely around their pretty faces, every hair obscured from view. How could they think in this heat, and why weren't they inside the university buildings?

After a while, Tariq appeared. Grey-haired, bespectacled and gentlemanly, his shoulders slightly hunched, and wearing a light jacket, denim shirt and light brown chinos, he looked like a college lecturer from just about anywhere. He smiled and grasped my hand in a firm handshake, looking intently at me with kindly but weary eyes, his head tipped to one side. I could see the likeness. This was Yasser's brother all right.

'Please, the heat is uncomfortable for you. Let us go inside and take a drink.'

He guided me by the elbow to the nearest building. As we entered, I was astonished to see, and smell, charred and blackened walls in what appeared to have been the foyer of a large library. Books ruined by fire lay in pathetic mounds all around, along with the remains of tables and chairs stacked up in corners and burned almost beyond recognition. Tariq seemed not to notice and produced a small knapsack containing a thermos and a couple of small, gilt-rimmed glass cups from inside the remains of a desk. He brewed the mint tea so intrinsic to the customs of hospitality in the Middle East, and handed me a little cup of the deliciously reviving drink.

I gave him the letter, the photographs and the package I had brought. He looked intently at the photo, then slowly opened the package. Clearly overcome with emotion, he murmured his brother's name, 'Yasser . . . Yasser . . .', and stroked the soft cashmere then held it to his cheek. I felt uncomfortable, an intruder but, as if he sensed this, Tariq soon composed himself.

'Anne, thank you for this. You may never understand the depth of your kind deed.' He hadn't yet opened the letter.

We went outside and joined some of his students who were having their lunch at a long wooden table in the shade of a beautiful old tree. I asked why they were taking lectures outdoors in the heat. One of the girls explained that three weeks earlier the Israeli army had entered the university, burning books, desks and computer equipment in retaliation for a protest march in which some of the students were alleged to have participated.

I asked if this was true. A young man answered, 'They can close our classrooms, but they can never close our minds.'

After lunch, I took a photograph of Tariq for Yasser. He stood to attention, staring straight into the camera. No matter what I said or did, I couldn't get him to smile. Then, just as Abed's taxi arrived, he asked me to take another photograph, and this time he managed a little smile and a wave to the camera. He shook my hand warmly, asked me to give his love to Yasser, and slipped me a one-page letter he had managed to write.

Back in Jerusalem, Abed walked me to the door of the convent, making sure I came to no harm. He would not take a penny more than the price we had agreed. As I drifted off to sleep that night, tears slid down my cheeks as I remembered the look on one brother's face, and knew I would soon see the same look on the face of the other.

I left the Lebanon in December 1984. Some several months later the Kfarfalous project was destroyed and the hospital left to go to rack and ruin, but there is a Rafik Hariri University Hospital, built in Beirut between 1995 and 2000.

In February 2005 Rafik Hariri was assassinated; a mindless act of violence that robbed the Middle East of a man with vision, courage and heart. I was in London the day the news broke on the BBC, leaving me stunned with shock and disbelief. I dug out the photographs of his hospital – 'my' hospital – and then I wept: for Mr Hariri; for the Middle East, and for the sheer stupidity and waste of the ongoing violence.

At least there is some comfort in the knowledge that Rafik Hariri lived to see a Beirut hospital commissioned and working, and that it bears his name and carries forward his dream of rebuilding for the people of Lebanon.

47

TRANSITIONS

When I left the Lebanon, I spent the next three years in the United Kingdom. My father's health was slowly deteriorating. Having suffered several strokes and a heart attack over a period of months, he finally passed away on Easter Sunday 1985. My stepmother, Edith, had cared for him for most of this time. By then she was partially blind and unable to escape into the pages of the books she loved. Now she listened to the talking books provided by the National Institute for the Blind.

My father's funeral was an ordeal of emotions and tensions, so many of which had been suppressed over the years. I wept for my long lost mother; for the loving father I had known in my early childhood, for the cruelties and sorrows of the past, as well as the joys. Now it was too late to say all those things we mean to say, but don't. On the upside, the funeral brought together five brothers and sisters for the first time since schooldays. There was solace in that.

I never saw my stepmother again. She died in 1997 at the age of eighty-five.

I took several professional courses, and joined a young company specialising in the care of the elderly. For two years I was the matron of a large nursing home in central London, which had been owned and run by Wandsworth Council until this private company took over. I was deeply shocked to find that elderly people were forced to live in filth and squalor, just a stone's throw from the trendy King's Road, Chelsea. The level of deprivation here equalled much that I'd seen in far-flung areas of conflict. The place stank to high heaven and medication took the form of the 'chemical cosh', which puts people into a zombie-like state. The Dickensian conditions were unacceptable to me in 1985 Britain, and my pioneering, fighting spirit came to the fore.

At a time when private companies were despised for 'taking over' council homes, we worked night and day to improve conditions. The local vicar, who turned up each Sunday to give Holy Communion to those who remembered what that meant, received the sharp end of my tongue. 'How could you tolerate these conditions, and not report it?' I asked him.

He replied, 'Matron, I can take you to a place not ten minutes walk from here, that makes this place look like Paradise.'

What the hell was going on? The way a country treats its elderly and infirm is the mark of a civilised country. Or so I had always assumed.

This was an instructive, worrying and depressing experience. During my twenty or so years spent nursing in foreign cultures, I had seen how the wisdom of age and experience was respected, how the elderly were turned to for advice; how they were cherished by all. I was shocked and angered by the contrast of our own culture, where the elderly are removed from familiar surroundings, leaving them in the hands of poorly paid and often unsuitable carers.

During this period I had to undergo an emergency hysterectomy. My natural exuberance and boundless levels of energy ensured that I returned to work way too soon, with the result that I quickly ran out of steam and, to my regret, was forced to give up my matron's job. After spending three months convalescing, I was offered a position in Saudi Arabia, which much appealed to my desire to experience and learn more about the world we live in.

No matter how efficient the briefing in London, nothing could have prepared me for the reality that is the Kingdom of Saudi Arabia. This vast, secretive country sits baking in the shimmering heat, patiently waiting for the twenty-first century to creep up.

The first surprise was Riyadh International airport, where the arrivals hall is a spacious and futuristic creation in marble, housing state-of-the art banks of computers manned by men in smart khaki uniforms. I fell into the group identified as 'unaccompanied females' and was immediately relieved of my passport and told to 'wait over there' by a stern immigration official. At last I was escorted to the customs area where my baggage was examined by a heavily bearded man who, without explanation, tossed the couple of magazines I had with me into a bin behind him. A pretty blue and white skirt I was particularly fond of followed, and he waved me on.

'May I have my skirt, please?'

'No. Go. *Mamnua*. This is forbidden.'

I told the hospital representative, who took me to the office of the airport manager, clean-shaven and elegant in his snow-white *thobe* and *ghutra*. He spoke fluent English, offered me mint tea, and told me not to worry; the problem with the skirt would be sorted out. He went off, looking annoyed, and came back without my skirt and looking infinitely more annoyed. He explained that the customs officer had seen a pattern of 'Christian crosses' on the skirt. This was deemed offensive and not allowed into the kingdom. And my innocuous women's magazines? Well, they had pictures of women exposing their necks, arms and legs. That was my introduction into the thought process of the *mutawah*, the ubiquitous and dreaded religious police of Saudi Arabia.

I realised I had a lot to learn.

48

NONE SO BLIND

Riyadh is an extraordinary city: many of its ultra-modern buildings are encased in mirrored glass which reflects the cloudless expanse of blue sky above. Whatever could be bought with petro-dollars in 1988 was there; the best architects, artists and designers were brought in to create the expanding kingdom. The only difference today is that a new generation of Saudis now study in overseas universities, colleges and business schools, in addition to their own impressive national seats of learning, and are calling their own creative shots.

At the two coastal extremes of the country – the Red Sea with Jeddah to the west and the Arabian Gulf with Dhahran and the Aramco oil fields to the east – the humidity ensures that the heat is omnipresent, oppressive and energy-sapping. In the central region, however, where the capital city of Riyadh stands, the heat is dry, oven-like and possibly easier to live with, despite reaching temperatures over fifty degrees Celsius – the kind of heat that sucks the air from your lungs.

In Riyadh I attended orientation sessions about the hospital and the city. Whenever these involved going out of doors, I found it almost impossible to focus on the flow of information that was being relayed; all I cared about was getting inside the next air-conditioned building! Labour laws clearly state that no one shall work when temperatures exceed fifty degrees. On the electronically controlled public information display in central Riyadh, the official temperature mysteriously never rose above forty-nine . . .

The hospital to which I was assigned was a satellite of the thousand-bed Riyadh Military teaching hospital and lay some sixty kilometres south in the town of Al Kharj, reached by a fast forty-five-minute drive from the capital. At first, the contrast with Riyadh was a bit like that between Dallas and Choke Canyon! But over time I came to prefer this area to the rushing city, so full of double standards. Al Kharj, fringed with lush, date-producing palms, was a dusty, archetypical Arab town with streets of one-storey buildings and a market, or souk, selling everything from brooms, spices and gold to prayer mats, worry beads and Michael Jackson albums. Several nearby farms grew alfalfa for feeding livestock, along with vegetables and fruit, using the central pivot irrigation methods with water pumped from underground reservoirs. Also in the area was a large camel farm where I first tasted camel milk, fresh, sweet, low fat and still warm from the animal.

The military hospital and staff accommodation blocks were based in a secure, guarded compound. The hospital served military personnel who staffed the only munitions plant in the country, and their families.

Southeast of the town lay the Rub al Khali, or 'empty quarter'. This is a harsh, unforgiving environment, where only the strongest can survive. Taking up a fifth of the Arabian Peninsula, this arid wilderness is larger than France. The enterprising Bedouin have survived there, juggling ancient tribal customs and Islam within a desert kingdom which has changed rapidly as oil riches from a very different world seep into theirs. From time to time, Bedou would come to our hospital. Often the patients were women, perhaps experiencing a difficult labour; or children, dehydrated from vomiting and diarrhoea and not helped by the time it took to reach the hospital. But for the most part the Bedou took care of themselves. For many years traditional bonesetters had been used, and still were for simple fractures, and babies were delivered by the *gabhla*, or village midwife.

When military men were at work or out, their women were often locked in. Nobody could get in and, more importantly, they couldn't get out. The emergency room at the hospital often received calls for help from women. They might have given birth on the kitchen floor, where they now lay bleeding and helpless and, as male ambulance attendants were not allowed into the houses, these were often messy, dangerous situations.

We knew that military security rules forbade hospital staff, particularly male hospital staff, ever to enter any of the homes. Women who needed help could phone for a Red Crescent ambulance, but these were staffed by men who couldn't enter the house of an unchaperoned woman, no matter how serious the emergency. So, unable to get help from the Red Crescent, women would phone our hospital. We had an efficient ambulance service, but it was there to transport our own patients, usually to Riyadh. It was beyond the remit of the hospital to provide a service for the general public in the area.

The male charge nurse in our busy emergency room was an efficient and experienced Armenian Lebanese. Married, with young children of his own, one day he took a call from a distressed young mother, screaming that her ten-month-old boy had stopped breathing. Dropping the phone, he jumped into an ambulance and ordered the driver to the woman's address, which was on the military cantonment. They had to break some shutters to climb in to get to the mother and baby. They tried to resuscitate the child on the spot and in the back of the ambulance on the way to the hospital, but it was too late and he died.

We had to do a lot of talking and defending to prevent the charge nurse being taken to prison. This was exactly the reason that our staff were not allowed to attend such emergencies. Hospital personnel, who have a strong drive to help and the skills to do so, find this very difficult to deal with. Failure to observe the laws of the country does bring serious trouble, and most laws in the Kingdom of Saudi Arabia are black and white. There is no grey, and you might wonder why anyone would choose to work in such a country. Like many places in life, including my own culture, you learn what is acceptable and what is not, adapt your lifestyle accordingly and get on with what you are there to accomplish. If you're unable to do that, you have to remove yourself.

All of these rules came under the jurisdiction of the powerful religious authorities, but not all Saudis are fundamentalist in their religious beliefs. Many of these proud and dignified people are forward-looking, wanting their country to compete in the modern world. I mostly enjoyed learning about this mysterious country and the complexities of its culture, and I remain in contact with Saudi friends I made there.

49

BEHIND THE VEIL

To those of us born into Western culture, religion and democracy, to be a woman in Saudi Arabia is not an enviable state. When outside of their homes, women must at all times wear a long, loose, black robe, the *abayah*, which completely covers neck, arms and legs. At no point must the garment cling to reveal the shape of the female body. In some places in Saudi Arabia, heads and faces must also be covered, but in the Riyadh area women have the choice of whether or not to cover up completely.

Officially the *mutawah*, or religious police, are not supposed to approach women or look into their faces, but you do not challenge the *mutawah* unless you enjoy meeting fire with fire. Situations could easily gather heat, with the hapless woman being taken to a cell, ordered to read the Koran, and possibly face a whole other world of trouble. Anyone, be they non-Muslim or Muslims from other countries, who tried to talk back, was usually deported after great deliberation in the Religious Enlightenment Office in Riyadh.

I now understood the absurd behaviour of the customs officer at the airport. The trick was not to draw attention to oneself in any way. If I saw the *mutawah* approaching, I found that the simplest remedy was to slip on the black headscarf I always carried in my pocket, and swiftly enter the nearest shop until the moment passed.

But the restrictions didn't stop there. Any woman, whether Muslim or not, and especially Saudi women, can only be out in public with a close male relative – father, husband, brother – and documents have to be carried at all times to prove the relationship. This is difficult to grasp until you experience the reality. Women are still forbidden to drive or take a taxi alone. For non-Saudi women to do so is to risk deportation, with the word 'prostitute' stamped in your passport. The driver also is punished. Saudi women are liable to the lash and jail.

As I write, in 2010, tiny shoots of change are appearing: at the new King Abdullah University of Science and Technology north of Jeddah, men and women can attend classes together, and women are allowed to drive within the boundaries of the large campus.

The limitation of a woman's role to that of wife – the bearer of many children – and the accompanying cultural attitudes was something I found very difficult to accommodate.

It was painfully evident that Saudi girls and women were taught nothing of their own bodies. Examples of this abounded in many ways. On two occasions in the labour rooms girls as young as twelve and thirteen, already married to very much older men, were divorced immediately because they had given birth to a girl rather than the coveted son. One young girl seen in the GP clinic was treated for depression brought on by her third divorce. First married off to an older man when she was twelve, her husband divorced her when she proved to be infertile. Married off again, and then again, each time she was divorced for failing to fall pregnant. The girl had never menstruated. She was ignorant of what the monthly cycle was, and her mother, too, seemed unaware of the most basic biological facts. It was obvious we needed to get someone into the girls' schools to educate them about their bodies.

Our beliefs and professionalism were challenged at every turn. Several midwives left, unable to cope with this level of what they considered child abuse. There were many times when I also wanted to leave, but had to consider whether my leaving would help the situation for all the other twelve- and thirteen-year-old girls in distress. Surely it's better to stay, to try and share our knowledge for as long as we are able to cope with the challenges. Many, many times the nurses were thanked by their patients. The women would emerge from behind their veils to smile a heartfelt thank-you that made our work worthwhile.

You come to realise that you can't fix everything. You just do what you can.

50

NAMELESS STREETS

Many of the hospital personnel, from doctors and nurses to security officers and telephone operators, were Sudanese. These people, mainly Arab Sudanese from the Khartoum area, were tall, athletic and graceful, distinguished by their air of quiet elegance. They were all Muslims, more African than Arab. Civil war had raged for thirty years and more, splitting their country into Muslim north and Christian south, but religion and politics were of no concern to us in our work; we were a dedicated international medical team, and that was what mattered.

Sister Aminah was an outstanding Sudanese midwife. Her calm demeanour and beaming smile made her a reassuring presence and popular with the women in her care. Her skin was much darker than most and into each cheek were slashed three deep tribal marks. When I felt she knew me well enough, I asked her at what age this was done to her. She said simply, 'When I was still too young to say please do not do this. I was seven.' Aminah spoke longingly of her husband and children back home.

I resolved to take a trip to Sudan. The capital, Khartoum, was barely a three-hour flight from Riyadh. In April 1990 I began the rather lengthy process of applying for a visa. The authorities seemed amazed that I would want to visit when I didn't have to, but eventually I was given a ten-day visa with best wishes for an enjoyable stay.

Word went round the hospital that I was going to Sudan for my holiday. Colleagues approached me, incredulous that I would want to vacation there! 'Are you really going? Really?' I offered to take mail, gifts and messages and as a result found myself inundated with soap, toothpaste, shampoo and powdered Nido baby milk. I couldn't possibly take it all, but I bought an inexpensive and very large suitcase, filled it to bursting, and explained that would be it. I was given many letters but few phone numbers. When I got there and saw the state of the phone system I understood why.

Mine was the only white face at Khartoum Airport. Immigration officials looked bemused by this unaccompanied female, but after scrutinising my visa, were polite and welcoming. The terminal building was air-conditioned and functional. Stepping outside into the blistering African heat, I was immediately swamped by dozens of taxi drivers. I chose the man with the smiliest face, who took the huge suitcase, balanced it with ease on his head and, straight-backed, cut a graceful swathe through the other cab drivers to his battered little taxi. It looked like all the others, except it had no doors. Not one. I spent the journey hugging my luggage and praying I wouldn't fall out.

A miniature plastic skull with a flashing red light inside it swung from the driver's rear-view mirror, along with his prayer beads. The route was lined with flame trees and purple jacaranda. This was the Africa that had triggered my light-bulb moment at age eleven.

The driver chatted away, frequently looking over his shoulder and laughing uproariously as he gave me a fulsome guided tour along the route. 'Very happy for you to visit our country, madam . . . Here on the left lived the soldiers of General Kitchener . . .' he said, as we flashed past long rows of tumbledown huts.

The driver waited while I booked into the Hotel Sudan, recommended by embassy staff. In prime position on the Corniche fringing the Nile, it had obviously once been very smart. Now the grand foyer was dark and bare and I was the only guest (which seemed to happen to me rather frequently on my travels!). When I was shown to a room whose bed offered a grubby old blanket and no mattress, I made my excuses and escaped to the better-equipped Meridien Hotel.

The next morning I met up with Fatmah, the sister of one of my doctor colleagues in Saudi. Fatmah was a larger than life character with a deeply rolling laugh that must surely have registered well up on the Richter scale. She ferried me around in her small car for the full ten days and I'd have been completely lost without her.

As soon as I saw the pharmacies in Khartoum, I fully understood the desperate need for simple toiletries. Other than a forlorn packet of aspirin here or a roll of gauze bandage there, shelves were bare, glass cabinets empty. Nothing to sell. Fatmah took charge of my large suitcase and ensured that the contents reached their various destinations.

I had planned to contact an Irish charity called Goal, who had a team of midwives working in the villages. Finding addresses wasn't easy: streets appeared nameless and houses weren't numbered. If you asked for directions, you were told something like 'Keep the Coca-Cola shop on your left and carry on till you see the man selling chickens, then turn right and continue till you see the goats grazing and you will see a fallen-down building . . .' and so on. Everywhere looked like it was falling down to me. Eventually, when we passed a police station for the umpteenth time, I said, 'Stop. I'll ask at the police station.' Fatmah said no one in their right mind would even consider approaching a police station. 'I'll just act like a foreigner. They'll see I'm clueless. Wait for me here.'

I walked up the broken path towards the dingy building with its barred apertures. Through the open doorway I could see several policemen playing dominoes, their automatic weapons lying carelessly at their feet. Some were stripped to the waist. Raucous laughter sliced through the heat.

Then I heard hoarse voices calling out, 'Madam, madam. Give us water.' To my right, partially hidden by undergrowth, I saw a large metal grille flush with the ground, covering what must have been underground cells. A padlock and thick chains held the monstrous bars down. Poking between the narrow openings of the grille were arms, hands, fingers and even faces squashed painfully against the metal; men packed in like rats, supplicating, desperate and drenched in sweat.

Two policemen shouted to me in Arabic and I greeted them as cheerfully as I could manage in these horrific surroundings. Without going closer, and trying to ignore the animal sounds of the incarcerated men, I called out, 'Please, I am looking for the foreign nurses. Do you know their office?'

The police looked nonplussed. I don't think anyone had asked them politely for directions for quite some time! I carried on being terribly British; it does help in tense situations, I find. A very tall policeman slowly looked me up and down then waved his gun vaguely to the left. 'Over there. Come back if you have problem.'

We did eventually find the headquarters of Goal – a large, stifling room with maps and anatomical charts on the dingy walls, some filing cabinets and a creaking electric fan perched precariously on an old table in the centre. Over a cup of mint tea, I was able to speak with an exhausted-looking but still cheerful Irish nurse about their project, which was to dissuade village midwives and mothers from circumcising young girls.

There are three types of circumcision, each progressively more extreme and sexually disabling than the last. I had learned something of this ancient, barbaric custom, both in Egypt and in Saudi Arabia where it is not practised but is seen among expatriates from other countries where it is. Traditionally, Sudanese girls are circumcised around the age of eight or so. Later, many suffer badly during labour, damaged to the point where the delivery of the first child is fraught with difficulties.

I admired what the midwives at Goal were trying to achieve and respected the way they were prepared to live and work in such difficult conditions, but I could see little prospect of significant progress being made by attempting to dissuade the female practitioners of circumcision. In societies where such things occur, it is the men who require a seismic shift in their ideas of what makes a girl marriageable.

In the tough, rural areas of Sudan, where people still cling on to their ancient tribal customs and beliefs, an uncircumcised girl will not get a husband. Since marriage is the only option open to girls, particularly in these rural areas, circumcision becomes a simple matter of survival and acceptance. Unmarried, you are an outcast. The more rural the area, the more strictly people adhere to such practices. It is believed that by removing the clitoris sexual desire is killed, so ensuring female purity and fidelity. Since the mothers want their daughters married, they condone the very ritual that they themselves suffered in childhood, and so the vicious circle continues.

51

HARSH TRUTHS

I went on an excursion with Christine, one of the midwives, to a traditional African village. This village consisted of eight round mud huts, topped with what appeared to be a thick layer of palm fronds forming a peak in the centre. There was not a blade of grass, nor the slightest sign of any other living thing, to be seen on the low horizon surrounding us in every direction. I waited in the car while Christine spoke with the village elder, asking permission for me to enter the compound. She turned, smiled, and waved for me to approach as villagers began emerging from their huts.

I felt transported into a centre spread of *National Geographic* magazine. Men, women and children wore not one single stitch of clothing. These people were very dark, their skin almost blue-black, with tribal markings – three round raised scars above each eye brow. These were identification, their unique mark, so much more accurate than an address in this environment. I thought of Aminah.

While there, I was struck by a tall young woman with high cheekbones, beautiful eyes and a gentle smile. Her body was ramrod straight, yet she walked with fluid, athletic and languorous grace while carrying a large tin full of water on her head. Not a drop was spilled. You never see Western women walking like this. I asked Christine where the young woman was fetching the water from, since there was nothing to see for miles around.

'There's a UN pump eight kilometres away.'

'Eight kilometres there and eight kilometres back?'

'Yes.'

'Why on earth did the UN put it so far from the village?'

'It serves other villages as well and is equidistant between most of them.'

I was astounded. In order to have water a woman – because it always *is* the women and girls – walked the eight kilometres, that's about five miles, pumped the clear water into her container, placed it on her head, and walked the five miles back. When I see supermarket aisles stuffed with every kind of bottled water, my mind travels back to that beautiful African woman bearing her tin can of water to her eight-hut village.

Then came the purpose of my visit. Christine took me into one of the huts, comparatively cool after the blistering heat outside, where a little girl of about seven or eight lay flat on the ground, naked, her ankles and knees tied together. As my eyes grew accustomed to the dark interior, I could see she was actually tied to a narrow board. I was taken aback by the dark abundance of pubic hair on so young a girl but, as I approached her, the 'pubic hair' flew off in a black cloud; flies, drawn to the blood and sweat from the circumcision performed the previous evening.

The little girl looked heartbreakingly vulnerable. She had undergone the most extreme form of the procedure, known as Pharaonic circumcision, whereby the tip of the clitoris and both the labia majora and minora are removed. Christine explained what I was looking at: three or four strips of Rizla cigarette paper had been stuck with sugar and water to the child's skin, or what was left of it, drawing together the raw sides of her flesh. To enable her to continue passing urine without soaking the papers, they had inserted a hollow reed into her urethra. She would remain in this position, tied to the plank of wood to minimise movement, for about six days.

I asked what instrument had been used for the cutting and was shown the blade of something resembling a serrated bread knife. This was one of the few times in a nursing career spanning forty years that I felt waves of nausea washing over me, and with every fibre of my being I wished I could scoop up that little girl and take her away.

There are no accurate statistics in a country like Sudan. I asked how many of these children died of infection and was told the number was quite significantly high, which I am sure it was – and is. I was appalled by the cruelty of the custom but, had I been born in rural Sudan of a loving mother, I would no doubt have ended up being circumcised. Then, wanting the best for my own daughters, perhaps I would have allowed someone to go at them with a rusty bread knife . . . I don't think so, but I can't imagine the situation because this is not one world.

We all start from who and where we are and, in the wise words of an old Native American proverb, 'Great Spirit, grant that I may judge no man until I have walked two moons in his moccasins.'

52

MOHAMMED'S LEG

At a champagne and twiglets do at the British Consulate, I met Marie, the wife of one of the diplomats. Marie was an Irish nurse who, feeling uncomfortable with the lifestyle disparities surrounding her, did something about it. She discovered that all Hansen's disease sufferers were banished to an area on the outskirts of Khartoum. Here, in 1990 Sudan, leprosy was still feared and lepers stigmatised. Shocked by the neglect and miserable living conditions of these tragic people, Marie raised money and set up a clinic for them, where she visited twice a week.

The day after the cocktail party, I went with her. Huddled under makeshift sacking, old sheeting and corrugated iron, men, women and children crawled out to meet Marie.

I watched with admiration as she dressed infected sores, cuddled children, as did I, and encouraged the women with her smiling presence and practical help of fresh bandages, fruit, cheese, bottled water and soap. To the awful grimness of their surroundings and lives, she was bringing good cheer and humour, validating their existence, and in doing so she was giving them the most valuable gift of all: some dignity and self-worth.

Following this visit, with the grateful community waving goodbye, Marie took me to one of the sprawling general hospitals in Khartoum, where a few days previously she had taken Mohammed, an elderly gentleman with an infected, leprous leg that needed amputating.

Mohammed, who gave Marie a cheerful wave as we entered, was a sweetheart, with a shock of white hair. His smile lit up the ghastly, overcrowded room, the 'quarantina ward', tucked away towards the rear of the hospital. Conditions were bad, with many sitting or lying on the floor, others two to a bed, with tattered sheeting covering bare springs. Not everybody in there needed to be quarantined; some just needed to be hidden from view – like the three young men who sat propped up against the back wall. All three, oddly, had both arms amputated above the elbow.

Quietly Marie explained that they were from the Christian Dinka tribes down south. A group of ten travelling to Khartoum for work ran into a patrol of 'government soldiers' who tortured them, leaving them for dead. These three were found alive, their arms tied behind them with wire bound tightly above the elbow. Gangrene was setting in, hence the amputations. They had also had their tongues removed. The look on their faces as their eyes followed us was haunting. I imagined a beaten dog whose spirit is finally broken. I wanted to weep; to drag whoever was running this damned country into this room and make him look long and hard; make him see what we were seeing; and then face swift justice in an international court of law.

But life is not like that.

It was high time Mohammed's swollen leg came off. At least we could do something about that. Marie, furious at the delay in surgery, demanded to speak with a staff member. I could guess the reason for the delaying tactics. They wanted baksheesh, a back-hander. I was familiar with this – it was a way of life in Egypt – but this was Marie's first experience, and boy, was she furious, and determined not to pay.

I looked into the old gentleman's eyes and saw seventy years of desert survival, dignity and the joy of life. 'How much do they want?' I asked her.

'One hundred riyals.'

I took out some Saudi riyals and held them out to her. 'No matter what you say, you won't change the situation,' I told her. 'Just take the money, and get the bloody leg off before it kills him.'

Within minutes, a male nurse in a once white uniform took the money and Mohammed, beaming, waving and thanking us profusely, was being whisked away on a trolley with us following. Incongruously, he wore a pair of hob-nailed boots; no laces, just a gaping boot on each leg – one brown leg skinny, the other grossly swollen and weeping with sores. The narrow, chipped, green-painted swing doors into the operating room had panels of splintered glass, the uneven floor looked filthy to me, and the old-fashioned operating table had one end propped up with piles of books.

Three men arrived. One wore a surgical mask and carried a bottle of ether; the other two had trays of instruments, including a saw. Mohammed, his leg about to come off, was still waving and smiling at us over his shoulder. We took a ten-minute stroll down the dingy corridors.

It was over quickly. The diseased leg, with bloody, severed end and boot still attached to the foot, was propped up against the wall in the corridor. Marie had promised to take the leg for burial in Mohammed's village, but first various forms had to be signed in triplicate permitting us to remove the limb from the premises. Otherwise, if stopped by police we could be in trouble. Pity the system was not this efficient when the leg was still attached to Mohammed!

Before departing, we went to check on Mohammed. Still smiling groggily, with the other hobnailed boot on his remaining leg, he thanked us profusely. My last glimpse was of him waving madly and shouting, '*Shukran, shukran* ('thank you, thank you'),' as we beat it out of there.

Marie drove some eighty kilometres across the hard, ridged surface of dirt. There were no landmarks, just the large expanse of sky and low horizon all around us, but she knew where she was going. We arrived at a village of ten huts that formed a perfect circle and waited for the headman to approach. When they understood we had Mohammed's leg, everyone started clapping slowly, swaying and singing.

Four women carrying dried reeds gathered from the banks of the Nile, which was nowhere in sight, approached the back of the vehicle. Gently, they lifted the leg, complete with hobnailed boot, and carried it reverently to the back of one of the huts where it was placed into a scooped-out shallow grave. For the next hour they sang, chanted, clapped and stamped their feet, throwing various mysterious items onto the booted leg: items such as spices, nuts and dried herbs. Then it was covered over by the earth. We drove back, content in the knowledge that Mohammed's leg was home, safe and blessed.

53

THE PROFESSOR'S KEY

Sudan could have been one of the wealthiest of African countries, but thirty years and more of civil war arising from ethnic and tribal persecution had reduced the country to penury. By 1990, the country was tethered by martial law, brought in after the 1989 coup, the introduction of Sharia law, and a vigorous programme of Arabisation which was victimising non-Arab tribes in the country and would eventually lead to displacement and the camps at Darfur.

What I was seeing all around me spoke of widespread government neglect and corruption, while resources were poured into the all-consuming military machine. Dollars spent on guns and tanks are dollars that strip investment in the future of a country's children. All this was pitifully evident; you had only to look at the state of the hospitals and schools, and see the bare shelves in the shops. If this was what the capital city was reduced to, I thought, God alone knew what was going on elsewhere in the Sudan.

Sudanese paediatricians in Saudi had spoken to me fondly of Professor Jaffer, the highly respected medical director of the Children's Hospital in Khartoum, and urged me to try and meet him during my visit.

The taxi driver dropped me at the front entrance of the large teaching hospital, my ID was carefully checked, and I was taken directly to what passed for the intensive care unit where several doctors were battling to resuscitate a six-year-old boy. What shocked me was the equipment and supplies they were using: sparse, basic, outdated. These skilful, dedicated men were not going to give up without a fight but the frail child did not survive. An older doctor with a head of white hair thanked the others, then turned slowly and spoke gently to the mother, squatting anxiously in a dark corner of the small room. She began wailing loudly, rocking back and forth in grief.

This was Professor Jaffer, the most hands-on medical director I have ever met. It was easy to see why he was so loved and respected. Other than occasionally getting away to speak at international conferences, where his opinions and teachings were highly valued, he had always refused to leave his beloved hospital and city, despite the steady deterioration of both. He looked exhausted, but immediately wanted the names of all the paediatricians at the hospital in Saudi Arabia who'had spoken of him. He remembered each and every one, and commented on what sort of students they had been. He was as proud as a doting parent, wanting to know how his former charges were doing. He took precious time to show me around, pleased that I was so interested in the welfare of children.

The professor was putting in twenty hours a day, battling the odds with too few staff and limited resources, which restricted him in trying to accomplish what he knew would have been possible in a properly equipped facility. Several hundred sick children needed help, yet he took time to show me every nook and cranny of his hospital, starting with his office, a Dickensian chaos of patient files and research papers stacked high.

From a thick leather belt around Professor Jaffer's waist hung many heavy keys on two huge rings. He selected one and opened a huge, old-fashioned metal safe. 'What do you think

I keep in here, Anne?' I had no idea. One key opened the heavy outer doors, then another opened a smaller, inner door. Inside the safe were two shelves. On one were four small packs of liquid antibiotic for injecting. 'This is my entire stock for the month, and each day I have to decide to whom I should give these.'

That cut me to the quick. In half of the world we are awash with antibiotics, taken for every trivial complaint to the extent that they have lost their efficacy and created new mutating superbugs which now endanger the developed world. In the other half of the world, a tiny, precious, life-saving cache is kept in a safe, and a doctor has to choose which desperately ill child he shall save while others are condemned to certain death. This dedicated man was forced into the role of ringmaster in a macabre circus of life and death.

To the rear of the hospital was an open area where concrete foundations had been laid. Long, metal rods pointed skywards. 'You're building a new section,' I said, tentatively. 'Yes, these are our plans.' He showed me the drawings for new wards, operating theatres, X-ray department. But the foundations had been laid three years before, and the metal rods stretching towards what was meant to be the next floor were slowly rusting. Money for the foundations had been provided by the British Save the Children Fund, but further funding from local businessmen had long since run out. It was just not happening.

Nearby stood a forlorn, dark blue generator, bearing a small brass plaque stating it had been donated in 1988 by Elspeth Howe, wife of Geoffrey Howe, then a Cabinet minister in Margaret Thatcher's government. It was used four hours a day, five days a week, to run the X-ray machines, but that's all they could stretch to. I thought of the generators in Qui Nhon that provided us with precious energy measured in hours and half hours, then of Western office blocks and shopping centres belching wasted energy into space.

We visited a ward where all thirty-two children housed in it were in the final stages of terminal illness. All were under the age of ten. Skin and bone, sunken-eyed with swollen bellies, they were a pitiful sight, as were their mothers, sitting quietly waiting for their children to die. Some were haemophiliacs, others had various illnesses, but all had been transfused from a batch of donated Austrian blood later found to be infected with HIV.

'There is nothing we can do for them,' Professor Jaffer said.

We went round to each child. Some were so emaciated and fragile that I couldn't pick them up – it was physically impossible to give them a moment's human contact because you would hurt them by doing so. But there were others I was able to pick up and cradle. You could feel the small heart thumping rapidly against your own ribcage, look into eyes that burned into yours. These children had been condemned to death through what should have been a life-saving transfusion. It couldn't possibly have been deliberate, but it might have been negligent. This overworked doctor had no energy to waste on anger, but the tragedy almost overwhelmed me in this place of many tragedies.

I'd spent two days at the children's hospital. It felt like two lifetimes. My visa was for ten days only and time was up. Those ten days have stayed with me.

54

THE GATHERING STORM

Back from my break, I felt grateful, fortunate, and more than a little guilty to be working in a modern, air-conditioned, well-equipped, technologically advanced military hospital. Sudanese colleagues were eager to hear my impressions. I left a lot unsaid.

It was soon after my return from Sudan that Desert Storm, the first Gulf War, broke.

Like British expatriates the world over, I regularly tuned in to the BBC World Service and particularly enjoyed the twenty-four-hour round-up of international news. In Saudi Arabia, the chimes of Big Ben signalling the start of this programme are heard at eleven p.m., rather late after a busy day. Nonetheless, I generally stayed awake to tune in, and it was one night in early August 1990 that I was instantly alert to a news item that unsubstantiated reports said Iraqi troops were massing on the Kuwaiti border.

There was nothing about this in the Saudi news, either Arabic or English, the next day, but since news and broadcasts were routinely censored, I made a point of listening to the World Service that night. This time the report was definite. In the morning I quietly asked one of the other British managers, a pragmatic, down-to-earth Scotsman in charge of the laboratory, if he'd heard the news; he had.

'Do you think they know what's going on?' I whispered.

'Why are you whispering? Of course they bloody know!'

'Well, why don't they tell us anything?'

'You'll be lucky if they tell each other!'

At my regular nine a.m. meeting with the military director of the hospital, I tentatively asked if he had heard anything. He said no.

Later that day Iraq invaded Kuwait and the rest is history – but still there was nothing on the Saudi news. Not until the second day was the situation acknowledged more openly. The atmosphere was tense with rumour and counter-rumour as non-essential personnel and dependents were instructed by their embassies to leave the Kingdom. Within days, particularly on the eastern seaboard with Dhahran and Al Khobar, Aramco personnel, this time essential, began to resign and depart. They were particularly vulnerable should the Iraqis decide to invade Saudi Arabia from Kuwait, targeting the lucrative oil fields.

Fear is contagious. Wealthy Saudi families began evacuating their families to homes in London, elsewhere in Europe, or the US. Most information came from our embassies rather than from the host country, which needed stability and must now have been shown how vulnerable they were. Most of the labour force in Saudi were expatriates; the departure of essential personnel was a clear demonstration that Saudis needed to start training their own people in order to create a strong national workforce at every level.

American, British and coalition troops began entering the Kingdom. Astonishingly, thirty-four nations contributed in some measure to the coalition, among them Australia, Canada, Denmark, the Netherlands, Greece and Germany and, from closer to home, Morocco, Bahrain, the United Arab Emirates and Egypt. This was an extraordinary turn of events in such a closed country. Was an international light about to expose its dark corners? The Riyadh skyline equalled anything Dallas could offer, yet bearded men with camel whips prodded women into covering their limbs and heads. Sleek limousines with blacked-out windows purred along crowded streets, taking their veiled occupants shopping in chandeliered malls bursting with Versace and Chanel, yet Bangladeshi workers, expected to survive on one bottle of water through a twelve-hour day in upwards of forty-five degrees, collapsed on building sites. Anything money could buy was available, yet most decisions appeared to be in the hands of those with a medieval mindset.

Even in peacetime the only means of access to Saudi Arabia for a foreigner was via a job contract and a work visa. These were issued on a selective basis, with strict vetting and policing at every level. I, and most of my colleagues, had gone through this process, and wondered just how many 'outsiders' would now be allowed into the country.

A vast airbase was created in the desert, where large numbers of US troops, military hardware and planes of every description were stockpiled. A field hospital was set up to receive American wounded. The army medical field officer liaised with our facility over what services we could make available if they were overwhelmed with casualties. Subsequently, the CO invited me to visit his field hospital to see their facilities. It was not until I saw the vast base that I became aware of the extent and seriousness of the situation. Planes of every description were parked on miles of runway. Stealth bombers crouched in large black triangles like giant science fiction bats, and I recognised the faithful old Huey helicopters from Vietnam days. A strong wave of *déjà vu* flowed through me, and my stomach lurched as I realised these guys looked set for one hell of a war.

*

I was asked by the British Embassy to act as a warden, liaising between embassy officials in Riyadh and British passport-holders in the Al Kharj area, of whom there were a hundred and eighty-four. The area was vast, scattered with farms managed by British or New Zealanders and interspersed with some palaces belonging to various members of the enormous Saudi royal family. I travelled to the embassy for briefings once, and later twice, a week. The ambassador, Sir Arthur Munro, and his staff, kept up an efficient flow of information, with clear lines of communication. This helped staunch the wild rumours that unnerved many hospital staff members who had no embassy to instruct them. Senior military advisors briefed all wardens, answering questions as fully as security restrictions allowed.

As the nursing representative, one of my duties was to sit on the twelve-member Major Disaster Committee. Our brief was to prepare the citizens of the town and surrounding area for the possibility of conflict and exposure to chemicals. I was one of two women in the group, the other being the director of nursing at the Ministry of Health hospital in Al Kharj – an experienced Jordanian woman whom I came to admire and respect.

We had almost five months to prepare, though we didn't know it at the time. So much emphasis was being placed on the possible chemical capability of Saddam Hussein and his army that everyone believed that immediately the air-raid sirens sounded chemicals would drop from the sky. I never believed this myself. We were a good four hundred miles from the Kuwait/Iraqi borders and Scud missiles, while certainly dangerous for those within a closer range than we were, were known to be wildly inaccurate; places as far afield as we were had nothing to worry about.

Nevertheless, the British and other Western embassies quickly issued all their personnel with gas masks. Smack in the middle of the forehead of mine was a big blue dot, which, as one of the American soldiers explained to me, identified me as 'civilian'. I tried not to dwell on the vision that came to mind of authorities picking round a load of corpses and sorting them by colour-coded dots. I tried on the mask in the privacy of my bed-room, looked in the mirror and hoped I would never have to wear it in public!

We were ordered to carry with us at all times a bag contain-ing our gas mask, a bottle of water and a flashlight. When the air-raid sirens sounded, no matter what the circumstances, the gas masks were to be put on immediately.

Sabre-rattling between George Bush Sr and Saddam Hussein went on until mid-January 1991, with tension mount-ing steadily. The international airports at Riyadh, Jeddah and Dhahran were intermittently closed, then opened, then closed again; there were false alarms and rumours flew. This was probably the most stressful period.

The Major Disaster Committee, under the chairmanship of a Saudi brigadier general, met in all about half a dozen times. Myself and my female Jordanian colleague aside, all the com-mittee members were military men – two Americans and eight Saudis. The Civil Defence Officer was impressively knowl-edgeable, motivated and efficient. He had been trained in both Saudi Arabia and the US and had great leadership qualities. If the worst-case scenario materialised, he would be the man to have around.

I was one of three people who actually had first-hand expe-rience of military conflict. This made the dynamics of the committee pretty interesting since women were always expected to take a secondary – and quieter – role. Discussion at the first two meetings revolved around chemical warfare and how to deal with its aftermath: the setting up of tents close to the entrance of the hospital, segregated by gender of course, where the contaminated were to be hosed down by male or female staff as appropriate. By the third meeting I sensed impending chaos for want of simple, basic planning, and decided it was time to inject some practicality into the situation. I pointed out that the first need was for clear public service announcements to instruct the population what to do and where to go if an emergency forced them to leave their homes. Everyone had access to television or radio; even Bedouins had radios in their tents. This was obviously a powerful medium for mass communication. I was asked to explain myself.

With the possibility of war looming ever closer, the fact that when the men were out the women in the area were locked in their houses was of very serious concern to me. I could only imagine the panic and chaos that would ensue if conflict came to the area and the women were trapped. This I expressed as clearly and forcefully as possible.

The chairman, however, simply reiterated the rule that women would not be permitted to leave their homes unless accompanied by a close male relative, and pointedly mentioned that I had been in the Kingdom long enough to know this.

The committeemen remained convinced that chemicals were going to rain from the sky, bringing instant death to many. Survivors, they said, would proceed to the hospital to be hosed down. I suggested the civilian population be instructed to proceed to a designated building nearby, such as a school, mosque or other suitable public venue, to receive further instructions. A wholesale rush on the hospitals would rapidly overwhelm staff and facilities. Those exposed to chemicals should be decontaminated in clearly defined areas well away from hospitals. Otherwise, I warned, there was danger of panic creating further contamination inside the hospitals.

My words were received in silence until the chairman said, 'Anne, you have been in Saudi Arabia long enough to know that unclean persons are not permitted to enter a mosque.'

I asked him for the definition of an unclean person. I knew

the answer, but wanted the two American officers to hear it. He carefully explained: women who are menstruating; women who are within the first forty days following childbirth, and anyone of either sex with an open wound would not be permitted in a mosque. It could not have been clearer that not only were the Bangladeshi, Afghan, Indian and Sri Lankan workforces – who had, notably, not been issued with gas masks – expendable, but many ordinary Saudi women as well. One thing was certain: if violence truly was going to break out, these people were going to get one hell of a wake-up call. But I left it at that.

Rome was not built in a day.

55

INVISIBLE

Tension and momentum increased as we prepared for imminent war. It was obvious that all coalition troops were on the brink of bombing the Iraqi army – they were only waiting for the 'go' signal. Many foreign nationals and Saudis had already left the Kingdom, but very few left our hospital; the staff remained steadfast. Even though people were clearly anxious, the situation felt reasonably stable.

As so often in difficult situations, there were humorous incidents. On one occasion when I went to buy some groceries in the local souk, about a dozen American soldiers were lounging disconsolately with their cans of Coke at some outside tables. One lad got up and approached me, asking politely and apologetically, 'Pardon me, ma'am . . . Could you tell us where the – um – action is around here? . . . Sorry to ask you, ma'am . . .'

I knew what he meant, of course, and I also knew that, despite their briefings, these boys had absolutely no idea of the reality of their situation, of what it meant to look for that sort of 'action' in Saudi Arabia. I smiled, and said, 'I hate to tell you guys, but you are the most action there's been around here – ever. Don't talk to females, like you're doing now. It is just not allowed.' Had the *mutawah* seen us talking, we – especially I, the female – would all have been in a world of trouble.

The funniest situations involved female American military drivers. With women not allowed behind the wheel in Saudi Arabia, the *mutawah* were apoplectic over this strange phenomenon and tried to stop it. These women, however, fresh from the land of the free, were not about to tolerate the mindset of the religious police. To describe the spectacular face-offs as a clash of cultural extremes would be an understatement.

As I have said, not all of the workforce were issued with gas masks. There was, and is, a definite pecking order in Saudi Arabia, and there was no question that Bangladeshis were on the bottom rung of it. They held the most menial of labouring jobs, subsisting on basic rations in order to send a pittance to their families back home. You saw them everywhere on building sites, scurrying up and down ladders and scaffolding.

When I first came to Saudi Arabia in late June of 1988, it was hotter than anything I had ever known. It was also the holy month of Ramadan and most Saudis slept through the heat, breaking their fast at sundown and feasting at night. But the foreign labourers kept going, with only one or two bottles of water and a few short rest periods in the middle of the day. These men frequently collapsed, falling to their deaths off building sites. Trolleys lined up in every hospital emergency room carried bags of life-giving dextrose/saline at the ready, to receive the dozens who collapsed with dehydration in the cruel heat. Doctors and nurses tried all sorts of delaying tactics to help these poor men because once they regained consciousness their gang masters would demand their return to work. All the gardeners tending the hospital compound, and I think in the town as a whole, were from Bangladesh.

One day, as I was walking 'home' round the back of a large wooden shed at the back of the admin block where I worked, and where the Bangladeshi gardeners would meet for their bowl of rice and a rest, I heard a man sobbing and the low hum of voices trying to soothe him. I stopped and knocked on the flimsy plywood door to find out what was wrong and whether I could help. The men were initially startled, then one said, 'Oh, madam, madam, our friend . . . please, it is our friend.'

I hate being called 'madam', but just now my concern was the distress this man was in. I didn't want to invade his privacy, but I did want to help if I could. One of the men explained that their friend was terrified of the big war coming, that everyone had the gas things, and they didn't.

At that moment I felt a surge of anger on a number of counts. This stupid war blowing up out of nowhere had half the world terrified over supposed chemicals. Young soldiers were climbing in and out of heavy protective suits in the fierce heat of the desert. I thought of how this collective madness we call 'war' affects ordinary people at so many levels that those at the top don't even begin to imagine. Ordinary people like this terrified Bangladeshi gardener: uninformed, unprotected and ignored, like the frightened friends who were trying to comfort him.

He pulled himself together and said, 'Madam, I have wife, three little children, I am not ready to die. What will happen to my family if I die? I have nothing to stop the gas.' I sat down next to him and said, 'Now listen, this is just talk, nothing terrible is going to happen here.'

'But, madam, you are safe, you have a gas mask.'

I put my bag down, took out the gas mask and said, 'I'm sure we are in no danger here. The danger of gas is near Kuwait. The bombs that throw the gas cannot come all the way here; we are four hundred miles away from where the Iraqi soldiers are. Nothing is going to happen here. And to show you I mean it, here, you can take my gas mask.'

He was shaken. He didn't want to take it, saying that I was an important person and I was needed if people got sick. That term of distinction – 'important person' – stuck in my craw. I asked him how well he thought we would all survive in this godforsaken desert without the green grass and the bougainvillea that he and his friends were growing. Did he not think what he was doing was important? I pressed the gas mask on him, and he continued to refuse it. 'Well, we can't share it,' I said, and everyone laughed.

I explained that the air-raid sirens did not mean chemicals were about to fall from the sky; if they heard the siren, they should go to the admin block. 'If it's during the day – you know my hours, from seven to seven – go straight to my office.'

'But the security men will not let us pass.'

'I will tell them I have given you permission.'

The truly awful aspect of this situation was that many such workers all over Saudi Arabia, whether from Bangladesh, Afghanistan, India or Sri Lanka, had no gas masks and no support from their embassies. It seemed no one gave a damn about these people; to all intents and purposes they were expendable. We were all of us so caught up in our own concerns that nobody had thought to include these unfortunate people.

Nobody ever thinks to include the invisible men who are so necessary to their wellbeing.

56

THE SOCCER PLAYER

On 17 January 1991, at about one a.m. Central Southern Saudi Arabia time, I was drowsing on my bed, partially in uniform because we had a strong idea it was going to be this night, when the air-raid sirens sounded. This was really it: the first siren that was not a practice run, and in the small hours of a dark night it was frightening. The sirens wailed, the power went off, and within ten seconds my major-disaster bleep sounded. I was out the door before I was even properly awake.

Six senior members of the hospital management team were on the major-disaster bleep, the first people to be alerted if something major happened in the area. We had a well-rehearsed procedure to follow, beginning with meeting at an agreed base in the hospital. We'd been trained to put on our gas masks immediately the air-raid sirens sounded, but it didn't enter my head to do so even though I was supposed to set an example to the nursing staff. But then never, from beginning to end of the war, did I ever believe chemicals were a real danger.

I sped over to the main building where the night staff were, of course, already on duty. Because I knew the obstetric unit was very busy, I quickly put my head round the door to reassure the midwives. In all six delivery rooms, every midwife was wearing a gas mask, though not the women in varying stages of labour whom they were tending. The whole thing was preposterous. They were inside the hospital in a sealed unit, and within the unit were individual labour rooms. Even if gas did fall from the skies, they'd have been safe for a while, but nobody had thought this through. The long, slow build-up to this war had instilled disproportionate levels of terror of chemicals. Imagine how terrified the mothers must have been to see a midwife at the end of the bed wearing a gas mask!

I offered reassurance as best I could: 'Look, I've just walked over here, out in the night air for six minutes, and I did not wear my gas mask. I'm perfectly all right. Please take your masks off. It's stressful enough delivering a baby without wearing a gas mask to do it.'

So, these admirable midwives, who had remained steadfastly at their posts, following strictly the orders given by the military, slowly peeled off the masks, perspiration dripping from them. Not for the first time I felt enraged by the stupidity of war, and what it does to ordinary people.

I went to the assembly point as arranged, but I was the only one there. All this time the siren was wailing, and if I'd known how to turn it off I would have done so. You couldn't hear yourself think. But I had to think. Where could the others be? I went to the switchboard area to look for them.

Most of the operators were Eritrean, excellent men with a strong work ethic and very good at their jobs. On duty that night was Mohammed. He sat at the switchboard wearing headphones – and a gas mask! The board, jammed with an overload of calls, was lit up like a Christmas tree. Mohammed, quite obviously terrified, was shouting unintelligibly through the mask so no one could understand a word he was saying. As he could not hear me, I placed a hand on his shoulder, scaring ten years off the poor man's life.

I had an insane urge to laugh, but didn't. 'Mohammed, please,' I said, 'nobody can understand a word you're saying. Please, Mohammed, it's quite safe. Please take the gas mask off so that you can speak!'

Coalition bombing began at three a.m. on 17 January 1991, and ended on 27 February, the forty-second day.

The field hospitals providing medical/surgical services to wounded Iraqi prisoners of war were organised and run by the Swedish military. Immediately bombing ceased, the Swedish government ordered their people to leave Saudi within seventy-two hours. Our hospital was one of several military hospitals on stand-by to receive wounded prisoners. All leave was cancelled, all routine surgery postponed, and any patient able to be discharged was sent home. The seriously ill were transferred to the Ministry of Health hospital and only women in labour or with obstetric problems remained, to be cared for in the maternity unit. All hands were on board to prepare clinical areas for the expected influx.

At three a.m. on 1 March, a cavalcade of military buses transporting the walking wounded began arriving, closely followed by ambulances carrying the more seriously injured – one hundred and twelve men in total. The buses pulled up and we saw the faces of the men inside as they squinted through the dirty windows, some looking anxious, others terrified. On seeing our uniforms, their relief was obvious, and quickly they passed the word around: *mustashfa* . . . hospital. These prisoners had feared that they might be on the way to the Iraqi border to be handed over. Iraqis did not have a reputation for being kind to their own captured soldiers. Some would be accused of desertion, and many might even be executed for dereliction of duty or incompetence.

The first twenty-four hours of their arrival was taken up with the attempt to settle them. Most had already undergone

surgery by the Swedish doctors. Many had external metal fix-
ators stabilising fractured limbs, and looked like a tribe from
another planet as they clambered off the buses in the half-light,
bewildered, dazed and exhausted. Tall, heavily armed Swedish
soldiers carefully guided them into the main entrance of the
hospital where they were handed over to the Saudi redcap
military police. Teams of doctors, nurses, porters and radiographers who had been on stand-by worked quickly and
efficiently to get the men processed – some severely injured,
a handful seriously traumatised and disorientated – into rooms
and calmed down.

Most were in fact ordinary civilians who had been rounded
up and pressed into uniform. Poorly trained and equipped,
they were a sorry sight. Many had lice. One had pulmonary
tuberculosis and was painfully thin; another, a bank manager
who spoke very good English, was embarrassed by his
colostomy and distressed because he had lost his glasses. I had
a pair of bifocals I hardly used and gave them to him. The
youngest patient was a boy of fifteen who had been running
from bombing in Basra when his right heel was blown off; the
eldest was a farmer aged sixty-six who had saved hard for
years to scrape together enough to buy a third-hand tractor. He
had been the proud owner of this piece of machinery for no
more than a few months when 'a bomb dropped from the sky
and blew up my tractor'. He was absolutely furious and stared
long and hard into faces as though he was determined to find
the person responsible.

Only seven men in the group were professional soldiers.
They were members of the dreaded Republican Guard. They
had to be secured, and separated from all the others, who were
obviously uneasy around them. One of these men was different from his fellow Guards. Ahmed seemed unable to relate
to anyone or anything around him; he did not eat, sleep, react
or respond to anything. His blue eyes had that middle-distance

lack of focus so instantly recognisable – the thousand-yard stare of eyes that had seen too much. He sat with his face to the wall, or stared at the floor. What this young man needed was time, gentleness and a semblance of normality. He would rejoin the world when he felt ready.

I left an exercise book at his bedside, with a selection of paints, crayons and pens. In his own time, I knew he would begin to draw, write or tear up paper angrily, anything to recover from the pain that afflicts a numbed soul when feelings begin to return. I had seen this work with the traumatised Vietnamese children.

One of the nurses called me the following day. Ahmed was beginning to write. Staring intently at the page, he painstakingly wrote the narrative of his experiences, which eventually covered eight pages in small, neat, Arabic script. When he had finished writing, he gave me the exercise book. I have had his words carefully translated by three different Arabic speakers. Slowly picking his way through the minefield of his emotions, he told of how he had originally joined the army because they had the best football facilities, which he believed would help him to realise his one dream – to play soccer for his country. Coerced into a never-ending series of military engagements during the eight-year conflict with Iran, he came to detest war. He described his horror at being sent to investigate the effects of chemicals used against the Kurds, of seeing the mothers and children lying dead.

Having had leave, he refused to rejoin the army and was slammed into prison for three months, only to be released straight into the thick of things to fight in the current war. Now, with two fractured legs, his dream of playing for the Iraqi national team was over.

To the civilian Iraqi population, Ahmed was a dreaded and hated Republican Guard. To the military authorities, he was a recalcitrant soldier with a reluctance to killing fellow human beings. He would be returning to his wife and daughter with two damaged legs, and his dream trodden into the dust of history.

I often wondered then what would become of Ahmed. I often wonder now whether he ever managed to carve out a life for himself, and whether he and his family survived the devastation of the next Iraq war.

Part Five

SQUARING THE CIRCLE

1990. From the air rice paddies glisten lush and green; too soon country-side gives way to the ugly sprawl of shantytown suburbs, and multiple emotions jostle for space in head and heart: threaten to overwhelm.

Humidity, heat and anxiety hover above nervous throngs of first-time returnees. Officialdom. Smart khaki uniforms, red-trimmed peaked caps pulled low over steely eyes. Identikit men, cold, expressionless.

To the victors the spoils . . .?

December 2004. The changes are quite astonishing. Huge inward investment has carried the country triumphantly into the new century.

The place now throbs with life, teems with visitors; businesses are booming, hotels are bursting with tourists, and buildings are shoot-ing up all over the city.

Tan Son Nhut International Airport in Ho Chi Minh City bears no resemblance to the overcrowded, sweaty, khaki-coloured building, regularly bombarded by mortars thirty-six years ago when the place was still known as Saigon. This is a modern, high-ceilinged, glass-and-steel building, where the floor is a vast expanse of gleaming tiles. The plastic seating is comfortable and the air-conditioning is efficient and almost too cool. Everywhere is spotless, and it is strangely quiet. There's a sort of softly purring efficiency about the place, which is curiously devoid of the frenetic activity associated with airports.

There are a few shops, but the display of goods is surprisingly sparse – mainly a limited selection of gaudy souvenirs – and the sandwich bar pushes the tooth-rotting fizzy drinks that are found throughout the developing world.

Flights are called: Qui Nhon, Danang and Hanoi . . . What potent memories are recalled by the very sound of those names.

'Would those requiring assistance to board with young children please make yourselves known and proceed now to gate eleven, where we are most pleased to help you.'

An unreasonable wave of anger: where were you when the legless ten-year-old Ba was being carried in a nurse's arms? Where was your help then?

57

INTO THE PAST

In 1990, while working in Saudi Arabia, I was granted a visa and made my first return visit to Vietnam. As the Air France plane made its final descent into Ton San Nhut, a collage of children's faces shimmered in my memory bank. Twenty years is a long time.

I went to a cashier's window to change dollars into local dong.

'How much you want?'

'One hundred dollars' worth, please.'

The intense, bespectacled cashier's voice shot up an octave. He took a closer look at me. 'You want one hundred dollar? You sure you want one hundred dollar?'

It didn't seem much for ten days, especially as credit cards were not yet acceptable. Only dollars or travellers' cheques could be used in hotels and for internal flights; the local dong was for meals, taxis and souvenirs.

'Yes, please. One hundred.'

From beneath the counter he produced a wad of creased and grubby old notes, held together by string and rubber bands, and easily a foot in length. 'What's this?' I asked incredulously. 'Fifty dollar, lady,' he replied, starting to push a second, identical bundle towards me.

'I can't take all that. I don't have room in my bag.'

'You want one hundred dollar of dong, you got one hundred dollar of dong.' I eventually settled for twenty dollars of dong. It was all I could manage!

The country was barely beginning to open up. Only with hindsight did I come to realise I had returned way too early for the kind of trip I had in mind. My movements were restricted to the centre of the city, and I was flatly told I would not be permitted to visit Qui Nhon by officials who seemed totally mystified as to why I would want to. I didn't even mention Kontum. The few non-Asians I saw were Russian 'advisors', there since 1975. What the hell they were advising on was not evident to me in 1990. The place was a mess. At the American War Crimes Museum I did meet two American service veterans – the two who persuaded me to visit the Cu Chi tunnels which reminded me of Pat Smith's hospital at Kontum.

The 'War Crimes' Museum was a tough one. The walls were covered with pictures of GIs posing with severed Vietcong heads and various body parts, accompanied by long explanations in Communist ideological prose beneath each image. Displayed in two glass cases were T-shirts allegedly removed from dead or captured US soldiers. The instantly recognisable Black Sabbath shirts, with their flying demons, vintage crucifixes and grinning skulls, were described as examples of Satan's work, carried out by the 'American running dogs'. Both shirts were stained, and had several slits and tears in them. I tried not to think about what might have happened to their owners.

As I strolled through the streets of the former Saigon, I was relieved to see that the beautiful Notre Dame cathedral was untouched. The Caravelle and Continental hotels were as I remembered them and I recognised many of the buildings along Tu Do Street. Crushing poverty was evident in the hordes of children scavenging through mounds of rubbish; groups of squatting women chewing on betel nut leaves and spitting into the gutter tried to sell pathetic little mounds of fruit and vegetables. Many ex-soldiers, redundant, and abandoned to make their own way, were identifiable from their permanent war wounds. The limbless, sightless or paraplegic were reduced to begging in the streets. Others, perhaps missing only an arm or one eye, were among the hundreds of cyclo drivers trying to scratch a living, waiting disconsolately outside hotels with few guests.

The once gracious British Embassy looked forlorn, the gardens overgrown. When I peeked inside, I saw Russian men playing squash and lifting weights, and discovered the building was being used as a gymnasium. The American Embassy, just down the street, was thoroughly run down and neglected, its former glory long forgotten. It felt as though I'd stumbled into a long-abandoned film set in a faraway universe. At one end of this once iconic building stood two rusty petrol pumps. It was only when a truck stopped to fill up that I realised they were in fact functioning.

Very noticeable to me, and a poignant reminder of the war years, were the Amerasians – those war babies of local girls and unknown American/Australian/Korean soldiers – now in their late teens and early twenties, drifting around like a lost tribe, junked and forgotten. Some were pale and blonde; some red-haired and freckled; others were dark-skinned, with the tight, thick curly black hair that spoke of Afro-Caribbean blood. Most of these youngsters were taller, their physiques quite different from the average Vietnamese. From a distance, or when seen from behind, you might think they were Westerners, until you saw their faces or heard their fluent Vietnamese.

I was approached on two occasions by young men who pressed almost worn out, faded scraps of paper into my hand, asking me imploringly if I knew this person. In both cases, these were old letters, now barely legible, one with an address in Houston, Texas, the other from New York. 'My father. My father. You know? You know?' It was hard not to break down and weep for these boys, still hoping their fathers would turn up and take them away from all this.

The authorities, strangely, gave me permission to travel to Hanoi. I had to think carefully. Many Americans had been captured, imprisoned and tortured there. Eventually I did decide to go and flew in a decrepit Russian Tupolev. I was glad I did.

Hanoi was very different from the brash din of Ho Chi Minh City, where the excesses and inequities of capitalism could still be found. Although desperately impoverished after years of aerial bombardment, Hanoi had an air of faded French elegance, distinctive amid the Asian sprawl. Here were placid lakes, strewn with water lilies, where ducks trailed lines of fluffy little ducklings behind them. Small, pastel-coloured temples, decorated with painted lotus blossoms and carved dragons that curled sinuously around their pillars, were tucked away in secret little places along the streets. This was a city I imagined Monet would have enjoyed painting.

There were few cars to be seen; many bicycles, some mopeds, and wooden carts pulled by oxen were the modes of transport in a Hanoi slowly coming to life. Now that Uncle Ho's dream of a united Vietnam was a reality, the only way was up. People everywhere were friendly and approachable.

I paid the requisite visit to the Ho Chi Minh Museum and mausoleum, and found the whole experience deeply moving. Were all those lost, ruined lives really worth it? From where I was standing, the answer was a resounding no, but this was not my country. Perhaps the Vietnamese would say yes. The new generation was inheriting Uncle Ho's dream of a united country, free from foreign rule. They would make it work; the hell their parents and grandparents went through was already beginning to fade from memory.

This is how it works, I guess, till the next bright idea comes along.

I stayed at the run-down but picturesque Victory Hotel, much of it built on stilts reaching out over a lake. In the vast dining room, I sat in solitary splendour at one end, while at the other a group of thirty Russians were boisterously enjoying their umpteen-course meal, washed down with copious amounts of vodka. The waiters, resplendent in smart black and white dress suits a size too large, bow ties at their scrawny necks, clustered around a small television set flickering in a distant corner. They were watching the football World Cup. I asked who was playing. They had no idea, but it seemed irrelevant. The sound was non-existent and the picture quality poor, but they cheered and chattered excitedly. The game connected these young men to the rest of the world, and that made me feel like standing up and cheering.

The Russian group turned their attention to me, calling out 'Eeenglish. Eeeenglish. Come,' beckoning me to join them. Oh God, how was I going to get out of this? I could hardly pretend I hadn't seen them, and when they sent over a vodka for me I bit the bullet and joined them. A chair was dragged up and I was firmly told to sit between the only woman in the group (who looked more masculine than many of the men) and the only man who could speak some English, who with gusto lined up several shot glasses in front of me. 'Eeeengleeesh. *Budem zdorovy. Budem, Budem*,' (Let's stay healthy). Others shouted '*Tabla Riddim, tabla riddim*'; this meant 'Virgins are no fun' which, thankfully, I didn't understand at the time!

Looking around the table, at the flushed, sweaty friendly faces, I noticed a younger man sitting at the far end of the table, part of the group, yet somehow isolated. The body language was familiar: a world of pain around the set of his shoulders, a disengaged look in his eyes, making no contact with anyone. It was unmistakable: it was the thousand-yard stare.

I asked my new friend who he was. 'He is Mikhail. When our soldiers come from Afghanistan, some are, how you say . . . crazy a little bit. American soldiers like this from Vietnam, they go to Mexico, find beautiful beach and beautiful bitch. Then they OK. Russian soldiers? They come to Vietnam. Find beautiful beach and beautiful bitch, then they OK.'

Everyone laughed. Linking arms, swaying from side to side, they sang songs loudly, harmoniously and with feeling, at the tops of their voices. Mikhail was silent. The emotional energy around that table suggested songs of the homeland. The hair on the back of my neck prickled and stood up, and I joined in with the Welsh national anthem, 'Land of my Fathers', and tried hard not to let the British down in the drinking challenge. I downed a few shots, to enthusiastic applause. Suffice to say, I did not intend ending up as anyone's 'bitch' and extracted myself from the raucous crowd while I still could.

The next morning, I travelled back down south on the decrepit but reliable old French train. It took forty-eight hours to travel through fascinating scenery; past the lushness of rice paddies, through small, dusty hamlets where children waved excitedly as they do the world over, and snaking along magnificent sweeps of coastline. Craters left by B52 bombing were easily identifiable, and in any case were pointed out to me by my government guide. He seemed more interested in practising his English than in keeping me on a leash; or was he? I was upset when the train stopped for thirty minutes at the teeming station in Qui Nhon and he strictly forbade me to disembark. 'But why? I loved this place. Can't I just take a short walk, my legs are stiff.'

'Not permitted, madam. Not permitted. I am sorry.' Funny, I have never thought of myself as a threat to anyone's national security.

Politics will do us all in one day.

Eventually, the train coughed in to Ho Chi Minh City rail station, five minutes ahead of schedule. I vowed to return as soon as I could travel freely to Qui Nhon and Kontum.

I would have to wait fourteen long years for the opportunity.

58

GHOSTS

December 2004. I was back in Vietnam and the changes that met me were quite astonishing. I was determined this time to revisit Qui Nhon and Kontum, places of such huge significance in my life both professionally and personally, but first stop was Ho Chi Minh City. In startling contrast to what I had witnessed fourteen years earlier, the buzz of capitalism was alive and well. Amid the hustle and bustle of progress, though, the Amerasians were still in evidence, well into their thirties by now, but many still nurturing the hope that they might find their father in the crowd. Wherever visiting American war veterans gathered for a cold beer, you would find the Amerasians.

Drawn like a moth to a flame, I again visited the American War Crimes Museum, now called the Vietnam War Remnants Museum, and walked slowly through a gallery displaying photographs of journalists and photographers who had either died or gone missing during the war. Looking closely into their faces, I reflected on the taste for danger, and the courage, that had brought them here to reveal the truth about the war. Many were, of course, American, but there were pictures of journalists from the four corners of the globe. Some of the photographs were labelled clearly with the date and circumstances of death; others had disappeared without trace.

Suddenly I saw a face I recognised, that of a freelance photographer named Dana Stone. He and his friend Sean Flynn, son of the famous screen actor Errol Flynn, had disappeared together in Cambodia in 1970. A little further along the wall, there was Sean, smiling, just as I remembered him.

These two young men, Dana and Sean, occasionally pitched up at the Minh Quy hospital in Kontum to see if they could help Pat Smith in any way. They would hang out for a while, taking some pictures away from the brutal heart of the violence. The last time I saw them they were talking about going to Cambodia and we all, Pat in particular, tried to dissuade them from doing something so foolhardy and dangerous, but go they did, and were never seen again.

Sean Flynn and Dana Stone were fine young men, kind and full of laughter, and they loved the Montagnards. I saw them clearly in my mind's eye, sitting in the sunshine, drinking water from a tribesman's gourd . . . Becoming tearful in the museum, I turned and blundered into a young man who steadied me, took me outside and we sat together on a bench.

He was an American lawyer, George Lewis, from Chicago, also much moved by the museum. His father had served and died in Vietnam and now, at the age of thirty-five, his son had plucked up the courage, as he put it, to take a look at this country, described so eloquently in his father's letters to George's mother.

Like me, George had come to lay a few ghosts. He told me about his father, an officer based in Vung Tao in the Delta, where he was killed. George had his father's medals in his pocket, and proudly showed them to me. He had been only three years old when his father died. I told him about the

Amerasians, about Dana and Sean, and about my time with the children in Qui Nhon. We spoke of life and death, enjoyed a cold beer together, then hugged and went our separate ways. The legacy of war has long fingers, still reaching out and touching people down the years.

The next morning it was back to the airport for the long-awaited return to Qui Nhon.

I turned out to be the only Westerner on the Air Vietnam flight. As I looked out excitedly and a little apprehensively at the landscape below, I thought I would recognise Qui Nhon from the air, but the plane descended inland and came to rest on the primitive runway of a scruffy inland airfield where grass grew between the flagstones.

It was a perfectly good landing, but this place was clearly not geared to tourists! No air-conditioned, covered walkway here, and the walk across the tarmac to a large barn of a building was quite a distance from the plane.

Slightly ahead of me, a gaudily painted Vietnamese woman, battling unsuccessfully to hold back the years, teetered along on white stilettos. She was quite a sight to behold in her sprayed on white trousers, worn with a tight pink top – neckline very low – lots of gold jewellery, and blonde-streaked hair permed into a frizzy mass. She carried a sparkly pink holdall and bitched the whole way to the terminal building.

'What kind of a horse's ass arrangement is this? I didn't pay to walk on this trip, honey.'

I tried to engage her in conversation. 'Are you from Qui Nhon?' I asked.

'You think I'm from this one-eyed town? No, I'm from Los Angeles.'

'Are you on holiday here?'

By way of a reply to the question, she spat out a wad of

chewing gum and said, 'You think I'd vacation in a shit-hole like this?'

With an image of the sweet, demure and beautiful Vietnamese girls in my memory, I could only wonder what life had handed this woman; why she needed to protect herself with a tough, rude, ill-tempered exterior, turning her into a caricature of what she might once have been.

At the terminal building everyone else piled on to a bus but I needed to find out exactly where I was. It certainly didn't appear to be Qui Nhon. I spoke to a ground hostess who explained that I was in Phu Cat, thirty-five kilometres from Qui Nhon.

'Are there hotels in Qui Nhon?' I asked. 'I have no reservation.'

'Oh yes. Which area do you want?'

'I want to be somewhere near the provincial hospital.'

'Are you sick?'

'No, I'm a nurse and worked in Qui Nhon during the war. I have come back to try and find some of the places I used to know.'

'There is the Life Resort Hotel where I think you would be comfortable, but it is expensive, one hundred dollars a night.'

That would blow my budget. 'Is there somewhere cheaper? I'd like to be close to the beach.'

'There is the Qui Nhon Hotel. It is a very nice hotel where the Vietnamese stay, and it is ten dollars a night.'

That sounded more my speed. The helpful hostess phoned up and reserved me a room, and I set off in a dilapidated taxi. The taxi driver spoke no English but he still chattered away and I recognised the odd few words here and there. The route the driver took was unfamiliar to me, but I could see that where I was headed was not part of the tourist trail. We passed simple villages where people appeared to live by raising chickens and ducks; I tried not to think about bird flu, or whether my back would survive the potholes over which we bounced and juddered or, indeed, whether my pilgrimage would turn out to be a fool's errand . . .

59

SEA OF MEMORIES

'Madam, this is Qui Nhon,' announced the driver. At last! But still I didn't recognise my surroundings until, with a sense of relief, I saw the sea: the sweep of the bay and the rocks on either side, and then the hill with the radio mast at the top. The taxi pulled into a driveway opposite the beach and stopped outside a huge, modern hotel with marble pillars on either side. A large green dragon was twisted round one pillar and a red dragon was sinuously draped around the other. Both had wide, staring eyes and bright red forked tongues emerging from their mouths.

I gave the delighted taxi driver a dollar, and walked into the vast lobby. Everywhere was tiled, cool and spotlessly clean. Two pretty Vietnamese girls behind the desk checked me in. Incredibly, I once again seemed to be the only guest! The vast dining room was easily large enough to seat two hundred people. The tables were laid with crisply starched white table-cloths, and each was adorned with a spray of orchids; there was a bar at the far end of the room and plastic palm trees in each corner, probably in an attempt to fill some of the space. But there were no guests around.

My room was beautiful, and also very large. It contained two double beds and a single. The bathroom was enormous, and there was also a little annex where I carefully placed my trusty rucksack, which looked rather sad in these surroundings!

I could hardly believe the price I'd been quoted and went back to the desk to check. It was correct – ten dollars. So, back I went to my palatial accommodation, where I showered and then settled in front of the huge television. I actually managed to find a movie channel and happily watched a Marlon Brando film dubbed into Vietnamese.

I then enjoyed a delicious but solitary meal in the vast dining room, after which I wandered out to watch the sun go down. The hotel was just a few feet from the strip of beach that I had known in 1967/68 as Red Beach, a designated in-country R&R centre for US soldiers. It had been secured and guarded so that young soldiers could relax by the sea in safety, when few such places *were* ever safe. The military authorities also allowed us to use Red Beach, and this is where we took our damaged children twice a week. Traumatised, maimed and paraplegic though they were, the beach rang with laughter and joy, as young soldiers built sand castles for the youngsters, gave piggy-back rides, and took little ones into the waves. Over to the right somewhere was where Mike and I had often sat and read poetry to each other . . .

I sat on the little wall, scuffing the silver sand with my toes, watching the sun set, and allowed my mind to drift gently back in time, remembering it all, and then to drift slowly forward again to the present. I didn't cry. There was a quiet, calm acceptance that that was then and this is now. Back at the hotel, I had a stiff nightcap at the bar, went back to my room and slept like a baby. I'd let go of a few things.

The next morning, I woke up with a sense of excitement. I had photographs with me of various buildings as they had been in the late 1960s and was hoping to find the Holy Family Hospital, but I no longer had any sense of where it was. The town was now a sprawling blur of bicycles, mopeds, fishing nets and red flags with hammer and sickle; small businesses had sprung up all over the place, yet the town wasn't exactly thriving. The money being invested in Vietnam was going to Hanoi, Danang, Hue, Nha Trang, Ho Chi Minh, and the delta in the south. These were the places that were expanding to attract trade and tourism. Qui Nhon was not one of them – not yet.

After a strange and certainly different breakfast of fishy rice soup and lots of coffee, I went to the desk to try and arrange for an interpreter. Xuong, one of the receptionists, said she would be happy to help, and though I kept calling it the provincial hospital and they called it the government hospital, she said she knew where it was. It was quite close and she would take me.

Xuong couldn't speak that much English and my Vietnamese didn't stretch to all the questions I wanted to ask, but she was sweet and pleasant company. We walked along a road where you had to have eyes in the back of your head to avoid being hit by bicycles and motorbikes. I was the only Westerner around. The people in the street smiled, children shyly giggled or stared at this stranger.

We reached a large, cream-coloured building with a few trees in the grounds. I don't know what I was expecting – thirty-six years is a long time – but this building looked unfamiliar, too new. (Later, I saw a few smaller, older, more familiar buildings to the rear.)

People milled about in an orderly fashion; this was the government hospital and I needed the medical director's office to ask for permission to be there. As we went in through the gates, Xuong took out a handkerchief which she pressed to her nose and mouth; she held it there for the whole of our visit. This is an Asian habit around sickness.

Inside, the building was clean, orderly and relatively quiet. All nurses wore the starched white dresses and caps that now seem dated in the West, but we all used to wear them in the 1960s and 1970s. There were a number of patients lying in hammocks strung across the corridor, some being gently fanned by a relative to help them in the oppressive heat, but the whole place had the buzz of an efficiently run machine about it.

We walked up two flights of stairs to an austere room where the medical director reigned. He sat behind a large, shiny desk, an authoritative figure in military uniform. Several gold stars adorned his red shoulder epaulettes; his peaked cap, pulled low, shielded his eyes. You just knew, even without seeing them, that those eyes were icy cold and expressionless. Xuong spoke to him, but he was giving nothing away.

He answered Xuong, glancing once, briefly, in my direction. I knew he wasn't missing a thing. He did not want us to go round the hospital, he wanted to know who I was, and I had the uncomfortable feeling that I shouldn't be there. For the rest of my stay, the closer I got to authority, the more closed things were. Unless you had papers with umpteen stamps all over them, you weren't going to get anywhere.

I took out some of the photographs of the children and tried to explain to the director that I was retracing my steps. Later, Xuong found someone in the hotel who could speak good English and I was told what exactly had taken place. The medical director had asked her why this woman was here. Xuong told him that I was a nurse who had come here thirty-six years ago to care for sick and wounded children, some of whom had come from this hospital. He asked her who the doctors were at the hospital and she told him they were New Zealanders. He said, 'Is she American?'

'No, she's British.'

'She is lying. There were no foreigners here thirty-six years ago. Only Vietnamese.'

He never looked at me but I saw that Xuong was uncomfortable. At that point he stood up, bowed his head briefly in my direction and walked out of the office. The interview was over, and we left.

I needed a rethink. First, a good interpreter was essential. The authorities were not happy with me nosing around. The difference in mindset between here and swinging Ho Chi Minh City was like night and day.

After showering, changing and collecting a cold beer, I strolled across the road to the beach. I sat down and gradually the calm of the previous evening returned to me.

I had so badly wanted to come here. I hadn't been able to get to Qui Nhon in 1990, and now here I was, in this place so full of memories for me. I had, for years, cherished a silent hope that I might find some of the children, although they'd of course be adults now, but I knew deep down this was unlikely to happen. In all probability most of them would be dead. Double amputees, children with internal injuries, their bodily systems ruined, how could they possibly have survived without specialised care?

I sat there, working out my plan. I had wanted to start at the beginning, with the children from the provincial hospital, but I clearly wasn't going to get very far there, even with a fluent interpreter. Our Children's Centre would, I knew, be long gone, but if I could find out where the military airfield had been situated, I'd at least find the location of the Centre. And there was bound to be a children's hospital or centre of some sort here, so I would go and visit there . . . And I absolutely had to go to the leprosarium, on the outskirts of Qui Nhon, on that exquisite bay fringed with palms. And this Life Resort Hotel – that, I thought, was worth a phone call to see if they spoke English.

I called the Life Resort Hotel and a fluent English speaker answered. I explained what I needed. 'We will give you Miss Margaret.'

Margaret was the Austrian manager. The company she represented were opening up a string of luxury hotels in beautiful places around the world. She had spent two years in Burma and had then been transferred to Qui Nhon, to open up this one.

'Anne, how long will you be staying in Qui Nhon?'

''Probably about eight days, but you're too expensive for me.'

'We can make a special deal for you. We'd be thrilled to have you here for Christmas. We don't have many guests and I need someone sensible to talk to. We'll send a car round.'

I was sorry to say goodbye to Xuong but I settled my bill at the Qui Nhon Hotel, where, within the hour, a conspicuously luxurious car swept up to the main door. The smartly uniformed driver took my rucksack with due ceremony – 'Is this all there is, madam?' I said, 'That's it,' and was whisked away in air-conditioned comfort to the Life Resort Hotel, about eight kilometres north of town.

'Do you know a place called the leprosarium?' I asked the driver.

He looked puzzled.

I bunched my hands into fists and held them up, and said it was a place for people who had lost their fingers like this.

'Yes, we will pass the road,' he said.

As we left the bustling chaos of town and passed through palm groves and brilliantly green rice paddies, I at last began to feel that I *was* actually in Qui Nhon. We passed the hill we used to call Telegraph Hill. Anyone who was in Qui Nhon during the war would remember this hill. My excitement was growing.

Then the driver turned a corner and there in front of us was the beautiful valley with a narrow road leading down to the leprosarium.

'Down there, madam, that is the place. The sick people you

are speaking of are there.' I was busting to go down, but it was too late in the evening. I'd save it for tomorrow.

A couple of kilometres further on he took a sharp left and we bumped down a dirt track, rounded a bend and entered a driveway lined with the most exquisite, tall palms that met at the top, forming an avenue of shade. We pulled up outside a sleek, luxurious hotel. I felt I had blundered, yet again, into a parallel universe.

A smart young doorman leapt forward, opened the vehicle door and helped me out. Again, 'Is this all your luggage, madam?' he asked, expertly extracting my rucksack from the plush interior. Again, 'That's it,' I replied, and inside we went.

The lobby was achingly cool in more ways than one. All coffee and cream tiles, orchids and colour-co-ordinated staff, glass doors across the lobby led to a sparkling infinity pool. Beyond that lay the turquoise South China Sea. The hotel half filled the entire bay.

'Are you Anne? Welcome, welcome to the Life Resort.'

A European woman, who of course was Margaret, bore down and enveloped me in a bear hug. She was lovely; a real homely, welcoming person who exuded warmth and earth motherliness, and I guessed she must feel a bit cut off and lonely in this place, exquisite though it was. Who, I wondered, stayed here? Margaret explained it was early days in the development of this particular project, but it had become a stopover on coach trips catering to the more intrepid traveller, en route from Hanoi to Danang, Hue, Qui Nhon, Nha Trang and Ho Chi Minh City – or vice-versa. They would stay one night at this lovely place – a whole busload of people too exhausted to truly appreciate what was being offered.

One glance at the accommodation reinforced the absolute conviction that I couldn't possibly afford this level of luxury. I needed to confirm the arrangement with Margaret. 'Stop worrying,' she said. So I did.

My room was larger than a Welsh cottage, for God's sake! It had a four-poster bed, a separate dressing room, a shower area and, needless to say, its own fridge and a huge television. We, it seems, are unable to function without TV to connect us to what is going on in the world. But then, how many of us do – really – connect with what is going on in this world . . .

Huge glass doors opened onto a balcony overlooking the ocean, a mere fifty metres away. Filmy, delicate curtains were all that separated me from the waves. To my left, in the sweep of the bay, would be the leprosarium. It was strangely comforting to know that.

Internet facilities meant I could immediately connect with family and friends. I resisted the temptation immediately to email my excitement to Mike and my sisters. No, tomorrow was soon enough. I could barely believe where I was, and suddenly I thought of the moon landings, and the reaction of the Montagnard elders. Some things should not be rushed. My soul needed time to catch up with my body.

60

LETTING GO

The following morning I told the hotel staff I wanted to visit the leprosarium. They seemed bemused – most of their guests were happy to sun themselves around the pool – but they were polite, and very helpful. All the receptionists spoke fluent English, and one young woman, Yeung, volunteered to be my interpreter.

Again, the hotel provided a car for me, a less obtrusive vehicle this time, and as we drove down the curving, narrow lane, I marvelled again at the beauty of the place. Memories came flooding back to me as anticipation grew. In 1967 the road had been a dirt track; now it was a much smoother trip down the cool, shady road edged by trees.

We arrived at the gates and Yeung jumped out to speak to the guard, who cheerfully raised the traffic barrier, saluted and waved us on. I immediately saw what had changed and what had remained the same. For a start, the hospital building was new. In complete contrast to the frosty reception I had at the government hospital, the friendly Vietnamese woman doctor in charge didn't hesitate to introduce me to all the personnel, which included two French nuns – a poignant reminder of the old leprosarium.

I asked how the treatment had changed, and she told me that there were now three leprosaria in Vietnam: one in the delta, this one in Qui Nhon and one close to Hanoi. They saw approximately thirty-five new cases a year. I wasn't sure if she meant throughout Vietnam or just at this place in Qui Nhon but, most encouragingly, she said there had been a huge change in attitude towards the illness and a big difference in how it was handled. Unlike the 1960s, sufferers no longer had to spend their lives in a colony, together with their entire families. Now, fresh cases were treated in hospital for nine months, then returned to their communities with a supply of the medications they needed.

While Yeung and I were strolling around, chatting and taking photographs, absorbing the scene, an old gentleman rode up on a bicycle. Half his feet were missing and the stumps covered in dirty bandaging; his fingers were missing too, yet still he managed to ride his bike. His nose was almost eaten away and he had the scarred, leonine face typical of the chronic Hansen's disease sufferer. He stopped a few feet away from us and looked intently at me. We went over to talk to him, and learned that he had been at the leprosarium since he was thirteen, when he came with his brothers and sisters to live with his parents, who both had the illness. He looked to be in his sixties now, though it was hard to tell.

'Do you remember the foreign doctors and nurses who used to come here during the war?' asked Yeung.

'Yes, yes, yes – I do, I do!' He got so excited I thought he'd fall off his bicycle.

'This lady was a nurse who used to come here then.'

He kept staring at me. Of course he's not going to recognise me, I thought. I'm sixty-odd now, no longer the young woman I was then.

He told the interpreter he remembered the big men. He didn't call them Americans, just said he remembered the 'big men' who used to bring sweets and operated on the limbs of his mother. These men helped the French nuns, who always had lunch with them. Then they would go for a swim.

The hair was standing up on the back of my neck. It was such a long time ago, and he remembered all of it. I moved towards him, and we hugged each other. These emotions are so powerful; they know no boundaries. It was a spontaneous and amazing recognition of humanity, each for the other, at one and the same moment. I reached out to him and he reached out to me. It didn't matter that we didn't speak the same language or have the same cultural background. In an ideal world, we would all keep our differences but reach out to each other with love. Yeung had tears in her eyes. She said later that she had learned something that day.

I often think that the more sophisticated and materialistic we become, the more we rob ourselves of less tangible, more profound values. That encounter held a great depth of meaning for me, like that extraordinary moment of connectedness that passed between the child Ba, the American soldier and myself on that military plane all those years ago.

I got back to the hotel and wrote Mike all about it, knowing that he, as always, would understand. I emailed him photographs, which he sent on to other veteran medics he was still in touch with. Their response was incredible – they just could not believe I was back there. The ripple of love just went round the world.

The next day, I showed several of the staff at the hotel my photographs. Yeung had described the visit to the leprosarium. They knew of it but had never visited. She had told them about the moment when I hugged the old gentleman who was so badly disfigured.

'Were you frightened to touch him?'

'No, not at all.' I explained that I was a nurse, that this was normal for me – and, anyway, it was perfectly safe.

The staff were all bright, young people in their twenties. Some were university graduates, some were working to make money to pay for further courses, others were interested in hotel management. I asked them whether they were taught anything at school about their country's wars with the French, then the Americans. The answer was no. The little they knew of these momentous upheavals in their history they had learned from their parents or grandparents. But they *were* taught in school what a great man Ho Chi Minh was. As the days went by, I realised that it was pointless trying to get information out of anyone under the age of forty. They were pleasant and friendly, but they did not want to discuss the recent past.

I spent several days attempting to find anything I recognised. Where the old military airfield had been was now a large market place. Wide, paved highways edged with Communist flags led to and from the area. We were able to work out that where the Children's Centre had been was now part of a covered fish market. There was nothing there to remind me of anything. That was then, this was now.

I felt certain that somewhere there must be a centre for children with physical disabilities and other special needs and, if indeed there was, I would love to see it. Yeung investigated and found Madame Yao's special school. A car ride through narrow side streets, crowded with vendors, chickens and ducks scattered in all directions, took us to a nondescript building with barred windows and a huge wrought-iron gate hung with sheets of corrugated iron. A guard let us in and took us to an office where we met the director of the school.

Madame Yao, a woman in her early forties, had set up the school in a small way some twelve years before, and had continued regularly raising funds in order to expand. Now she had room for a hundred and thirty children, ranging in age from seven to fifteen. Some were profoundly deaf, some were blind, some had orthopaedic or neurological disabilities, or other special needs, either medical or emotional – or both. They were being taught life skills, computer skills and handicrafts as well as their lessons.

I showed Madame Yao my photographs of the children I had nursed all those years ago and asked her if she had any idea what might have happened to them.

Her face shut down. 'I don't know. I think they would have died. The soldiers would have put them in a special place.'

I pressed on. 'The children were disabled by war wounds. This is Ba. She was ten and she lost her legs. There were many children like her, victims of mines. This little boy had a catheter because his genitals were destroyed. It is conceivable that he would have died without nursing care.'

'Yes, he would have died.'

'You don't know any women in their forties who have no legs?'

'No, they would all be dead. They would not be here. They would send them away.'

I needed much longer. Something like this could not be done in a few days. Her expression told me this was a taboo subject. I had to let it go.

Despite Madame Yao's rather stern and detached demeanour, I spent a surprisingly enjoyable day at the centre, where we were treated to a hastily put-together concert. A young blind boy named Trung, eighteen years old, played keyboard and harmonica while two girls sang. He played some Buddy Holly songs, and then some Beatles tracks. Trung said he loved the Beatles. I complimented him on his English and he explained that he had taught himself by listening to the BBC World Service. He asked if I had a favourite song. 'Do you know "Hey Jude"?' I asked. His face broke into a wide grin, 'Oh yes, I do.' He sang and played it perfectly, bringing a sudden tightness to my throat as I recalled Denny and Hiao in Kontum.

Then ten children wearing the traditional dress of the hill tribes danced energetically.

'You know they are completely deaf. They cannot hear the music,' said Madame Yao. 'Watch.' She turned the tape recorder off but the children carried on dancing, counting their steps in unison. Madame Yao turned the music back on, 'You see? They can hear nothing.' She flicked the music off and on several times while they carried on, never missing a beat.

Then she took me to a different room, where I was confronted by teenagers and young adults with gross lower-limb deformities. Madame Yao said one or other of their parents had been exposed to Agent Orange: 'The gas that took the leaves off the trees also took the limbs off the children.' That's how she put it. 'My parents told me about this,' she said, adding 'and children are still being born now with these deformities. I can take you to some houses in Qui Nhon where you can meet more. You can take photographs of them.'

'No, I don't feel right doing that.'

'I can take you. You can take pictures of them.'

She was very pragmatic about the whole thing, but by now I was emotionally drained. I also accepted that I wasn't going to find anybody I once knew and that was OK. I'd just remember them as they used to be.

We said our goodbyes. Yeung told me how much she had enjoyed the visit, and that I had given her some insight into how strongly nurses feel about the people they care for.

61

ROADBLOCK

I never made it to Kontum. I had the official paperwork, a guide, and a driver. We made a start on the journey at six a.m. but just as we'd begun the climb up Highway 19 into the Central Highlands, we encountered a roadblock. For all their apparent politeness, the two policemen manning it were never going to let us through. Amid lots of smiles and salutes, and despite my documents, they insisted that I, a foreigner, could not be permitted to continue on into dangerous territory. I was disappointed, of course. Very disappointed. But I somehow wasn't surprised – certainly not nearly as surprised as the hotel staff when we arrived back just a few hours after we had left!

I invited Thanh, the guide, to share brunch with me in the hotel so that we could talk.

'What's really going on?' I asked.

'Well, we hear rumours . . . we know they are killing the ethnics.'

'But why?'

'Because the rumours say that the ethnics are being funded by American Catholics who are encouraging them to over-throw the government.'

It was only the serious look on his face that prevented me

from laughing. My memories of the Montagnards at Pat Smith's hospital were so warm, touching and life-changing that I simply could not get my head around what this young man was telling me. Even after all these years, it was hardly likely that the gentle Montagnards had become subversives and revolutionaries. Still, I knew that it was brave of Thanh to say anything to me – he could have stuck to the official line we'd been fed about danger to foreigners – but perhaps he'd realised that I wouldn't swallow the cover-up.

'Who were those two plain-clothes men with the policemen at the roadblock?' I asked.

'They are the secret police. They are in many places.' He looked sad. 'We are not bad people.'

I looked at this pleasant, intelligent student of English Literature, and tried to grapple with what I had brushed up against.

'You're a bright young man. Your English is fluent. You must speak with a lot of tourists.'

'Most tourists are not like you, Miss Anne. They are on vacation. They know nothing of this country. They are not interested.'

'Well, Thanh, many people will not have had my experience of living and nursing here. They work hard, and they come here to enjoy the beauty of your country and have a good holiday. They *are* interested, that is why they come, but they only see what they are meant to see. It is like that in many countries. I'm different because I'm retracing the steps of my memories, that is all.'

'Yes, I understand that, Miss Anne, and I wish my government was more open.' Thanh wanted so badly to speak out but he, and I, knew that he had to be careful.

'I have seen how much Ho Chi Minh City has changed,' I said, wanting to help him feel better. 'Your government is working hard to develop Vietnam and make life better for all of you. The tourist industry is a big part of their plans, and you are very important to that industry. Maybe when I come again, in a few years' time, you will have a hotel of your own.'

We both laughed, and then Thanh said, 'My fellow students think of Vietnam as being shaped like a bamboo pole with baskets at each end, like the ones you see in the market place. Those two baskets represent Hanoi and Ho Chi Minh City and they are full to breaking. The centre of the bamboo pole that rests on the shoulder is bending to the point of snapping. That represents Qui Nhon. We are in the middle, between the two major cities, and we have nothing here. The government knows this, so they are planning factories and industries in this area to build computers and make components for them. Qui Nhon will become like the Silicon Valley in America and the bamboo pole of Vietnam will grow strong again.'

I was touched by his analogy. We carefully did not mention the Highlands and their people again.

This luxurious hotel, the Life Resort, so close to the leprosarium and built by a Dutch company with such vision, was no doubt a little premature, but when the anticipated boom in this central area of Qui Nhon arrived, it would come into its own.

That evening, I had a drink at the bar with Margaret. 'Some of the staff think you're a CIA spy,' she casually told me.

'My God! What did you tell them?'

'I told them they were watching too many bad movies. Some said, "Why is she asking all these questions?" I told them to use their brains, that a spy would not be showing them her photographs and asking questions so openly. I told them you're a nurse, not a spy.'

I felt a bit uncomfortable after that, especially when Margaret said, 'You need to know that is what a couple of them think.'

'But why would they think that?'

'Oh, because their heads are full of wild stories. I have found Vietnam is full of rumour and counter-rumour. Since I've been here, I rarely go out of the resort. I keep myself to myself and just focus on my job here. To tell the truth, I'll be glad to leave, I don't much like the atmosphere in this country.'

'I'm sad to hear this,' I answered.

'No need. It's been interesting having you here, Anne, you're an unusual guest, and your openness and passion for the children you nursed in the war is obvious. It has really touched some of our younger staff. They'll remember you and your photographs long after you have gone.'

The next evening was Christmas Eve. There were only eight guests at the hotel, but a huge brightly lit Christmas tree dominated the marbled foyer. Next to the tree was a gingerbread house, filled with Margaret's home-baked Austrian cookies. Their warm, cinnamon smell spread throughout the lobby, as far as the open terrace doors, from where you could see the beautiful swimming pool sparkling in the moonlight. I decided to go for a swim and, as I floated gently in the warm water, I could hear a small choir of hotel staff singing carols around the tree. There it was again: Vietnam weaving her surreal web around me, just as she had all those years ago.

Listening to the singing floating out on the evening air, my thoughts drifted to a limping Montagnard, somewhere up there near Kontum, softly humming 'Hey Jude'. Tears don't show in a swimming pool.

Next day, I was invited over to join the Hillingers, a couple with two young children, for Christmas lunch at their table. He was from New York, his wife was South Korean, and they'd lived in Ho Chi Minh City for the past seven years. I was amazed to hear that Gary Hillinger was a coffee trader – I had had no idea that coffee was grown in Vietnam and I asked him where.

'Up in the Central Highlands, around the Kontum area. It's ideal coffee-growing country.'

I told him of my connection to the area and how the authorities prevented me from going there in 1990. Gary explained that the country only started to open up and attract major investment in 1994/95. Since then, things had really taken off and Vietnam was now buzzing. He told me of the plans to create a techno-industry in the Qui Nhon area, which Thanh had referred to, and I recounted my experience at the road block.

'Yes,' he said, and exchanged a smile with his wife. 'We heard all about that. They think you're a CIA spy, did you know?'

Oh Lord. There it was again.

Gary went on. 'When I first arrived, they thought that of me. They think that about any foreigner here in unusual circumstances.'

That made me feel a bit better.

'I heard that Montagnards are being killed. I wonder if you've heard anything when you're in Kontum?' I asked.

I sensed he was deftly side-stepping my question when he said, 'I've never been to Kontum myself, I have local middlemen who take care of that, but you hear stuff, I guess. It's partially a land rights thing . . . I reckon it's best not to say anything.'

It had taken a lot of effort to get the necessary stamp of approval for travel to Kontum, and what a charade it had turned out to be. Had my permit been another example of the Asian reluctance to say no, which causes them to say yes, even to the point of issuing written approval that will ultimately be ignored by some implacable official?

I wasn't sure what it was all about. I knew I'd brushed up against something secretive and threatening, that I'd been barred from one of the most beautiful areas in the world, and was unable to revisit some of the most beautiful people in the world. I still grieve about that, but I'm anguished at the thought that those gentle people I'd loved thirty-six years earlier might no longer have been alive.

Boxing Day was curiously solitary: I swam and sunbathed in beautiful surroundings, but there was hardly anyone around. I spent the afternoon walking along the beach and, as the tide receded, I was able to walk around the headland and clamber over rocks to the bay where the leprosarium was. There was the white sandy beach, fringed with palms, and fishing boats bobbing out in the waters. A peaceful scene, where all was well. I walked back, conscious of having had a lovely relaxing day, my last before departing for Cambodia.

Back in my hotel room, I showered then flicked on the television. It took me a while to grasp what the rolling news channel was telling me: A gigantic tsunami had hit Thailand that morning, with untold damage and loss of life.

At dinner in the hotel dining room nobody mentioned the disaster. Perhaps they were smarter than I and knew not to disturb their vacation in paradise by viewing CNN. As I watched the sun set, it was hard to take on board the havoc unleashed just the other side of this Southeast Asian peninsula.

Back in my room I decided that if anything was going to happen here, the windows wouldn't save me from it, so I left them wide open as usual. I drifted off to sleep with the sound of the sea lapping gently just below my balcony.

62

SOLINA

My flight south to Ho Chi Minh City from Qui Nhon was uneventful and I felt content in myself. I had half expected to feel sadness at departing from Qui Nhon, particularly as I'd failed to track down any of my former charges. As it was, frustration at having been kept from visiting the Highlands aside, I accepted the new realities and felt at peace, ready for the next leg of my journey into the past. I was to be met at Phnom Penh airport by Solina, my interpreter, right hand and friend from the refugee camp days at Sa Keao.

When I left the camp in Thailand in 1980, I also had to leave Solina. Damaged by her horrific experiences in Cambodia and depressed by her situation as a refugee, Solina was desperate to emigrate to a neutral country. I hated deserting her, and asked my sister Susan if she would become a pen friend to Solina, a suggestion to which she instantly agreed. I had thought of this because, wherever in the world I found myself, Susan's regular, newsy letters kept me reassuringly in touch with the ordinary, daily happenings and routines of family life in England.

Susan would describe the flowers and birds in the large garden where she and her husband have always grown their own fruit and vegetables, and tell me what she was busy pickling, bottling or freezing for the winter months to come. She talked of her six happy, healthy grandchildren and reported the news of the village. Those slices of home sealed up in an envelope kept me going through the worst times, when turmoil threatened to overwhelm.

Subsequently, Solina told me how important Susan's letters were to her, helping her hold fast to the thought that there was a world of peace and normality out there. Now I was about to see Solina after almost twenty-five years. I could picture her clearly in my mind's eye, but that was as she was then. Would I recognise her now? Would she recognise me?

I need not have worried. As I emerged into the melee of the arrivals area, there she stood, no longer the starved, anxious torture victim I met in 1979, but a well-nourished middle-aged lady, beaming a warm smile of welcome in my direction.

We hugged excitedly and I felt tears pricking my eyes. All those years ago, in that stinking camp, she had quietly sworn to return to Cambodia to help her people, and vowed to walk me through her story. I thought it a pipe dream then, but here we were. Her faith had been rock solid, far stronger than mine: I hadn't dared, in such terrible circumstances, to raise what might have been false hope.

Solina guided me expertly through the crowds, out into the fierce heat and across to her little Korean car. Chattering excitedly, we bumped along the dusty, potholed roads heavily populated by a vast tide of motorbikes and bicycles. We eventually turned into a side road where every building seemed more dilapidated than its neighbour. Solina braked hard, three inches from large, double wrought iron gates across which two sheets of corrugated metal hung drunkenly, providing some privacy from prying eyes.

We entered a small flagstone courtyard where a sprig of pink bougainvillea blossomed in a ceramic pot beside a wooden bench, and a line of brightly coloured sarongs had been hung out to dry. The two-storey, whitewashed house was a simple building where Solina and her two nieces rented the ground floor and a family of American missionaries lived on the floor above. Inside, the apartment was invitingly cool, sparely furnished and welcoming. In the large sitting room, two hammocks were slung across the corners, and the bamboo chairs again brought a sharp flash of memory back to my childhood and the chairs my father had sent from Singapore.

A small bed, mosquito netting draped at the ready, had been put in Solina's office, now prepared as a bedroom for me. On the wall, written in decorative script on a large whiteboard, were the words:

Sister Anne
Welcome to Cambodia

I was deeply moved. I knew I was about to be led by the hand, stage by stage, through Solina's past, and that it was profoundly important to both of us.

When I left Sa Keao camp in 1980, physically and emotionally drained, the Red Cross authorities were busy tracing relatives of the displaced Cambodians, and had begun the lengthy process of screening suitable candidates for resettlement. Solina, like so many others, was eventually accepted into Canada, but not before enduring many months of tension, uncertainty, and the upheaval of being moved from one transit camp to another. Once in Canada, she had settled with a wonderful family in Ontario, where she attended Bible school and trained for missionary work.

In 1999, she returned to Phnom Penh. Observing the grinding poverty, chaos and trauma of the post Pol Pot years, she reaffirmed her decision to help her people, and had remained there since.

With her fellow missionaries of the Overseas Missionary Foundation – OMF – Solina was carrying out vitally important work in this troubled place. Together, they set up orphanages, took homeless children and sick people off the streets, and were providing an anchor to women in distress: those who'd been forced to prostitute themselves to survive, or who were victims of domestic violence. In addition to all that, they helped young people to find work and encouraged and supported small, entrepreneurial projects that would give hope, dignity and an income to those in need.

A small handful of other charities also did what they could, but there didn't appear to be any other effective programmes in evidence. The social problems were so enormous that only well-co-ordinated, properly funded and determined government programmes could have made a positive impact. I admired enormously the efforts made by missionary organisations, even though I wasn't always comfortable with the evangelising aspects of their work.

A couple of days later Solina and I left at seven a.m. on the six-and-a-half-hour bus journey to Siem Reap, the location of the Angkor Wat temples.

The bus was comfortable, and its air conditioning mostly worked. Crossing Ton Le Sap Lake on a crowded, noisy ferry that in no way met international safety standards was one of life's more buttock-clenching experiences, but the trusty bus continued undaunted along Route 6, the paved highway that wound through the countryside, sometimes sun-baked and tinder dry, other times lushly green. People toiled in the rice paddies or fished on the banks of the small rivers. Sleepy water buffalo pulled creaking wooden carts loaded with melons or straw along dusty roads.

Frequently, through thick jungle foliage or rising behind a cluster of thatched dwellings, I spied the glinting roofs and turrets of Buddhist temples, so resonant of Southeast Asia. Enraptured by these beautiful structures, which I kept excitedly pointing out to Solina while I attempted to photograph them from the bus, it took me a while to realise that my friend was unusually silent and unresponsive. Eventually she said quietly, 'Anne, we do not like the temples. We hate them. The Khmer Rouge tortured and killed people in those temples and so they represent pain and certain death to us. They are not beautiful to us.'

I took no more photographs.

I remembered now that when Solina was tortured by the regime, it happened in a temple, but I hadn't realised that this practice was widespread. What a clever way to poison and kill the foundations of a society: make the people fear their places of worship, eradicate religion. That would certainly speed up the plan to return the country to Year Zero.

I asked Solina, 'Don't you sometimes look into older people's faces and wonder whether they were killers or victims?'

'This is the reason so many Cambodians are still afraid to return,' she replied. 'When I first came back, with all the hideous memories, I did think that way, but I hardly ever think about it now. I have put it out of my mind. I do the Lord's work and that protects me.'

Times change, things move on, not always for the better. As the bus rumbled towards Siem Reap, I mentally prepared myself to deal with disappointment, which was just as well. I remembered Siem Reap as a village with one hotel. Now we were confronted with a multitude of bars, cafés and restaurants, and the hubbub and noise that went with them. Backpackers, touts, prostitutes and persistent hawkers – many of them ragged children – trading in every kind of tat jostled for position amid the crowds who jetted in briefly from Bangkok to 'do the temple thing'. I learned later that five thousand visitors a day come to see the temples.

At the modest rooming house where we had booked in for two nights, we were joined by three of Solina's missionary colleagues from Singapore and we set out to see some of the temples. I was relieved to find them just as they had always been. Inside the Angkor Thom temple, I found the carved face to which, in 1968, I'd made my promise to return. I placed my hand on the huge stone cheek and whispered, 'I said I'd be back. Here I am.'

I found a quiet place for myself and sat down on one of the gigantic gnarled old tree roots to reflect on what had passed here. I remembered the children I'd cared for, passing like a ghostly army through my thoughts; I thought of the young soldiers on all sides of the conflict, so many dead and maimed; and the politicians – Lyndon Johnson, Richard Nixon, Ho Chi Minh, Henry Kissinger, Pol Pot. Could they really have thought it was worth it . . .

I rejoined the others and we watched a magnificent sunset before returning to our guesthouse. All I wanted to do was go to bed and have a darned good sleep. Solina, however, had other plans for us.

63

ECHOING VOICES

The sun was setting in a scarlet and gold-streaked sky as we bumped and jolted along the potholed lanes in a tuk-tuk to the home of people I'd never heard of.

We arrived at a small, modern whitewashed home to be greeted by a smiling middle-aged man with a kind, bespectacled face. This was Reaksa. Behind him, shyly hanging back, was his heavily pregnant wife, Sophaly Eng, and their three-year-old son, Philos.

I was instantly made to feel very welcome. This was a warm, loving family home, suffused with Christian belief. As a child in Wales, I had been made to go to church and Sunday school, but it was no more than part of the discipline of our upbringing. Here, I felt almost embarrassed, an outsider in the presence of true faith, as I observed the ease with which this group of people shared the comfort of their chosen religion.

Amid the cheerful hugs and chatter, we enjoyed a delicious meal of grilled fish with stir-fried vegetables, followed by huge platters of locally grown fruit. As the young missionaries helped Sophaly Eng clear away, Solina, Reaksa and I sat quietly together. Reaksa was a handsome man in his mid-forties, but despite his open and friendly face I recognised immediately and unmistakably the look in his eyes. Years must have elapsed since the experiences which gave rise to it, but there it was, still discernible to anyone who had seen the like before.

Solina explained how our paths had crossed in the camp in 1979, and told Reaksa something of my travels and experiences as a nurse. As she spoke, it seemed like yesterday to both of us. Reaksa listened intently, perhaps understanding before I did my need to hear his story. I desperately wanted to know and understand how he and others had survived their holocaust, how they had got their lives back together and found the strength to face their painful memories and return to their changed country.

Having treated people in those times of dreadful conflict, trauma and loss, I had a deep need to believe that the survivors of the desperate conditions in which I had known them would somehow manage to find, against all odds, a meaning and purpose to their lives. Perhaps I was seeking reinforcement of my hope and faith that at least some of my patients of long ago had moved on into a future that had helped shape a better present. I wanted to know how their transformation from victims to leaders happened. I suppose I sought some kind of validation of our work in their stories.

With quiet intensity, Reaksa told a story typical of what had happened to Cambodians under the Khmer Rouge. He described how they rounded up his schoolteacher father and businesswoman mother, his seven brothers and his two sisters, herding them off to a primitive, segregated village in the jungle. There, ruled over by illiterate and vindictive teenage peasant boys, who held the power of life and death over them, the family scrounged the means to survive.

After two years of living hand to mouth, Reaksa's father was arrested on trumped-up charges and the whole family taken by ox cart to the outskirts of the village where a big pit had been dug by terrified villagers, forced to dig their own graves. Six

Khmer Rouge watched and laughed as Reaksa's family kissed each other farewell in preparation for death. One by one they were forced to walk to the edge of the grave; one by one they were struck on the head and neck with heavy farming hoes, adults first as their screaming and terrified children looked on. Then it was the children's turn.

I listened to this, hardly daring, or indeed able, to breathe. How could this man possibly move on from his terrible pain? If the eyes are the mirror of the soul, then his soul was in torment. Yet this man had about him a still calm that belied what I saw in his eyes. Perhaps it was my own reflected shock that I was looking at.

We all know what happened in the forced labour camps in Germany during World War Two. I had visited the concentration camp at Dachau in 1971 to see for myself the full extent of the horror, but I had never before sat listening to someone who had survived such cruelty and yet could talk of it with such impressive dignity.

Reaksa recounted how he had managed to climb out of the grave, how he survived, and how he came to escape to Canada. Grief at the loss of his family turned to burning anger with their murderers; anger gave way to depression and despair, but he had no faith in professional counsellors and psychologists and sought answers in the Bible. Eventually he found his Christian faith and a vocation and went back to Cambodia to seek out the killers of his family. He found only one of the six Khmer Rouge responsible, the others having died or moved elsewhere, and confronted him with what he had done.

This man pleaded for forgiveness, saying that he and his comrades had been forced to carry out orders. This man had children, but there was no school in his village and he couldn't afford to pay for schooling elsewhere. Reaksa felt his hatred and bitterness dissolve and, in an extraordinary act of Christian generosity, raised funds for a village school, and for enlightened teachers who would educate the pupils to learn from the nightmare of the past. Reaksa had written about his experiences and gave me a copy of his book.

I have remained profoundly affected by Reaksa's story. The Christian missionaries argue that forgiveness is a positive commandment, following the example of Jesus who forgave those who put Him to death: 'Father, forgive them, for they know not what they do.' Forgiveness, of course, doesn't exonerate the evil deed, and there should surely be consequences for the perpetrators.

If we do not forgive, we risk living with anger, hatred and a desire to hurt which eventually will destroy us emotionally, spiritually and even physically.

Inner peace lies in forgiveness.

But should genocide be forgiven? Surely the deliberate, wanton, cold-blooded mass killings such as seen in Nazi Germany, Cambodia and Rwanda requires justice to be firm and decisive if it is to be meaningful. A line representing decency and humanity has to be drawn, and when that line is crossed, justice must prevail. All life is precious and no one has the right so brutally and cruelly to crush it.

The following morning I felt out of sorts, strangely tearful and angry.

The heat felt oppressive, despite it being early January, and I had not slept well the night before. Images of Reaksa's eyes competed for space in my mind with the memory of his words. In between, I was haunted by visions of Ba, Hue and the many other maimed Vietnamese children who I felt in my heart had not lived; and of the children and young mothers ravaged by illness and starvation in the border camps .

I was anxious, too, for news of the tsunami that had struck the day before I left Vietnam, but no one here seemed particularly interested. Even the missionaries, patiently chipping away at the desperate poverty and trauma in their own country, dismissed the plight of those struck by that massive tidal wave as sinners punished by an angry God.

But if they were ignoring it, so would I – for the time being at least – especially as Solina and I were to leave after breakfast for Battambang, a journey of some one hundred kilometres south-west of Siem Reap. We travelled the dusty, damaged roads in a taxi shared with several others, and I managed to put the blues behind me.

We, Solina and I, passed the next three days in a blur of heat, dust, laughter and intimate exchanges about our lives – two women from different ends of the earth, yet in tune with each other like long-lost sisters.

Next day, I allowed Solina to lead me where she wanted to take me, without having the slightest idea what we were going to see or why.

We reached our destination on foot, up a wide dirt road which passed beneath a wooden archway on which Khmer script was painted in large letters above the entrance. The grounds were neatly manicured and orderly. We walked slowly along an avenue lined on either side with short palm trees, their trunks painted halfway up with whitewash. Scarlet bougainvillea tumbled over the walls and low roofs of several buildings. There was no sign of other people and the place had a mysterious, sultry stillness about it, as well as being beautiful.

Solina was silent and expressionless, and still I didn't know why we were here. I saw, here and there in the lush foliage, painted sculptures, almost garish, which suggested strange kinds of mythical, winged creatures to me. As we walked up to a low bamboo and thatch bungalow surrounded by a wooden veranda, Solina spoke.

'This is the Buddhist temple where I was brought after my

arrest. My arms and legs had been tied behind my back, and I was transported here in the back of a cart pulled by oxen. When the cart passed beneath the entrance, I was sure I would be killed in this place. This is where I was tortured for eight months, Anne.'

I stopped. 'We don't have to be here, Solina. Let's go.'

'No. It is important for you to see my story.'

In the camp in 1979, she had spoken briefly and brokenly of being tortured because she had refused to marry a local Khmer Rouge leader. Now she explained how rumours had abounded that if you were taken into the temple, you would not come out alive. That was why, when the ox cart entered the temple grounds, she felt her life was over.

In the months of sustained torture that followed, at times plastic bags were tied tightly over her head until she lost consciousness; at other times, her hands tied behind her back, she was left immersed up to her neck in a large stone jar filled with foul water, where she was bitten by vermin, for days and nights at a time. That was not all that she had to endure. She was accused of spying for the CIA and electrodes were attached to sensitive body parts . . .

As we walked slowly around this place, we came upon a deep well. 'They threw people down there when they had finished with them,' she said quietly.

We left after half an hour or so, and walked in silence to our patiently waiting taxi. There was no need for further words.

Our next stop was at the tiny village where Solina was born. We strolled in the sunshine between wooden dwellings built on stilts. In the shade beneath sat women and young girls weaving colourful reed matting to sell at market. This was one of the self-help business projects encouraged by the missionary organisation, and Solina chatted easily with the women and children as we passed by. The women were covering their costs and making a small profit, but their greatest gain was the restoration of their dignity.

I instantly fell in love with that small village, a feeling cemented by the marvellous sight of a man strolling by with his pig on the end of a long piece of rope, 'Taking him for daily exercise!'

While there, Solina visited an elderly uncle of hers who lived in a simple bamboo and thatch house on the banks of a river. It was entered by a series of small steps that had been carved into a tree trunk. I sat outside in the shade of a beautiful old tree until Solina came out and beckoned me inside. I took off my shoes and stepped carefully into the long, dark, comparatively cool and airy room.

As my eyes adjusted to the dim light, I saw an elderly, emaciated gentleman lying beneath a brightly embroidered cotton cloth. He was clearly very ill; his breathing was laboured, shallow and slow, his skin hot and dry to the touch. Around him squatted his wife, his three adult children, a number of grandchildren and other extended family. Some fanned him with palm fronds, others spoke gently to him, or to each other. A teenage girl sang softly. It was a loving scene.

Then Solina, who knew what Western medicine could do, presented me with a huge dilemma by asking if I could help her uncle. Here was an elderly dying man, whose wife said he hadn't eaten for days, neither had his bodily functions worked. My Western training whispered, 'Fluids, Frusemide, manual removal of faeces, etc.' What I saw before me shouted, 'Let nature take its course.'

I thought of how, back in my supposedly civilised country, we warehouse our elderly as soon as they become inconvenient or embarrassing to have around, paying strangers a pittance to care for them. Here, I saw a family tending their patriarch with love and respect in his own home. Though wisely reading the situation, his family were suddenly introduced to a foreign visitor, and suddenly their situation had acquired a different dimension: could this be a miraculous intervention that might buy them a little more time with him?

The pressure of those anxious eyes boring in to me, seeking help, was unbearable. I examined the shrunken old gentleman, who watched me carefully with his wise eyes. Improvising, I found some plastic that doubled as a protective glove and removed the impacted contents of his bowel. Then I bathed his face and showed his wife how to trickle water over his parched lips and tongue without causing him to choke and risk inhaling fluid into his failing lungs.

He seemed a little more comfortable after these ministrations, and I then got our trusty taxi driver to take me to a local pharmacy where I bought, for mere pence, some Frusemide which would, hopefully, stimulate his kidneys to function – worth a try, but I knew and the old man knew that these were meaningless actions which would at best delay his passing by a few hours. But we also both knew that it might reassure his family that they had done everything possible to ease his journey.

64

JOYS AND SORROWS

Back in Phnom Penh with two days left before my return to London, Solina had another surprise in store for me: Vichuta! The impish fourteen-year-old girl who had worked for SCF in Sa Keao was now a forty-year-old woman, yet she was instantly recognisable among a group busily working at computers in a small office. We hugged each other, almost jumping up and down in our joy and amazement at being reunited, and went off to catch up over lunch at a local restaurant. It was a very long lunch – twenty-five years is a very long time to catch up on – and I was bursting with eagerness and excitement to hear Vichuta's story.

The daughter of the Chief Justice of Cambodia, who was executed along with most of his family when the Khmer Rouge took over, Vichuta had been at school the day they came for her father. Neighbours ran to warn her that they had taken her family. Ten years old, she fled to distant relatives on the outskirts of town. Three days later Phnom Penh was emptied, its people forced out of the city to work as peasants in rural collectives. It was four years before Vichuta and the remains of her family escaped to the border camps in Thailand.

Like Solina, Vichuta had been resettled in Canada, where

she'd graduated in law at university in Montreal. She first found the courage to return to Cambodia in 1999, but was so shocked by what she saw that she couldn't wait to leave. Once back in Canada, however, she was unable to forget the plight of women and children in Cambodia that she'd witnessed, and she returned to start up her own charity. She and her team provided legal services for victims of domestic abuse as well as survivors of people trafficking.

Young people of both sexes were trafficked into the sex trade in Cambodia and Thailand, often into paedophile rings operated by men from all parts of the world – Japan, Europe, North America, Australia – bought from their poverty-stricken families with lies and money. Young boys around the age of ten were also taken to work on the fishing boats. Again, families with no prospects were given money, and the promise that their sons would be employed and well cared for; offers difficult to refuse for those with nothing.

I looked at Vichuta and Solina and remembered how traumatised and physically debilitated they had been when I first met them. Now, mature women back in their own country, they were dynamic, professional, single-minded, and determined to help others less fortunate than themselves. I was overcome with respect and admiration.

Vichuta said, 'We learned so much from Dr Ivan and Dr Mark, and from you, Anne, and the other nurses at Sa Keao. You all showed us that it is worth taking a stand against things that are wrong. You all stayed to help us when you could have left. Don't think that we learned nothing from you, because we did.' I was deeply touched by this, and felt that the validation for our work that I seemed to have been searching for had been given, freely, and once and for all.

During lunch there was much reminiscing about the days in the camp. 'Anne, do you remember how I used to wait for you at the main gate in the mornings?' Vichuta said. 'You always gave me a ride to work on the back of that old bicycle of yours.' I had forgotten that. To spare myself the long, hot walk through the camp to my mother and baby clinic, I bought this trundling old bicycle from the son of our Thai cook. I used to leave it at the front gate at night and pick it up early in the morning. I knew the Thai guards used to ride around on it after hours, but that meant it was quite safe.

Vichuta reminded me of a small English/Khmer dictionary I had given her. 'It was blue,' she said, 'and I still have it. Now it is well marked, and I know all the words, but I will always keep it. You also gave one to Solina. Hers was yellow.' I asked them both whether they felt Cambodian, now that they were back.

'I feel like a Cambodian Canadian,' replied Solina, but Vichuta, who had only been in her teens when she moved to Canada, said, 'No, I feel like a Canadian Cambodian.'

Her thoughts still on the past, she said, 'When we rode through the camp on your bicycle, the Khmer Rouge used to shout things out. Do you know what they were saying? I never told you.'

I did remember, but had instinctively known it was best ignored.

'They were shouting at me, Anne. "Look at you, running after these American dogs. We should have killed you when we had the chance, but don't worry, we will kill you when we all return to Cambodia. Be sure, we will all return and then we can finish the killing." Many bad things they used to say.' Throwing her head back, she laughed heartily. 'I would like to see their faces now. *I* drove *you* here – in my white, air-conditioned Toyota! I would love them to see that. You see how things can change?'

When I opened my purse to pay, Vichuta quickly picked up the bill. 'Anne, you and the SCF team gave me an extra twenty-five years of life and learning that I could never have dreamed I would have. Now, at least allow me to give you lunch.'

It was a marvellous reunion. The shared love, joy and laughter around that table was one of life's truly enriching moments.

The next morning, Sunday, was the last of my trip. After our usual delicious breakfast of green mango, fresh baguettes and strong, black coffee, Solina announced, 'Now we will leave for the church and a short service. You can sit in on my women's group, and then we will pop in to the Killing Fields.'

You don't hear a sentence like that every day.

'Excuse me? The Killing Fields? *POP IN?*'

'Yes, it is the last part of the Khmer story. It is important that you see it and tell others.'

The church service was beautifully simple, the familiar hymn-singing robust. The people were placing so much trust in their new God, I could only hope he was listening – no one else seemed to be. Alice, a motorbike-riding seventy-year-old missionary, was there, playing her violin alongside several young male musicians, some of them playing the three-stringed instrument often seen in Cambodia. The sound they made was richly melodious. In this land which had suffered so much, the clashing extremes of brutality and exquisite beauty regularly took my breath away.

Solina's women's group met weekly. The sessions offered companionship, moral support and practical help. Some of the women were victims of domestic violence, others had been 'rescued' from the sex trade and were finding it difficult to readjust to normal life. Several older women were still trying to come to terms with the trauma they had suffered during the Pol Pot years. The meeting was all in Khmer, but body language crosses international borders, and I was able to perceive the moods and emotions of the group.

The Killing Fields lie in rural countryside about fifty kilometres outside Phnom Penh, reached by a seriously bad road. Every now and then as we drove, I noticed roadside vendors beneath shade trees selling clear glass bottles of yellow fluid. I asked Solina what it was.

'It is petrol. They steal it, fill up their bottles then sell it very cheaply.'

'They're doing it so openly,' I said in surprise. 'Don't the police catch them?'

Solina looked at me pityingly. 'They give the police a bit of money to look the other way. Everybody does it.'

'Do you buy from them?'

'Of course, it's very cheap. That's how I can afford to have this car.'

After some while, out in the middle of nowhere, Solina announced that she'd missed the turn-off to the Killing Fields. Ahead of us on the road, which had now become a narrow dirt track, were two stocky men wheeling bicycles. They wore what had been the 'uniform' of the Khmer Rouge: black pyjamas and red-and-white checked cotton scarves.

Solina pulled up alongside to speak to them. They turned and looked at us, their faces expressionless, and I saw they were well into their fifties. During Solina's exchange with them, the atmosphere was so palpably charged with cold hostility and tension that I found myself almost shivering despite the heat.

The conversation over, the men went on their way and Solina turned the car round to retrace our way. I knew something was wrong.

'What did they say?' I asked.

'Nothing.' Her jaw was set firmly, her eyes glued to the road, her body taut.

'Solina! What did he say that's upset you?'

'Nothing.'

'Was it about me? Was it rude?'

'It was nothing to do with you.'

'What did he say?'

Solina slowed down, half turned to me and said, 'When I asked them for directions to where we are going, he said, "Do you want the village, or the place where we put down the degenerated people?"'

In that frozen, shocking moment, I realised I had brushed up against history. I thought of Mohammed in the Lebanon, the family man who so proudly displayed a photograph of Adolf Hitler on the wall of his home, and how I'd ducked the chance all those years ago to ask the questions that needed to be asked. Now – here – was another opportunity to try and understand.

'Solina. I apologise for asking this of you, but I have to. I would like to talk to those two men – try to understand what all that was about – but I need an interpreter.'

'No!'

I had known the answer before I asked the question. It would have been mine too, but I had to ask.

We bumped along in silence, then Solina said, 'Do you think they would be interested in anything you have to say? To them you are just another degenerated person.'

That kept me quiet for the rest of the drive to the site known as the Killing Fields. Some things you have to let go.

There were few people around this place. Solina told me that there were a lot of tour buses there during the week, but not on Sundays.

The area of land where eight hundred skeletons were found buried, many still with fragments of clothing on them, lies against the bank of a river. Bizarrely, given the circumstance, I was immediately reminded of the Glaslyn, the wide, clear river which runs through the village of Beddgelert in the heart of Snowdonia. This vision of the area I had grown up in as a child flashed into my mind very clearly as Solina and I walked across the grounds towards the rippling water:

Like the Glaslyn, large shade trees dotted the banks at intervals. Unlike the Glaslyn, some of the tree trunks had signs nailed to them: *Against this tree women and children were bound and whipped . . . Men were hanged from this tree . . .*

No, not like Wales at all.

In the centre of the site is now a tall, modern glass structure which holds the skulls. At the very bottom of the several sections of this structure are kept a pathetic collection of ragged clothes, black pyjamas mainly, which were found on the bodies of those buried here. This beautiful place had several mass graves. Many such places exist throughout Cambodia. This one has been kept as a memorial – and a reminder.

'Do you think Vichuta's father could be buried here?' I asked Solina.

'Probably. Most of the people here were the intelligentsia and their families.'

'Has Vichuta visited this place?'

'No. She will never come here. She focuses on her work. Nothing else.'

The only other visitor we saw was a Westerner, a woman, who was looking closely at the skulls and making notes. I struck up a conversation with her and learned that she was a retired dental surgeon from Denmark, who was calculating the ages of the skulls by studying the teeth.

'I wish people in my country could see this. We have become so spoiled, and still they complain about how hard life is.'

My head hurt from trying to figure out the human condition. I left her to her calculations and joined Solina, who was sitting outside in the sunshine, talking to a man I had noticed when we arrived. He politely left us, and she told me that his entire family had been murdered and buried here, and he lived and worked as a caretaker of the site in order to be close to them.

After a little while, we left the Killing Fields. As we drove away, I did not look back. This was a place that I never wanted to see again.

The next morning, in a blur of tears, hugs, exchanges of gifts and promises to come back soon, I left for the airport.

As my plane took off, soaring higher and higher over Phnom Penh, I looked down at the sprawling mass beneath, spreading out into the emerald green of the paddies, and thought of the myriad human tragedies that had been played out down there. My mind was blown, my heart felt bruised, but then I thought about Solina and Vichuta, and all those wonderful people who were battling the poverty and sadness to make a better world.

That made me feel better. I settled back into my seat and mentally prepared myself for the long journey home.

65

RESOLUTION

In a departure from my usual work, when I left Saudi Arabia back in 1995 I went to teach life skills, art and English in a school for children with special needs in Kuwait – a society where such children were usually regarded as an embarrassment and hidden from view. Aged between five and eighteen, they suffered variously from the full spectrum of special needs, including autism and Down's syndrome. The school's dedicated owner wanted an experienced nurse to take a class of seven children with motor problems – cerebral palsy, neurological deficiencies following head injury – to reinforce the work of the physiotherapists alongside their classroom lessons. I loved the work, but after two years I'd had more than enough of the Middle East and felt it was time to go home.

Over the following eight years, I worked in a series of private duty posts in London and slowly began putting my memories, experiences and stories on paper. I quickly slipped into the daily routines of work, and a life concerned with so many of the things we think are so important, but are actually quite inconsequential. But the sights and sounds of my sojourn in Vietnam and Cambodia simmered quietly just beneath the surface of my mind. I felt though, that I'd finally laid the ghosts of Southeast Asia to rest.

Mike, of course, had been a significant part of that time and, happily, has stayed a close and good friend. We have grown old apart, yet together, sharing our separate lives with each other through sporadic letters, emails and phone calls. Mike's unflinching love for his wife and family remained intact always; the progress of his children and grandchildren proudly shared. At the same time, he has enjoyed vicariously my adventures, and cheered me on from the sidelines.

I had much to be thankful for, but now there were ghosts closer to home occupying my thoughts and plans.

In the summer of 2005 Joan, my youngest sister, was on holiday with her family in Snowdonia. While there, as she (and Susan and I) had done several times in the past, she visited the overgrown graveyard of Ynys Cynhauarn church just a mile from our childhood village, where our mother had been buried in an unmarked grave. On this occasion Joan found herself suddenly angry and upset at the enormity of what had happened, but she used her turmoil to set the record straight.

Using the research skills she had acquired through her interest in genealogy, Joan painstakingly trawled through Parish records, spoke with local officials and was able to identify the spot where we believed our mother to have been buried: In 1950s Britain, suicide was illegal and deemed to be a shameful act, to be kept secret. Despite being a churchgoer, Mum was buried, without fuss, in unconsecrated ground.

This particular space is now hallowed and fully integrated into the churchyard. Once Joan had the necessary details, we three sisters decided it was time to do something positive to confront and counteract the tragedy that had silently dogged us for fifty-six years. We had arranged for a headstone and now the moment had come when we would relive those childhood emotions, numbed with shock and trampled on with such disregard so long ago – and, in so doing, heal our painful wounds.

My sisters and I arrived at the remote, beautiful old church of Ynys Cynhauarn at one p.m. on 2 August 2006. Rainclouds were scudding across the sky, and an unexpectedly cool wind tugged at our suddenly inadequate summer clothing. Sheep in the surrounding fields raised their heads lazily to take a look as we drove along the narrow farm track to the old lych gate of this ancient church; cows mooed softly as we walked up the path.

Between us we carried a bush of Mum's favourite herb, rosemary, and some of the flowers she had loved: snowdrop and bluebell bulbs, forget-me-nots, and a lily of the valley plant, all dug from Joan's and Susan's gardens in Cornwall and Norfolk respectively. We had braced ourselves for the stirring of painful memories and the feelings of distress they would bring but, as we approached the site of our mother's burial place, the sense of calm that pervaded the surroundings descended on all three of us.

Clara Rosetta Watts nee Douglas
Loving wife of Arthur Frederick
Beloved mother of
Anne Patricia
Susan Carol
Joan Rosemary
Forever in our Hearts

The first sight of the headstone, a beautiful blue-grey slab of Welsh slate placed two weeks earlier, looked as though it had always been there.

In setting out to arrange the dedication that was about to take place, we had met the Reverend Aled Jones-Williams, a young minister whose kindness, wisdom, calm and innate sympathy and understanding had seen us through our initial tears and brought us to this moment. He had fitted seamlessly into this emotional journey of ours, advising that we plan nothing specific for this ceremony, but allow time and space for whatever was going to happen to unfold.

Aled arrived, carrying four folding chairs, a few sprigs of rosemary – the herb of healing – and a candle. We helped him get these out of the strong wind into the shelter of the church, where we arranged the chairs in a circle in front of the candle-lit altar. Inside the circle, Aled placed his candle at our feet, encircled with the sprigs of rosemary, and lit it.

We were nervous, but he set the mood perfectly by suggesting that we just sit quietly, allowing our thoughts to drift until they settled, and formed themselves into anything we might want to say – silently to ourselves, or shared out loud. The young minister started us off with a short prayer and then said, with visible emotion, that he found this little gathering one of the most loving and moving events on an intimate scale that he had ever seen.

We sat, awkwardly at first, each of us lost in our own thoughts. We almost stopped breathing, afraid of how things would move on. I, for one, was not at all sure I could control my emotions and felt a sudden wave of panic.

It was Susan who first broke the silence, suddenly and quite spontaneously. 'I want to thank you, Clare, for adopting me,' she said. 'If you had not been so kind, I don't know how my life would have turned out. Thank you.'

I was deeply touched, and her words gave me the strength I needed to find my own voice and speak to my mother directly, as Susan had done: 'Although you disappeared from view, we know that you've always been with us . . . at our elbow, nudging us along . . . encouraging us along life's highway and saying bravo.'

Then I read out a poem by Mary Carolyn Davies entitled *If I had Known*. I had trouble getting through it.

Perhaps the most moving of all was when Joan, only a child of two when our mother left us, found her voice and said, 'At last we have acknowledged her existence on this earth. She was here, and she was loved.' Then the tears came, softly healing the hurt of so long ago.

We had walked into the churchyard as three grieving middle-aged women. We walked out of it, our arms linked, as three little sisters who had found redemption for their mother and resolution for themselves.

The story is written. I read again from the beginning.

'No daughter of mine will spend the rest of her life wiping other people's arses.' Now, with pride and humility, I can say: 'See, Father. My life has been, and is, so much more.'

I am sixteen. My father, who I know loves me despite everything, is very angry. We are arguing, both of us with great passion, about poverty. My teenage naivety touches a nerve. Father shouts: 'You know nothing! In Calcutta I watched people lie down at night in the gutter – people born in the gutter, raised in the gutter, who marry, work and die in that same piece of gutter. When you have seen this, we can discuss poverty, and not before.'

Tears stream down his face. I am shocked, silent.

Eighteen years later I am in Calcutta, my rucksack fastening broken, a strap on a favourite sandal frayed.

A painfully thin man sits cross-legged at the side of the filthy, teeming road. In front of him, spread out on a small piece of leather lies his livelihood; small piles of tin tacks, nails, needles and thread. He smiles brightly, looks carefully at sandals and rucksack. 'Come back in thirty minutes, madam.'

When I return, the sandal is reinforced, re-soled and polished. Better than new. The leather fastenings on my rucksack are strengthened. He asks for two rupees. I am thrilled with his work, I give him four. He returns one and a half rupees. A fair price, he says.

I love and respect my father. I see now the source of his tears, his anger and frustration. He would always say, 'When you are older, you will understand.'

Now I am older, more than halfway through my sixties, and I still don't understand.

Flickering across my mind's eye are children, always children – African, Vietnamese, Cambodian, Brazilian – all over the world, suffering. Children who have never sat down to a good meal, or had safe water to drink; who are maimed or orphaned by war, drought, disease . . .

No, I cannot understand. Surrounded by plenty, I cannot understand why one part of the world has too much while others have nothing.

I've experienced humankind at its worst and its best, seen the terrible and the beautiful as I've travelled through life. The idealism of a teenager still burns inside me. It's not difficult to bring comfort through kindness and caring to the world's forsaken. I know each and every one of us can make a difference.

Index